Endangered Spaces, Enduring Places

Endangered Spaces, Enduring Places

Change, Identity, and Survival in Rural America

Janet M. Fitchen

With illustrations by
Sandra Rosenzweig Gittelman

Westview Press
Boulder • San Francisco • Oxford

Copyright © 1991 by Westview Press, Inc.

Published in 1991 in the United States of America by Westview Press, Inc., 5500 Central Avenue, Boulder, Colorado 80301, and in the United Kingdom by Westview Press, 36 Lonsdale Road, Summertown, Oxford OX2 7EW

Library of Congress Cataloging-in-Publication Data
Fitchen, Janet M.
   Endangered spaces, enduring places : change, identity, and
survival in rural America / Janet M. Fitchen ; with illustrations by
Sandra Rosenzweig Gittelman.
      p.   cm.
   Includes bibliographical references and index.
   ISBN 0-8133-1114-4. ISBN 0-8133-1115-2 (pbk.).
      1. New York (State)—Rural conditions.   2. Farm life—New York
(State)   3. Rural poor—New York (State)   4. Community organization—
New York (State)   I. Title.
HN79.N4F58   1991
307.72'0973—dc20   90-19908
                                                                                        CIP

Printed and bound in the United States of America

The paper used in this publication meets the requirements
of the American National Standard for Permanence of Paper
for Printed Library Materials Z39.48-1984.

10   9   8   7   6   5   4   3   2   1

Contents

Illustrations

Acknowledgments

Producing this book has been a labor of love; what has kept it from being sheer labor has been the solid support and assistance of so many other people. I would like, first of all, to express my deep gratitude to the hundreds of people spread out over rural New York who gave time and thought to my research, answering numerous questions, offering unsolicited insights, and eagerly suggesting people and facts to track down. Some have followed up, sending me written information or keeping me informed of local news; others have been patient as I followed up with repeat interviews. Some of these "field informants" have also served as critics of earlier drafts of portions of this book, and I thank them especially, if anonymously, for that. I emerge from this five-year project with files stuffed full of notes; with memories of special interludes on farms and in small towns, schools, offices, and homes; and with a deep respect for the people I have met, for their insights and their efforts.

As the writing progressed, I gained substantially from the encouragement and comments of a variety of scholars in rural sociology, anthropology, and other fields. In particular, I thank Don Dillman for his encouragement and very helpful review of an earlier draft of the manuscript and Sonya Salamon and S. M. Miller for their perceptive and pertinent critiques. I owe a generalized debt to many scholars in rural sociology and agricultural economics, at Cornell University and around the country, who have listened and responded, questioned and made me question. And there are also scholars-in-training, graduate students with whom I have had helpful and insightful conversations: In particular, I am indebted to Jenifer S. Heath, with whom I conducted some of the research reported on in Chapter 13, and to Mark Cohen, a fellow researcher in rural New York.

I am grateful for the institutional sponsorship that has underwritten parts of the project. The research that forms the basis of Chapter 13 was conducted while I was a collaborator on a grant from the National Science Foundation: Ethics and Values in Science and Technology (Grant RII-8409912) at Cornell University, for which June Fessenden-Raden served as principal investigator and project coordinator. Research during summer 1988 was supported by an Ithaca College summer research grant. Recent material on poverty was collected while I was starting a new research project funded by the Aspen Institute on Rural Economic Policy and by the Ford Foundation.

To my friend Sandra Rosenzweig Gittelman, social worker, and illustrator of this book, I express deep appreciation for caring so much about this project and for her illustrations, which, as readers will see, effectively capture and convey the spirit of what I am trying to say. I also want to thank Fred Estabrook of the Instructional Resources Center at Ithaca College for his maps.

Then there are the personal and intellectual supports without which this project could never have seen completion. I am indebted to my colleagues in the anthropology department at Ithaca College for their continuing friendship and their colleagueship in its best form as well as to my students for their interest in my work. My sister, Nancy Mathews, "my woman in Washington," has provided reports and information, and more than that, consistent encouragement. Doug Fitchen, husband, friend, and partner-in-life, has been a figure behind the scenes throughout this project. When I return home from a few days of interviews, he is there to debrief me and to share my excitement or concern; when I have been preoccupied by writing, he has been patient and thoughtful in discussing the material. I am deeply appreciative.

Janet M. Fitchen

Endangered Spaces,
Enduring Places

CHAPTER ONE

Introduction: Rural America in a Time of Change

From time to time in this urbanized, postindustrial society, images of rural and agricultural life flicker across the screen of national consciousness, evoking memories and myths of an agrarian past and provoking a passing awareness of current rural realities. In the mid-1980s, the farm crisis rose to the forefront of national attention, featured in the nightly news, television documentaries, commercial films, and print journalism. It was a gripping story, with homicides in heartland and grim prophesies of "death of the family farm." Gradually, however, farm families and family farms both faded from public attention. As the farm crisis slipped out of awareness, so too did rural America. Though its vast stretches and thousands of small communities hold over one-fifth of the U.S. population, rural America's problems are scarcely able to hold the attention of the rest of the nation.

One reason for the limited attention paid to rural issues is simply that urban problems seem so much bigger and closer to most citizens. Second, most Americans have only a minimal knowledge of rural America to serve as a background for the media stories of rural events and crises. Each event is just happening somewhere out there in the vast unknown of rural America. And third, each rural issue or problem that we hear about comes to us separated from every other issue or problem affecting rural places. Thus, even those people who are concerned about rural America develop little sense of the whole, little sense of the way the problems and events interact with each other and how together they affect the lives of people and communities.

This book provides the needed context and wholeness for understanding changes presently occurring in and to rural America. It does so by taking a local-level approach, focusing on actual rural places and specific changes. For example, what happens to rural workers when a small-town factory closes down and moves away as part of a national trend toward overseas assembly? How do national and regional housing trends cause poverty to become worse in some rural communities? And as the nation looks for places to house its growing prison population and to store its waste products, why do some rural communities campaign to receive a prison and others mount protest movements against radioactive wastes? Although such changes, issues, and problems sweeping across rural America are national—even international—in cause and scope, it is in actual communities that the impacts of changes for individual lives and social institutions are felt. Hence, research for this book *about* rural America has been conducted *in* rural America.

Many rural spaces, the settings of rural life, are now endangered by a variety of societal forces. Some rural places, the social matrices of rural life, are now in serious stress or decline, and some will disappear. But many rural places will manage to adapt and survive into the twenty-first century, although transformed and redefined. They will endure as communities because their people are working hard to preserve what they value in rural life and at the same time adjust to an increasingly urbanized society.

A TROUBLED DECADE IN RURAL AMERICA

The turning over of the calendar to the start of the last decade of the twentieth century, revealing the looming presence of the twenty-first, provides an appropriate occasion for taking stock of the directions of community life in rural America. It is a time of reflection and questioning in many rural communities, and a time in which even the identity and meanings of rural life and rural community have become issues. The deep and pervasive impact of the decade of the 1980s on rural America has been summed up by former Secretary of Agriculture Bob Bergland as follows: "At the end of the decade, it is clear that the troubles of rural America have deeper roots than comparatively short-term crises such as drought and farm foreclosures. The economic restructuring occurring in rural America in the 1980s has had dramatic social and economic consequences that are contributing to the decline of the quality of family and community life in rural areas" (Bergland 1988, p. 29). In one rural New York county, an economic development specialist concluded, "Like it or not, we're going through gut-wrenching change here." A probation officer in another community pondered, "Can we really consider ourselves rural any more?" Like so many others, these people wonder, Will the communities to which they devote such time, energy, and love still be around as functioning communities by the time their children mature? And if so, will their children stay? These are the personal ways in which the larger issues facing rural communities are often phrased. These comments reveal the kinds of local perspectives on rural change that are woven together in this book.

Change is nothing new in rural America. Broad societal trends and restructurings have been affecting rural areas since the founding of the nation, and the shape and fate of rural places has long been tied to what happens in urban areas. Now, however, many changes are occurring in a compressed period of time. The cumulative effect of this quickening pace challenges not only what goes on in rural communities but what people think about their communities and about their lives. In many rural places, the entire image of rural life is being called into question, and rural identity is becoming blurred.

THE FAST PACE OF CHANGE IN THE LATE 1980s

To keep the scope of this study manageable and to maximize familiarity with the context in which changes are occurring, I concentrated my research within a single geographic area, upstate New York. To introduce the study, I begin with a few brief vignettes from field notes taken between 1985 and 1990, during the course of research. Together these five glimpses indicate the kinds of changes and problems that will be discussed in depth in separate chapters of the book. They also illustrate the local-level, community-centered focus of the book and the effort to show how the changes touch and alter the lives of people living in rural places.

Performing Arts in the Cow Pasture

A center for performing arts was recently established on former hillside farmland in central New York State, attracting day visitors from the New York metropolitan area, along with weekend tourists and nearby vacation-home owners. The narrow dirt road that leads to the center bisects one of the county's waning number of economically viable dairy farms. On performance weekends in 1988, over 1,000 cars a day drove up the road right between the house and the cowbarn of this farm that has been in Pete's family for four generations. In Pete's view, the center is symptomatic of what is happening to farming in the area. He sees a future with further clashes between farms and the encroaching city. He forecasts that the current generation may be the last to farm in this valley: "My younger son is studying animal husbandry in college. I don't know if he will—if he should—take over the farm when he finishes."

A Village Factory Closes

In central New York, a factory that had been a mainstay employer for several hundred families in surrounding small towns suddenly announced at the end of 1988 that it would soon shut down and move its operations to Mexico. Through spring 1989, workers awaited their pink slips and began looking around to find other jobs. Martha, whose mother before her had worked in this factory, could only find a night-shift job in a smaller plant at a pay loss of $2.50 an hour. Her friend Ellen took a part-time job in a local fast-food restaurant for just over minimum wage. With the factory closing, each woman had lost a good job and had little hope of a satisfactory replacement. On a larger scale, the real loser was the community, which lost not only its major employer but a major community institution as well.

Housing Problems for Poorer Residents

In another central New York village, just as 1989 began, an owner of a large block of low-rent apartments suddenly announced that he and other landlords had arranged to sell over 100 apartments to a developer from the New York metropolitan area, who planned to renovate the buildings and sell the units individually as condominiums. Instantly, 100 low-income families were faced with losing their homes, trying to find a place to live at a price they could afford—in the middle of the school year and in a rural area where there is almost no other low-rent housing available. Sandra had already been looking for a better place to live before the announcement came. The kitchen in her apartment has a ceiling panel missing where water leaked from upstairs, a broken window pane that had been covered with cardboard for months, and paint peeling from the walls. Outside the apartment, Sandra fears for the safety of her children and finds neighborhood social problems, sometimes exacerbated by alcohol and drugs, "depressing." But now she is frantic because "there just isn't anything else around that we can afford."

New State Prisons Spur Rapid Community Change

In the extreme north of New York State, local political, business, and economic development leaders had eagerly sought a state prison for the jobs it would bring to their depressed area. As spring mud turned to the dust of summer, one new prison at the edge of town was open, a second under construction. The entire village appeared to be a construction site: Main Street was completely torn up as part of a major project to ease the traffic congestion related to the new prisons. A lifelong resident looked out of the window of the just-completed new county office building and commented thoughtfully on the meaning of all the construction in the streets below. "This town's growing so fast now. The speed of its growth makes it seem like *everything* is changing. They tell us that as soon as Main Street construction is done, in two years, we'll be back to the way we were. But we won't; I know we won't. Too much is changing for things ever to go back to the way they have been. And it will take a long time for this county to get used to all these changes."

Rural Lands at Risk, Rural People Protecting Their Space

In the southwestern end of New York State on a wintry night in 1989, 5,000 people, 10 percent of the county's total population, showed up at a small-town high school for a public meeting. Farm families and college professors, businesspeople and school youngsters, local government officials and long-term unemployed residents—all were concerned and angry. The state of New York had just announced that some overgrown farmland in this county was being considered as a potential site for the state's low-level radioactive waste dump. This night marked the start of a long and active rural protest movement.

These five items taken from field observations indicate the span of this book: the whole array of changes occurring in and affecting rural communities in several regions of New York State in the late 1980s. Dairy farms were going through a very difficult period, and many family farms were lost. At the same time, the national trend of offshore manufacturing and the transition from manufacturing to service employment was delaying and weakening economic recovery after the recession, hitting hard in some unsuspecting rural communities. For rural people lacking up-to-date education and job skills, inadequate income increased their vulnerability in a tightening rental-housing market. In some communities, new state prisons were being sought and welcomed, though their social impacts made many residents uneasy. And some communities suddenly found that their rural spaces were wanted by outside forces as a repository for dangerous materials. Although not all of these changes are occurring in any one community, most of them can be found in virtually every rural county of the state. Together, they are transforming the physical and social environment in which rural people live, the lives they lead, and their perceptions of their communities and themselves.

RURAL NEW YORK IN A TIME OF CHANGE

What Is Rural New York?

The phrase "rural New York" may strike some readers as an oxymoron, but it really is not a contradiction in terms. True, New York is undeniably an urban state, with one of the world's largest urban areas. New York City dominates the perception that most Americans, including many New Yorkers, have of the state. Nonetheless, the state still contains a lot of rural territory and many rural people, most of them spread over a vaguely defined region called "upstate," which also contains several metropolitan areas. Forty-four of the state's sixty-two counties are officially classified as "rural" (see Map 1.1). These officially rural counties contain 3 million people, representing 17 percent of the state's population. But rural New Yorkers for the most part are more densely packed than rural people in other states, and their greater proximity to metropolitan areas has major consequences in hastening and magnifying some of the changes now affecting rural life.

This large state contains many small places. There are 727 townships in rural New York, each with a governmental structure and municipal functions and responsibilities, and 324 incorporated villages. Some municipalities contain very small populations: One township has under 100 people; over 180 villages have populations under 1,000. One whole county contains only 5,000 people, and thirteen more have fewer than 50,000 people. And despite waves of consolidations forced by financial considerations, state pressures, or both, there are still ninety-one hospitals in the forty-four rural counties, and around 300 rural school districts, including some with fewer than 300 children in the entire school, kindergarten through twelfth grade. The small populations of these places, their small-scale governmental units, and their small institutions definitely convey a sense of rurality.

Ruralness in New York is not just a matter of numbers of people or communities, however, but also a matter of space and the uses of space. Over a quarter of the state's total land area (28 percent, or 8.5 million acres) is farmland. Agriculture composes a major sector of the state's economy, and New York ranks third in the nation in milk production and at or near the top in the production of several dairy products. Rural New York has much undeveloped countryside, including mountains,

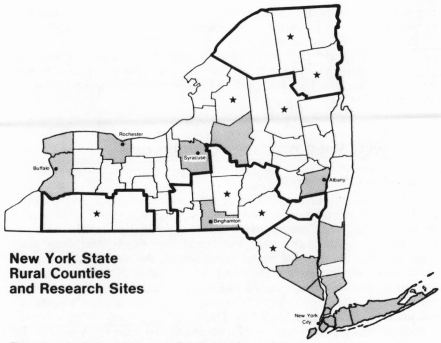

New York State
Rural Counties
and Research Sites

The 44 unshaded counties are officially 'rural' counties.
★ indicates the 8 counties classified as 'most rural' (Eberts and Khawaja 1988).
Bold outlined areas indicate the 16 counties where research was conducted.
The 18 shaded counties are metropolitan counties.

MAP 1.1

forests, and remote wilderness. Throughout upstate New York, there are miles and miles of back-country roads without any houses. More than 60 percent of the state's land is in forest cover, much of it actively maintained and harvested, some state owned, and some simply overgrown former farmland. In the 1980s, however, it suddenly became apparent that many chunks of undeveloped rural space were becoming developed—either for recreation and retirement homes or for new uses, such as waste disposal.

Ruralness in New York is also an identity, a way of life, and a state of mind. Residents of the small places continually refer to themselves as rural people and their communities as rural places. The ingredients of rurality vary with the territory, and "ruralness" is relative to whatever else is nearby. However, whatever it means to be part of "rural" in New York is now changing and becoming even less clear in the face of the many changes currently taking place.

Researching in Rural New York, Generalizing to Rural America

In focusing on research settings within New York State, we are examining rural areas that exist within the context of the highly urbanized Northeast, and within a diversified state with a relatively healthy economy and reasonably strong rural education, roads, and services. The case presented here is certainly not a worst-case scenario of rural America, but in many ways it can be considered a harbinger for rural America. Rural New York is experiencing now some of the economic, demographic, and sociocultural changes that are or will soon be affecting rural places in other regions. Understanding the impacts of change on communities in rural New York may help us understand what is happening in and to rural America at large.

The selection of a single state for research does not eliminate diversity, however. From community to community in rural New York, there are fundamental differences of a geographical nature, differences in topography and terrain, in climate, in soils, in proximity to urban areas, and in layout of settlements. In some rural areas, signs of growth and development are everywhere: new houses, either singly or in subdivisions, active construction of vacation homes, and farms that appear prosperous and well kept. In other areas the familiar signs of rural depopulation dominate: overgrown fields, abandoned and falling-down barns, large rural cemeteries with more people buried in them in any nineteenth-century decade than are currently living in the area, consolidated schools out in the countryside bearing generic or hyphenated names on their buildings, and empty stores along village Main Streets.

In order to sample some of this variation, field research was concentrated in three separate regions of the state (see Map 1.1). The central region's character, and its recent loss of dairy farms, is increasingly shaped by proximity to the New York City metropolitan area. The western Southern Tier, more remote from urban influence, has its own mix of community characteristics, with manufacturing playing a major role in local economies. The North Country, dominated by the mountains and the huge Adirondack Park, has a distinctly different set of economic and demographic parameters, including seasonal tourism and vacation residents. Even within each area, county-to-county differences are readily apparent, for example, in the geographic patterns of rivers and hills and in backgrounds and distribution of people. Some counties contain a dominating central place, whereas others have a bipolar division between two central places, and in others there is a more even scattering of population with no dominant centers. There may be differential agricultural prosperity in each section of a county or industrial development patterns that vary from one end of a county to the other. Superimposed on this foundation of variation, there are also important differences in the kinds of changes now occurring, in the force of change, and in the responses of people to the changes.

THE PURPOSES AND PLAN OF THIS BOOK

The major task of this book—and of the several years of on-site research that preceded it—is to portray and explain in a holistic manner the interrelated changes that are currently occurring in rural America. The book's larger purpose, though, is to describe the context of these changes, so that there will be a better basis for understanding their effects on rural people and places. The book focuses on the impacts of change, the social consequences for people as individuals and within families and especially for communities. It explores local perceptions and local responses, but it also urges state and national attention to the impacts of these changes on rural places.

The main body of the book consists of seven parts, each with two paired chapters and each devoted to one aspect of the changing rural scene. I start, in Part One, with a consideration of the farm crisis, its effects on farm families and their responses, and of the impacts farm problems and farm loss have had on communities. The farm chapters are placed first because of the central role dairy farming has long held in rural New York and also because among all the changes sweeping rural communities in the 1980s, the farm problem was the one most noticed by local residents. In Part Two I consider changes in the nonfarm economy, the loss and downsizing of rural manufacturing and the erosion of economic well-being as a result of the further transition to service-sector employment. Here, too, I examine the effects of the changes on rural people and rural places. Part Three describes some significant population changes and discusses local perceptions that may make it more difficult for rural communities to respond effectively to such change. Part Four is devoted to examining the worsening situation of rural poverty, its causes and consequences, from the point of view of people who are poor and of the rural communities in which they reside. In Part Five I discuss recent trends in providing community services to rural people, some problems, and some local service innovations. In Part Six I look at changes in the composition, responsibilities, and financing of local governments, and at some new problems now facing rural governments. Part Seven points up the increasing vulnerability of rural spaces to becoming the dumping ground for the nation, using as specific examples the proliferation of state prisons in rural areas and the attempt by the state to force certain rural areas to accept a new role in storing the state's radioactive wastes.

The final chapters of the book, in Part Eight, deal with identity and survival of rural communities. These chapters pull together some threads that run throughout the book, offering some overall observations as well as some suggestions for ways that the impacts of present changes might be smoothed. These concluding chapters describe the cumulative assault that all these changes have made on the rural identity, and the ways in which people in rural places have worked or could work to make sure that the places they call "my community" will endure. Here I emphasize the need for state and national attention to rural and community development.

The Research: Caveats and Commitments

Throughout the research and the writing of this book, I have tried to be two people: a listener-recorder who presents just what is observed and heard, and also a social science analyst who interprets and integrates what has been observed and heard. The events, perceptions, facts, figures, and words of rural people are presented as accurately and objectively as possible. The interpretation, however, is my own. To help the reader distinguish between analysis and field data, specific ethnographic material from interviews and observations in the field is generally set off visually by indented treatment. The main body of the text contains interpretation and analysis of the data as well as overview material on local trends and state, regional, or national trends.

For readers who would like to learn more about the multifaceted research that underlies this book, about the combination of strategies and processes utilized as I crisscrossed the state for nearly 400 individualized interviews and observation opportunities from 1985 into 1990, there is a discussion of methodology in Appendix One. For readers who would like to gain more historical insight into rural New York and New England than could be included here, many relevant materials are available (Gates 1969, Hedrick 1933, MacLeish and Young 1942, Vaughan 1929, and Fitchen 1981, pp. 31–57).

MAP 1.2

The ethnographic details presented and analyzed here, unless otherwise noted, all come from within fifteen counties in the three regions outlined (see Map 1.1). Within these regions, the majority of the research material comes from four core research counties, Allegany in the western Southern Tier, Chenango and Delaware in the central region, and Franklin in the North Country (see Map 1.2). Other counties in the three regions also provided significant research sites and opportunities. In conducting fieldwork, I followed issues wherever they seemed most clearly delineated, wherever stories were breaking, and where I had become familiar with the backdrop against which events were unfolding, where I knew both the locale and the locals. In presenting interview material from these diverse sites, I have generally not named the individual people or the locations, primarily out of a commitment to protect the identity of people among whom I do research. Occasionally I have identified a person by her or his public role in a community but not named the community, and usually I have used fictitious first names. I have identified some programs and groups by name or locality where there is no reason not to or where the news media have already made a story public. I have identified specific counties, however, in presenting demographic, economic, and agricultural data already in the public domain. Selected data from the four core research counties are presented in Appendix Two.

The main reason for not identifying specific communities, however, is that this book is emphatically not a community study: It is not a study of a particular community, or even of several particular communities; rather, it is a study of changes and issues as they affect and are perceived by people in *many* rural communities.

As an applied and committed anthropologist, it is my sincere hope that the analysis and suggestions presented in this book, as well as further work stemming from this research, will enhance understanding of the changes currently taking place in rural America, that it will contribute to a better understanding by rural people themselves, by the public in general, and by planners, practitioners, and policymakers of New York and the nation. I also hope that this book will stimulate other scholars to probe more deeply, perhaps in other places and with different methodologies, into the issues and concerns raised in this book. If the insight gained through social science research is made accessible outside of the scholarly disciplines, perhaps it can be socially useful. Although knowledge alone will not make the world a better place, lacking a sound research-based knowledge will prevent us from doing a good job of improving the world even if we want to.

In the early stages of my research, one interviewee, a rural township supervisor, urged that I use both my writing and my teaching of cultural anthropology to help people understand rural Americans. He pleaded, "In addition to teaching your students to understand people around the world, teach them to understand that not all Americans are alike either, and to understand that some Americans don't want to live like everybody else." "Teach them," he urged, "to understand rural communities." A commitment to this challenge has infused this book.

PART ONE

The Farm Crisis and Its Challenge to Rural Community Life

CHAPTER TWO
Dairy Farms in a Time of Change: Struggle for Survival

Of all the changes taking place in rural New York in the mid-1980s, the farm crisis was the topic most conspicuous and most widely discussed in communities around the state. Especially in 1985 and 1986, the status of local farms was a common topic of conversation and a source of publicly expressed anxiety. Many farms that were normally considered good, solid, and successful operations were now in financial difficulty, and many families finally had to ask themselves for the first time the painful question of whether to give up farming. In those years, as most farm people went about their seasonal activities, some cornfields went unplanted and hayfields uncut; a growing number of barns stood quiet and eerily empty. With weekly farm losses documented and publicized in the listings of auctions and sales, the farm crisis was real, dramatic, and preoccupying in many communities. The farm crisis, in fact, became the symbol and metaphor for all else that was changing.

The aim of this chapter is to portray some dairy farms sufficiently to give an understanding of what the financial problems of the mid-1980s meant and did to farm families. Based on interview material from forty farms I visited in 1986 and 1987, this chapter will examine the strategies farm people used to cope with the stress and to hold on, and the circumstances under which some of them let go of their farms. I do not present financial analysis of individual farms, however, as that is a task better left to agricultural economists.

THE FARMING WAY OF LIFE

Farm families in upstate New York not only *live on* their dairy farms, they *live* their farms. Brief vignettes of two diary farms, both considered by county agricultural specialists and by the local farming community as "good operations," will illustrate the tight interweaving of farm and family.

Two Family Farms That Rode out the Tough Times

"Side-by-side Farming"—1987 and Beyond

When Charlie and Rhonda married in 1976, he left his father's farm, rented the place next door, and started farming on his own. His father and his

brother continued to farm in partnership. Rhonda took off-farm jobs for a few years to raise cash so that they were able to purchase this farm and make some needed improvements, such as putting up silos to store corn ensilage and upgrading the cowbarn. Charlie and his dad still help each other out now and then and own one piece of equipment in common, but on the whole, Charlie and Rhonda's farm is separate. Now, a decade later, they have 60 milking cows and 60 youngstock; they own 80 tillable acres and rent another 100 acres. In addition to hay, they raise corn for silage and for grain, which helps reduce feed costs. They have no regular employees, getting by on their own labor supplemented by part-time summer help in haying time, and increasingly by the capable help of their bright preteen son.

The farm is a partnership, both in the formal business sense and in the labor and decisionmaking: Rhonda called it a "side-by-side farm"; much of the work they do is separate but complementary. She takes care of the calves, occasionally helps with the milking, does a share of hay mowing and all the hay baling. She does the barn cleaning and washing up, feeds ensilage to the milking herd and also writes the checks and does most of the bookkeeping. Charlie does the milking, feeds the cows and the youngstock, does a share of the mowing, and spreads manure. He does a larger share of the tractor work, including plowing and planting. He also fixes the machinery, although either one "runs for parts." Charlie says, proudly, "one important factor in survival of a farm in these times is the wife. If the wife doesn't support the farm, either in her working on it or in working off it, if she is not behind her husband, willing to take the long hours he puts in, the lack of vacations, the expenditures for the farm rather than the house, then the farm may go under."

During the 1980s, Charlie and Rhonda made a number of small but effective changes in their operation. They provided individual calf hutches that reduced the spread of disease and built a separate heifer barn for the stock not yet of breeding age. They also initiated a "breeding wheel" system that keeps closer track of when to breed each cow, when to dry her off, and when she is due. They purchased a used, automatic electric feed mixing cart costing only $1,500, as opposed to about $5,000 for a new one, and this, too, has increased production. As Charlie said in demonstrating the cart, "Increased production leads to increased profits, and that's the name of the game."

Rhonda talked of their off-farm activities. The "lack of social life," a problem for some farm wives, had been hard for her to get used to at first, as she had not been raised on a farm. "It's not that farm people aren't friendly, they're just busy," she explained. Charlie and Rhonda are very active, both separately and together, in a number of farm-related organizations, including Extension (the agriculture committee and 4-H), the Farmers' Home Administration Committee, the milk cooperative, a feed and equipment supply cooperative, and the Holstein Club. Both agree that meetings, as well as crop field days and dairy shows, are doubly important in their lives: They provide needed ideas and information on new farming techniques and trends, and they provide a chance to see and talk with other farming people. As Rhonda says, "Social life on a farm *is* meetings."

By summer 1989, despite a very rainy spring that had delayed planting and left some corn quite stunted, the farm operation was going well. Charlie, always looking for a challenge, is talking about long-range plans but is still keeping his eye on short-range management "to keep the operation tight." With their new baby over a year old, Rhonda is back into the full swing of farm work. She hires a teen-age babysitter in the summer and will have the sitter continue for after-school hours. "I'd really like to buy a tractor with a cab, so I could take the baby along when I'm doing field work. But used prices are high right now."

The Largest Herd in the County: A Family Farm
Thriving on a Conservative Approach

As we sat around the kitchen table on a rainy summer afternoon, devouring generous portions of ice cream and cake topped with fresh-picked strawberries, Harold and Kate, both in their early sixties, talked of the changes they'd seen in their area over the years. Three grown sons operate the farm together with their father, and two of them joined us for the food and conversation. It was a mix of information, opinion, and humor. Question: "What time do you milk?" (meaning, at what time of day do you do the milking?) Answer: "All the time"—which is about the case, for on this farm with 350 milking cows, one milking almost runs right into the next. Each milking takes about five hours, and the evening milking doesn't end till 11 p.m.

Even with two full-time regular hired men and one part-time farmhand, family members work long hours. "The boys" are done with work two nights a week at 8 p.m., which is regarded as early. Harold, the father, works every night for the full milking, in part because he insists on retaining cows that don't adjust to the milking parlor, so he takes responsibility for milking them individually. The youngest son said that if the decision on these cows were his, he would "do like most farmers, sell those cows. But if Dad is willing to do that milking, then it's OK with me." There aren't any real vacations in this family, only a few hours off now and then, and two or three entire days for each son. The hired help gets Sundays off, so the family finds Sunday its heaviest workday. The family's standards for amount and quality of work are high, and hard to match in hired labor. "It's getting harder and harder to get good labor nowadays."

Harold had grown up on this farm, and after the early death of his father in 1941, farmed the place with his mother. He purchased the farm twenty years later, and now it is a family enterprise. Each son has his own cattle and machinery and his own home, but not his own farmland. The land the family owns, including some purchased as neighboring farms have gone out, is far too limited in acreage and quality to support the large dairy herd, so they must rent more than half of the land they need. They are well aware that they cannot count on this resource indefinitely, as demand for vacation homes and housing development will make it more difficult to rent land for farming: "Developers don't want cows grazing on their investment." They also know that no one outside the family would ever buy this place for a farm because it has too little good farmland: "The land that is owned is not up to the buildings, in quality or quantity."

Few other operations in the county could either support four families or hold their loyalty, commitment, hard work, and long hours. Family members all recognize that theirs is an unusual arrangement, that few of the young men who graduated from college with the sons had returned to farm, and that when sons marry and have children, as two have done, the potential for conflict between each family and the joined enterprise may increase. Inevitably, succession will become an issue. They also know that when the operation is shorn of its rental lands, they will have to scale down the herd below the size needed to support four or even two nuclear families.

During the mid-1980s, when so many people were talking of the farm crisis, this farm enterprise did well. The main strategy, they say, is that they have kept the debt load as low as possible, hardly borrowing at all and doing their expansion gradually, on a pay-as-you-go basis. Harold maintains that through keeping borrowing to a minimum, he retains his and the enterprise's "independence," which is vitally important to him: "I want to be in the driver's seat." "The barns we've built were built without loans. If it will take three to four years to pay for a barn, you build it gradually, paying as you go along." The newest extension on the milking barn was still in progress, proof that Harold practices what he preaches. Harold believes that the problem for other farmers is that they were overextended and that "the banks have been too lenient with them, making the problem worse because the debts only grew." For himself, he says, "The banks come to this farm two to three times a year to see if we want a loan. But my philosophy is: If I can't pay for it, I don't need it. I'm real conservative." Kate pitched in: "Make that ultraconservative!" Kate hasn't generally worked on the farm, giving her creative energies instead to serving the needs of her family and her township. Indirectly, though, she has been a major strength in the operation.

BACKGROUND: THE FARM CRISIS
AND DAIRY FARM LOSSES

In the summer of 1986, the anguish of the moment overshadowed the longer view. In fact, in New York, as in the Northeast as a whole, there has been a century-long trend of decrease in the number of dairy farms and increase in the average size of those remaining, a trend that paused during the 1940s, paused again in the 1970s, when conditions were so good "you almost couldn't help making money in dairy farming," then picked up speed in the 1980s.

As the price received for milk fell quite steadily through the 1980s, debt problems of serious proportions began appearing for many commercial dairy farms in New York. Farmers received less for their milk in 1987 (only \$11.55 per hundredweight) than they had in 1979, yet input costs had risen significantly and continued upward. As a result, more farms than usual went out of business, and most went not by choice but by debt. Overall there was a 16 percent loss in total number of farms in New York State from 1983 through 1986, though counting the number of farms lost is a very tricky business because of differing definitions and inadequate data (Stanton 1987).

Farm financial stress and farm loss have been very uneven, with marked variation both within and between counties of New York State. Some of the diversity can be explored by looking at the overall dairy farm picture in the three rural counties where the farms described above are located: Delaware County, in the western Catskills in the central region of the state; Chenango County, just northwest of Delaware and contiguous for a few miles of their borders; and Allegany County, in the state's western Southern Tier (see Map 1.2). The three counties are all classified among the seven "most rural" counties of the state's forty-four rural counties (Eberts 1984, pp. 10–13). None of the three is among the top agricultural-producing counties. The agriculture in these counties is almost entirely dairy, and each county had around 500 commerical dairy farms in 1980. In all three cases, the county as a whole offers a less-than-ideal natural environment for agriculture, with hilly terrain, poor soils, and a short growing season setting the parameters for the kinds and scales of agriculture that can be practiced. Each county does, however, include some excellent river-bottom flatland, some areas of more gentle climate, and some good soils. Most farmland in these counties produces only pasture, hay, corn for ensilage, and in some cases corn for grain; most farms purchase most or all of their feed grains from the Midwest. On the whole milk production per cow (mostly Holsteins) is below breed averages, but some local herds have consistently set production records. There is a considerable range in size of operations (from 35 to 350 cows) and capitalization, in degree of modernization of buildings and strategies (from old wooden-stancheon barns to one farm with a computer modem in the milkhouse), as well as in productivity, farm profits, debt levels, and operator income. Superimposed on this variable base there are, of course, discernible differences in management styles and capabilities of individual farm operators, and also differences in their backgrounds, purposes, and long-range goals.

The long-term trend of decrease in the number of dairy farms in the state and the region is clearly mirrored in the three counties, which experienced a net reduction of 60 to 65 percent in the total number of farms from 1950 to 1980. Delaware County still had nearly 550 commercial farms in 1982 but subsequently lost many farms to a combination of farm problems and a strong land-development market. More Delaware County farms went out through the mechanism of the Federal Dairy Termination Program ("the buyout" or the "whole-herd buyout") of 1986 than was the case in any other county in the state. Nearly 20 percent of Delaware County's farm operators, eighty farmers, submitted bids, and half of these were accepted. By July 1988 the farm count in Delaware was down to 360 and falling. In neighboring Chenango County, farm numbers were slightly lower in 1980 than Delaware's, but farm losses since then have been much less precipitous. Allegany County, in the western Southern Tier, has lost fewest farms of the three. There, no active farmland is being converted to residential development, and farmland prices are low enough ($400 to $500 per acre for good, tillable land, down to $100 an acre for pasture) to attract farm operators squeezed out by high land prices, development pressures, and tax burdens elsewhere. The complexity and multiplicity of factors putting farmers out of business can be indicated by reviewing the cases of the twenty-one farms that went out of business in the first five months of 1988 in Chenango County. The farmers listed are in all cases men, reflecting that still today almost no statistics are kept on farm women, even those who are full legal partners with their husbands.

> The age range of farmers going out was from thirty to sixty-five or so, except for the farm where the operator, in his seventies, died. At least two of the farm operators who went out had gone into farming fairly recently when times were good, and then slid downhill ever since. One man in his mid-fifties was a very successful operator, but his grown children had left, and his health was not good. Three hilltop, marginal-land farms went out, in one case after a family tragedy, in another case after the loss of a heifer barn in a fire. One young farmer reportedly "never had his act together," but many of the others had been successful, though with a tight financial situation. At least two farms had been operated by men who were retired from nonfarm occupations.

> Two neighboring farms that both went out of business in 1988 make an especially interesting comparison. On one, the operator had poured considerable money from his primary nonfarm occupation into updating and enlarging his barns, to the point where the barns were better than the cows they housed. His neighbor, conversely, chose not to modernize his barn, turning his attention and investments instead into developing an excellent herd that took top prizes for production.

FARMS IN STRESS

In most cases, the "decision" to get out of farming was really a long, slow process, with many decisions along the way. As has traditionally been the case, the actual cessation of farming may be precipitated by "bad luck," by a death, a storm, or a fire, and in many cases the timing of such an event is a key element. In some cases, but by no means a majority, getting out of farming came at about the age when nonfarm people retire and was prompted by the apparent—or adamant—preference of grown children to do anything other than run a farm. In a number of cases the cash-flow problem dictated expansion just while the farm-family labor force shrank or when good hired hands became scarce and expensive.

Some farm families decided to give up farming even though their farm was not yet engulfed in financial problems. The realization that they had been working so hard and making less income than they could have made had they simply invested the value of their assets in the bank—and done no work at all—compelled them to sell out before they were forced out. But even when the exit from farming was "by choice," and a farmer was "ready for a change in his life," actually quitting was by no means easy, especially on farms that had been in the family for generations, where the decision to quit also involved guilt and self-doubt.

> Both James and Tricia grew up on farms, and their present farm has been in his family for over a century. Tricia's brother and sister had both gone out of farming within the last year, on the federal buyout program. "I think it almost killed my mother to see them go out. I'm the last person in my family to be farming. And now we're thinking about going out, too. But if we went out, *we'd* be the ones that put this farm out of business—after more than a hundred years in the family." Balanced against the guilt was one inescapable question Tricia posed, "How long should we go on earning only $9,000 a year—for a family of five?"

Some families kept hanging on in hopes that the prospects would get better and because "giving up" was not an option they wished to entertain, but eventually their situation became so bad that there was no longer any alternative. In one case the entire dilemma crystallized in a single, immediate decision, a small decision that would ultimately determine the future of the farm.

> A farmer in his late fifties had been in financial trouble for at least a year. The county Cooperative Extension agent, a specialist in farm management, had gone over his farm financial picture and had indicated that, in the long run, selling out might be the best move, but the farmer had resisted. A year later the farmer telephoned the state's emergency farm crisis hotline for advice, and the central office passed his message on to the Extension agent, who immediately drove out to the farm. The farmer was now in an emergency cash-flow situation. His immediate question was, "I'm down to my last few dollars and my last few gallons of gas in the farm tank. Should I put the gas in the tractor to do the haying? Or should I put the gas in the truck to go to town to look for a job?" Suddenly the months of thinking about the big question of whether to sell the farm were reduced to these two short-

range options, leading in such different long-range directions. The agent's answer in this crunch was, "If if was me, I'd put the gas in the truck. Never mind cutting the hay. Let the cows graze in the hayfield for the summer— it'll make good milk and you won't have to buy feed. After the summer, sell the cows, an then you won't be needing any hay."

For people who did give up their farms after a long struggle, the final reality is encapsulated in memories of "the day the cows went."

On George and Helen's hilltop farm, the cows went on one sad autumn day, all except for one cow that earned a postponement because she gave birth on the day the truck came—to twins. With sadness Helen whispered, "It's so quiet on the farm now."

Two Farms That Survived Deep Trouble

Some farmers, such as the two described below, entered the 1980s in a sound position and as efficient managers in a strong market. Both had decided to expand their operations. Subsequently, both were hit hard in mid-decade by a cost-price squeeze and rising interest rates.

Overextended and in Trouble

Earl summed up the farm crisis as follows: "A few years ago, the farmer was living on inflation: You'd buy a tractor, use it five years, then sell it for the same as you'd paid for it. . . . Now, well, it's a whole different story."

Earl grew up on a farm down the road. He started "from nothing—with just $500 in my pocket," purchasing a sidehill farm. Over the years, he bought up fourteen of the twenty-three small farms along the valley while his brother bought up the rest. During the 1970s, Earl felt forced to expand, as the bank wanted him to be better able to meet debt payments. "The bank would give me a line of credit of a quarter million, just for the asking." He bought out his brother and set up one of his sons in farming. Another son now works with him. Earl added buildings, several big, blue tile silos, and more cows—up to 110 now on the home farm and about the same on the other farm. He has one full-time hired man, plus part-time young workers, whose lack of dependability is a source of frustration. Earl is now fifty-one, has back problems, but is still extremely hard working, almost driven. His wife, Martha, always part of farm life, has now felt it necessary to get a college degree and take a job, at a daily commute of 60 miles.

Looking back on his years as a farm operator, Earl now sees the purchase of his brother's farm as the greatest mistake. If he had ignored the advice of bankers and experts to expand, he wouldn't be in the tight situation that he now is. With some irony, Earl proclaimed, "The new Chapter 12 bankruptcy is the best thing to come along for farmers in decades." He anticipates that the refinancing of his enterprise will be more effective than under the old system. He'd like to sell the second farm, as soon as land and cow prices go up sufficiently for him to get enough for it to clear the debts. "The worst thing with farmers," Earl says, "is their pride. For example, they buy new machinery to impress. I've learned, now, not to go for the shiny paint, not to buy new equipment." . . . A year later his farm was still in business, thanks in part to the new bankruptcy laws.

A Farm Nightmare That Lasted Three Years

"It was so bad that when you'd wake up in the morning you didn't know if today you were going to have to call the auctioneer. I'd never want to have to live through that again."

Peter grew up working on this farm and took over its operation just after graduation from high school, when his father died. A few cows that he had raised himself as 4-H projects became the nucleus of the fine herd he gradually built up over subsequent years. As the 1980s began, "things looks good in farming," so he married Cathy, who had grown up working on a farm, and they started a family. They took out a bank loan for expanding the barn so that they could enlarge their small but high-quality herd. Then, almost without warning, the farm crisis hit and "everything went haywire." Six months after the addition to the barn was completed, the milk market went down. They couldn't keep up with the loan payments, but neither could they obtain any new loans to buy more cows to fill up the new barn. They were trapped, unable to increase their cash flow for meeting their debt.

The three years of 1984, 1985, and 1986 were "a living nightmare." Cathy, who had already taken a teaching job in the local school, took on a part-time job on the side, and then two other part-time jobs as well. Peter managed the farm alone, with his elderly mother helping out with chores as well as babysitting and high school boys helping part time in the summer. They came very close to losing the farm. "Everything we did, we had to think about what would happen if we lost the farm. We even put the house in my name," Cathy related, "so that if the farm was taken away from him, they couldn't take the house too." "We often wondered if we could afford to buy groceries and pay the electric bill. That's how bad things were."

Eventually their shaky financial position bottomed out and began to improve. They refinanced their loans to stretch the debt out longer with smaller payments. They purchased the needed additional cows from an uncle on a "pay-back-when-you-can" basis, and some of their own youngstock matured to calving, which increased milk production. They were able to rent some land at low cost from a neighboring farmer-friend who went out of business. Cathy looked back on those years from the slightly more secure summer of 1987: "Even though we're not on easy street, things are much better now." She treasures the small signs of their improved situation. "This summer we've been able to buy some toys for the baby. Last summer I couldn't even buy toys or clothes for her. And I just bought this [plastic] tablecloth—I couldn't even get little things like this before."

Two years later, in haying season 1989, the bad times appear to be behind them: They still own the farm; the barn is now full, with nearly 60 cows; and "our herd is really getting good,"—as close as Cathy dared come to a boast. In fact, Peter had just received coveted recognition for several cows, an honor with some money attached. Referring to the now-recognized top quality of the herd, Cathy says, "A little seed we planted several years ago is now starting to blossom."

"*Still* we're not on easy street yet," says Cathy as she hangs laundry in the back yard: "I still can't afford disposable diapers, and I still shop at garage sales rather than getting new." The older child hands toys to the "new" baby, now just over a year old. Cathy has cut her extra work to just one small part-time job—in addition to teaching school, farming, and taking care of her children. She tried to quit her remaining part-time job, but because it covers car payments, she finds it necessary to continue. She's doing more farm work now this summer, leaving the children at the same nearby sitter who cares for them during the school year.

Cathy didn't say so, but it was clear that their own strengths, personal and professional, were critical in pulling this farm through, with the marriage still intact, a fine milking herd, and the farm still owned. "We were *tenacious* about keeping the farm. Peter had grown up on this farm and in farming. He had built up the farm for ten years. I'd always known I wanted to marry a farmer and to be a farmer—and I wasn't going to let it all go." Cathy's ability to earn an off-farm income that is relatively high for this poor township was also a factor, and she specifically mentions her ability to do several jobs at a time and Peter's willingness to let her do that instead of farm work. Also important is her expertise in the business end of farming (partly a result of her college studies), and his expertise with the cows. "Peter's an *excellent* cow man," Cathy said with real pride.

Two Farms That Went Out

Many of the farms that went out of business during the farm crisis, including the two described below, had been regarded as good operations, well managed, financially successful, and with good milking herds. In both cases, the operators had anticipated many more years of farming, even after their children had grown up and left home. But financial problems suddenly made it necessary for them to quit farming.

A Family That Decided to Quit Farming: "Couldn't Keep It Going"

"I grew up on a farm, and I *never* wanted to marry a farmer—I swore I wouldn't. But," says Yolanda with humor, "I did. And we've been running a *family* farm ever since. Now it's gone. We couldn't keep it going."

Yolanda emphasizes the family part, describing the work she and the children did on the farm along with her husband, Len. She has always done the milking alongside her husband. Some of the jobs were hers alone, such as "running for parts" and bookkeeping: "Bookkeeping for the farm is in your marriage license," she quipped. "A lot of our success as a family farm was Len's attitude. He always pitched in on the farm jobs he knew I disliked," such as washing the milking equipment, traditionally the farm wife's job. She also hated taking the culled or excess calves to town for slaughter, so Len did it. "I was never able to take a businesslike attitude to parting with the calves I had hand-fed for their early weeks." "And whenever Len purchased something for the farm, he also purchased something for the house." Yolanda ran a small sewing business on the side, and she and the kids were active in school activities, 4-H, and other farm organizations.

The tightening of the farm's financial situation coincided with their emerging awareness that their children did not want to go into farming. "For us, 1986 was a rough decisionmaking year. Our son finished school and decided to leave home; the part-time workers we could get weren't good; and then the milk hauler added a surcharge for his every-other-day pickup because our farm was the only one along a back road." As Len explained it, "The only way to deal with all this would be to expand. Back twenty, twenty-five years ago, a family farm could survive with 25 cows, but nowadays you have to have at least 50—and we simply couldn't do all the work ourselves for our herd of 40, 45 milking cows and 30 or so youngstock." Len and Yolanda sold the cows in the federal buyout, then had an auction for the equipment, and finally sold the farm to a man from the city who says he wants to run a farm but has had no experience.

The Playpen in the Cowbarn:
A Family Way of Farming

A family farm was their dream. Though neither Connie nor Tom had grown up on a farm, his teenage experience in farm work and their shared commitment to farm life as the best way to raise children led them to purchase a somewhat marginal farm that had been let go over the years. Their commitment to their dream kept them going through "twenty years of struggle." When they moved to the farm, Connie says, "I put my college degree in the drawer and pitched into farm work full time." As the family grew, Connie integrated children and farm work: She would often interrupt her milking work in the barn to sit down on a hay bale and nurse an infant or to talk to a baby in a playpen set beside the cows. The children grew up doing chores on a regular basis, and all were active in 4-H, showing animals and going on to develop their own businesses with their animals.

Tom and Connie resisted even thinking about giving up the farm when their financial situation worsened. They tried to cope with the problem by cutting expenses, eliminating part-time hired hands, and working harder themselves. They gave up any but the most necessary of household expenses. But cost-cutting was not enough. As the financial situation grew tighter, they debated, with a real sadness and emotional turmoil, whether to get out of farming: "Is all the input worth it?" Connie had felt so right about being home with her children all these years, so good about the closeness of the entire family, all working together on the farm. But two daughters were off in college now, and in a few years the third would be through high school, leaving only one at home. They really didn't want to find themselves further in debt despite a tremendous amount of hard work. Before the year was up, Connie had taken a job in a county agency and was enjoying its challenges, as well as the paycheck and health benefits. She now had limited time for farm work, so the milking herd was reduced. Two years later, with the financial future of the farm still insecure, they sold the remaining cows, but they maintained the hope of continuing farming by going into sheep raising.

FAMILIES IN STRESS

It was a time of incredible tension in many farm homes, as the generalized national farm crisis enveloped an individual's own farm, family, and life. Farm observations and lengthy interviews in three counties often tapped the same deep emotions that had been reported among midwestern farm families (Heffernan and Heffernan 1986a, 1986b; Norem and Blundall 1988). Some people were hesitant to answer the telephone or the door because they feared it would be yet another creditor or bill collector. In interviews there were long pauses, sighs, tears, and clenched fists. Those who were mourning the loss of a farm told of the decision they had made to get out and of the incredible emptiness they felt on "the day the cows went."

The emotional side of the farm issue was also referred to openly in the community, often under the rather loosely defined term "depression," and farm stress was even acknowledged in the ritual and pageantry of county fairs.

> In 1986, at one county fair, two of the five contestants for "Dairy Princess," as well as the outgoing princess, centered their public speeches on the stress and strains affecting farm families. In fact, two candidates and the reigning princess had all watched their family farms go out of business.

> A feed dealer reported that he saw "mental depression in every farmer that came through these doors, especially in 1982 through '86. But," he added, "once the decision is made and the farmer gets out, they seem to feel now they are going to be OK; they're happier; they're beginning to believe that there may be life after the farm is gone."

Eventually, as the studies of other social scientists had found, the stress level came back down for many individuals as they did what they had to, sold the herd and machinery, or maybe the whole farm, and got on with a new way of life (Graham 1986).

Independence and "Making It on Our Own"

To a large degree, each family was working its own way through the farm crisis, neither publicizing its situation nor expecting assistance from others in the farming community. In the more normal crises, such as farmer becoming injured or ill or losing his barn in a fire, neighboring farmers traditionally joined together to get in his crop, do his milking, or offer space in their barns. And they still do. But in the farm crisis there was isolation and separation more than mutual assistance, a pattern also found in other farm-crisis regions (Mermelstein and Sundet 1986; Wright and Rosenblatt 1987; Martinez-Brawley and Blundall 1989).

In part, farm people were too busy working longer, harder hours to pay much attention to their neighbors, too worn out for talking with neighbor farm people about something that was almost unspeakable anyway. But there were deeper reasons as well. As several farm people explained, "We're very independent people—perhaps too darned independent for our own good." One farmer explained, "When you hear someone is going under, people don't offer to support him. There's a sense of feeling that if it was you, you'd be embarrassed to face others—so you avoid seeing them." Another said, "There's a feeling that it could be contagious,"a fear that by associating with a farmer in trouble, one's own operation might also become affected. Other farmers alluded to the traditional competitiveness: "We're always looking at the other guy's corn, to make sure it isn't taller than ours, looking at the kind of hay he's baling, seeing what production levels his herd made last year." Farm people tended to rationalize a sinking farmer's plight in terms of that man's own shortcomings as a farm operator: "I was wondering how he was going to pay for those new tractors—two tractors in one year," and "Well, he was a hard worker, but he never seemed able to keep on top of things, to make the decisions, to do the planning."

If farm families in financial trouble did not turn to one another, they were even less likely to turn to local services such as welfare or medicaid for financial assistance. Many hard-hit farm families would have been ineligible for standard assistance programs because of their farm assets, but for most, it was their pride that kept them from seeking the kind of assistance that they had always criticized as "government handouts to the poor." They preferred to make do on their own, accepting at most some help for the farm itself in forms that relatives and friends might offer, such as loans of equipment or cows, or a low rental charge for land.

Emotional strain was also held within the family for the most part. Mental health agencies and workers in these counties reported no noticeable increase in farm family requests for counseling, although there may have been some undercounting, as intake records do not necessarily reflect farming occupations. In one county, a group of farm wives formed and met regularly during the height of the crisis. Such a support group provided a safe place for farm women to talk about their farms' problems without their husbands present, to find out that other farms were in the same difficulty, and to gain the comfort of knowing that other women were also concerned about their farms, their husbands, their children, and their futures. Few farmers in trouble turned to their clergy or church for emotional support either, although ministers also reported that the farm crisis did not noticeably cause farm families to stop coming to church. The state-operated anonymous hotline, FARMNET, did receive requests for information on where to turn for professional help with emotional stress, either the caller's own stress or that of a spouse. One farm person commented that the anonymous hotline was preferable to "turning myself in at a local mental health clinic." Trained counselors in one special program set up to assist farm families reported that there were many cases of depression but that it was not easy to "find" such emotionally stressed farm people: "They do not walk in or phone in requesting counseling or assistance." They could be found and helped only through careful, sensitive outreach work, through casual conversations at a county fair or farm auction, through quiet networking away from the office. In general, farm people downplayed their emotional stress: If the farm financial situation would only improve, they reasoned, any emotional stress would dissipate. And so they concentrated on the utilitarian, on trying to strengthen the farm operation itself.

STRATEGIES FOR FARM SURVIVAL

Cutting Family Expenses to Save the Farm

As the financial picture became very tight on these farms, families cut down on household living expenses in quite patterned ways, such as putting off medical or dental work if possible, discontinuing health or life insurance, and reducing cash outlays for clothing, groceries, home furnishing, and home repairs.

> "We used to make a couple of day-long trips in August to the big malls to get school clothes for the kids; now we just order one or two sets of clothes for each kid from the Sears catalog."

Next came cutbacks in spending for social and recreational activities, resisted as long as possible, especially for children, and painful when they came. Much of farm social life—barbecues, evenings of cards, bowling, and church activities—is with other farmers. Some farm families reported withdrawing from these events because they felt embarrassed to interact with other farmers who appeared to be doing all right. More withdrew because they simply had no discretionary money left over for leisure activities.

> "We used to try to hire an extra man to come in every other Sunday so the family could have a whole day off to go somewhere. We can't afford that any more."

> "You stop participating because you have no money to do things with. You can't pledge at church, you can't make a contribution to the bluegress festival in the town park, or to the church's strawberry fair, so instead you stay home. Even activities at school, if admission is charged, you quit going— unless your own kids are in it, and for that you'll squeeze out the money somewhere."

As many farm people knew, and some stated clearly, cutbacks in household and family living expenses could not save the farm, but the cutbacks were necessary anyway because there simply wasn't enough money to cover everything.

> "All these little savings and cutbacks in family and home expenses—they're just a tiny drop in the bucket compared to the huge amounts we're always spending on the farm. They hardly make any difference at all. And they are not easy on us: We feel that we're pinching pennies in our personal lives,

for the house, for the kids, for ourselves—while spending thousands of dollars for the farm."

"Whatever little I save on the grocery bill goes for parts for the farm machinery. I might save $50 on groceries one month, but that month's load of feed costs $500. I have a hard time justifying the big amount of money for the farm compared to our very small household expenses. And it seems like personal wants are always sacrificed for farm needs."

In several families, as money got even tighter, friction in the family increased. And because the family must operate as a unit to keep the farm going, tension is economically as well as emotionally disruptive: All members of the family have to work together as well as live together. "We can't walk away; we can't avoid each other."

Clinging to Familiar Farm Strategies: Cutting Costs and Working Harder

Much of the necessary adjustment was made in the farm enterprise itself and in farm practices. To some extent, these paralleled adjustments made on midwestern grain farms (Rosenblatt 1990), but the speed and range of alterations dairy farmers can make in response to fluctuating market prices is limited, circumscribed by the nature of dairy farming. One cannot simply stop milking, nor can one instantly purchase a new herd and resume dairying when the milk price improves. In a time when other farmers are going out of business, one cannot sell a herd of cows at anything near their true worth. Dairy farm operators can only attempt to improve their cash-flow situation in small increments by taking measures to boost production to earn a bigger milk check or cut production costs or both.

Farm management practices were tightened up in various ways: improved feeding practices tailored to each individual cow; milking three times a day, even in summer if labor was available; eliminating any excessive use of costly fertilizers and pesticides; rotational grazing on pastures; cutting the hay early when protein content is highest; rental of more farmland; and improved soil practices, using expertise and sometimes loans from various agricultural programs. Most operators tinkered with their herds, culling out weak producers and carefully weighing the pros and cons of buying replacement cows versus using only home-grown replacements. On some farms, however, there was nothing specific that the experts could recommend to turn a farm's financial picture around.

One farm couple recalled, "When we first found we were tight, we had a whole financial analysis done to see what we were doing wrong. We found out that we're not doing anything wrong. We're doing all we could do. But still, there's not enough money coming in."

Most farm families made efforts to reduce the cost of their labor force. Extra seasonal hired help might be given up, or, instead, a full-time year-round farmhand might be let go, with hired labor used only on a part-time basis in the summer. On some farms, the wife became a full-time farm worker, perhaps replacing the hired man to relieve cash-flow problems.

Many farmers postponed repairs of buildings and facilities, and most kept their machinery and implements going for yet another year with replacement parts; when parts, too, became unaffordable, machinery was held together with the proverbial "baling wire and chewing gum." These postponements were nothing more than delayed expenditures, and at some point it would no longer be possible to avoid replacement. Even in the short run it could be counterproductive to put off replacement because machinery breakdowns, for example, might seriously interrupt the brief, time-dependent harvest seasons. "If you have to spend a good haying day running for parts and then putting the baler back together, you might find that you lost the one good hay-drying day in a whole week." Farmers who did have to purchase equipment got it more cheaply at auctions, or went comparison pricing among overstocked dealers offering bargains. In this way, the misfortunes of some farmers and dealers provided the opportunity for other farmers to get what they needed at a lower cost. Even the blue Harvestore brand silos, once a mark of prestige on many farms and costing around $60,000 to $80,000, could be purchased for dismantling and moving away for as little as $5,000—but few farms had even this cash to spare. As an agricultural Extension agent put it, "Those blue status symbols have become tombstones on many farms around here."

Many farmers contemplated increasing the size of their milking herd, for if a farm's buildings and forage crops could support expansion this was one way to increase cash flow and make payments on debts even when milk prices were low. This strategy was driven, in part, by the government and commercial lenders, based on the generally accepted belief or "myth" that "bigger is better" (Strange 1988). For some farms expansion worked, but in other cases it simply increased the debt problem and prolonged the exit from farming. For most farmers who took this route, it was not what they'd have preferred because it increased their already heavy work load.

> "The last thing I wanted to do was increase the number of milking cows because it was all the hired man and I could do to keep up with the ones we had. But it was the only way that I could generate enough cash to keep the creditors from my door. So, we added 10 more to the milking herd, and we're working harder now than ever before."

"Working harder," in fact, was really the main strategy farmers used to keep their farms going: Men and women, farmhands, and farm youngsters all reported working harder in the summer of 1986. Some occasionally wondered *why* they were working so hard, and some grew discouraged and frustrated that despite working so hard, the farm financial problem still wouldn't go away. The overload of work in those years kept some farm people from participating in their normal level of community activities. Exhaustion, along with worry about losing the farm, drained them both physically and emotionally. Several women reported that they were worried about their husbands' health, several mentioned newly arising problems in their marriages, and some mentioned being short-tempered with the kids, as well as just plain too exhausted to give them the attention they needed.

> "Tiredness and tension, that's the way things are around here this year. How long can this go on? How long can we take it?"

Nontraditional Farm Animals and Crops: Acceptable and Unacceptable Alternatives

Given the forecasts for future dairying trends, which include both continuing consolidation into larger farms and greater concentration in certain favorable regions of the state and nation, another set of strategies for saving the family farm involves turning to alternative animals or crops, either as a sideline supplement for dairying or as a replacement enterprise. Now, as in the past, "running beef cattle" or "going to sheep" are common sidelines on dairy farms and acceptable alternatives because they are well adapted to marginal hill land, are not capital intensive, and can be combined quite well with off-farm employment.

In contrast, the "new alternative agricultural products" suggested by many experts as a necessary adjustment for dairy farmers in the Northeast to consider, if they want to stay in agriculture, were much less acceptable to local dairy farmers. From growing miniature-ear gourmet corn, snow peas, or kiwi fruit to raising fallow deer, these specialties for urban-market niches had little appeal. Although some farmers claimed that such alternatives were not appropriate to them because of the characteristics of their soils or elevation, their distance from urban markets, or high start-up costs, there seem to be deeper "cultural" or image problems in these alternatives. Men and women who have spent years developing a top-quality dairy herd, culling, breeding selectively, and tending carefully, are enormously proud of their accomplishment. Their herd is their identity, their pride, and their status in the farming community. From the time they were youngsters showing calves at the county fair and on through their adult lives as farm operators, they are looked up to, respected, and rewarded by all the agricultural groups and agencies on the basis of their herds. Family reputations can be made on a farm's herd, and the highest compliment one can pay is "He's a superb cow man." The fairs and agricultural shows that families attend all reinforce commitment to dairy farming and the crops that go with it. The magazines they read all emphasize fine dairy herds, good breeding lines, and top production levels. Local newspapers as well as specialized agricultural newsletters feature "honor rolls" of local farms with top producing cows. Every year the county Extension gives awards to a "Young Dairyman of the Year" and a "Dairyman of Merit" (who, despite the terminology, is sometimes a woman farm operator).

> On one farm, the kitchen shelves are crowded with trophies won for the high productivity of individual cows and of the herd as a whole. This farmer, extremely proud of the dairy herd he built up over the years, asked with considerable disdain and disbelief, "Can you imagine me raising kiwi fruit?"

As dairy farmers talk, it appears that these alternative crops are looked down on as not fully "masculine," as not "real" farming, as something "the experts" dreamed up, and as something appropriate only for "city people who have moved out here and are pretending to be farmers." (In this connection, one might note the title of a recent book: *Real Vermonters Don't Milk Goats*, Bryan and Mares 1983.) Furthermore, farm people gain satisfaction knowing that the product they provide, milk, is a basic, essential food. To switch from milk production to some specialty product, such as the miniature "yuppy corn" for a fickle, affluent gourmet market in the city is perceived as a descent into playing a less fundamental role in feeding America. Despite the loss of many dairy farm operations in recent years, the definition of farming is still dairy farming. And in New York, as elsewhere, attitudes about farming as a way of life are just as important in shaping decisions as economic rewards (Barlett 1986, Coughenour and Swanson 1988).

Selling Off Land to Support the Farm

Where demand for land for vacation homes is strong, selling a 5-acre parcel of woodlot or unused pasture at prices up to $3,000 an acre could help with debts and taxes. In some places, development pressures provided a tempting way to get out of farming entirely: A farmer could sell most of the farm to an investor or developer, and let the buyer deal with development costs and zoning regulations. The ready market for land in Delaware County explains why more farms there than anywhere else participated in the federal buyout program: They could afford to enter reasonably low bids for selling their herds because they knew they could raise considerable cash by selling land.

STRATEGIES FOR FAMILY SURVIVAL

For many families, the farm crisis was a period of renegotiating farming dreams and family roles. Families went through a period of serious questioning of what the farm meant to them and what they meant to each other. In some families, even if the farm was not in jeopardy, the farm crisis sent women into off-farm jobs and pushed more sons and daughters toward college and other careers.

> Karen and Vic had "lived well" through most the 1970s: "We survived a barn fire and rebuilt; we could have what we wanted, even go out to eat occasionally." Karen gave up her teaching job to stay home with the three children, who grew up into farm chores and responsible farm work, for which they were always paid. But after the early 1980s, the farm situation turned downward, and they often wondered how much worse it would get before they were forced to sell out. Karen said, "We want our kids to have options. We assume they'll go to college. But how will we pay for college, with tuition what it is, even at the state universities? It's no longer possible to send a kid to college just by selling a few cows."

> "Just at the right time" a full-time job opened up for Karen. She was reluctant to separate herself from the farm and the close working interaction of the whole family on the farm, but Vic encouraged her and she took it. The cash—and the medical benefits—were helpful indeed, and Karen came to appreciate also the opportunity to use her own particular talents. With this income, plus Vic's expertise in farm management, they survived a period of tight finances, frustration, tension, and some depression.

> Coming into the 1990s, the farm had survived financially and appeared stable. It was still the center of family life, but it was no longer their *whole* life. The family, too, had survived, though with each individual member on a separate path. Karen had been promoted to a position of major responsibility and major demands; one child was in college and the others preparing to go.

New Roles for Farm Women

Farm wives seeking off-farm employment consider jobs in county government offices, community agencies, and schools especially desirable because they provide family medical benefits. However, many of the jobs available in these rural areas pay low wages or provide no benefits; and "good" jobs may require long commutes from the farm. Most wives with off-farm jobs continue to do some of their traditional farm work, such as feeding the calves and doing the bookkeeping. But their other labor contributions to the enterprise, such as milking and driving tractor, are curtailed because of timing conflicts between farm chores and off-farm work schedules, throwing a greater burden of work onto husbands and teenagers. Other impacts are more subtle.

> One farm woman has a full-time job and is taking courses at night to prepare for a better job. There is no time for keeping the herd's breeding and production records. "The fine-tuning isn't being done any more. This hurts the operation; our production slips a bit. And it also hurts one's sense of satisfaction: The herd just isn't what it used to be—a source of pride."

Farm women taking off-farm jobs were following a marked trend of increasing participation of rural women in the work force. (Women who work without pay on their family farms are still not counted as being in the labor force until they take off-farm jobs.) Even without the stimulus of the tight farm financial picture, many families probably would have gradually moved in this direction as the children grew into adolescence and thought about college, careers, possible moves out of farming and away from the community. However, having to rethink the role of the wife-mother in a farm family has been painful in many families because they had previously thought that their family roles were so good, so right, and so lasting. When expected role patterns had to be questioned or could not be followed, there was a real sense of dislocation. For women who had defined themselves not simply as a "wife," but as a "farm wife," loss of the farm or loss of her farming role was an assault on her self-definition. For farm women taking off-farm jobs sooner and more precipitiously than they had anticipated, their outside employment was clearly a result of the farm crisis. The necessity of taking any available job rather than gradually selecting, preparing for, and entering a nonfarm career made the change seem more negative and the farm crisis more terrible.

New Anxieties for Farm Men

Role questioning and anxiety was even greater for some farm men, especially if the family was considering getting out of farming altogether. For many men, farming was the only thing they had known or done in life, and they felt they had no employable skills, "no resume." In fact, men who did quit farming and found jobs were almost uniformly praised by their first employers as being unusually hard-working, skilled, and responsible high-caliber workers who would be sought after by a variety of other employers. In cases where a farm had been in the family for generations, anxiety about giving up farming and seeking other work was exacerbated by a sense of obligation to continue a family farm. For some men, this generated an overwhelming sense of self-doubt and failure.

> "If my grandfather and my father could make a go of it, how can I let this farm go?"

> "This farm belonged to my mother's father, and to his mother's father before that. Am I wrong to be selling off some of the land now?"

> "Not everyone is going out. Some of the farms around here are doing OK. So what's the matter with me? What am I doing wrong?"

For farm men as well as women, the questions and decisions about whether to keep the farm or how to alter individual economic roles to enable them to keep the farm are far more substantial than a mere "career change" or "mid-life crisis" that many Americans now take for granted. Precisely because they never expected to have to make any major changes at this point in life, it seemed to many farm people to be wrong to even have to think about it. Many of them had not done this kind of thinking until absolutely forced by financial circumstances to do so.

THE CRISIS RECEDES—FOR NOW

The farm financial problems of the mid-1980s hit unevenly in the rural Northeast, both spatially and temporally. Even within New York State or a single county, there was considerable variation in the extent to which dairy farms were in trouble. In the three counties studied, local Extension agents estimated that about one-third of farmers were not in serious financial trouble during the 1980s. In fact, some farm operations weathered the decade reasonably well and a few quite profitably, though not without strain. If 1986 was bad for many local farmers, 1987 was somewhat better. Some of the same farmers who had barely held on now expressed a little carefully hedged optimism as the debt problem and the cost-price squeeze let up a little, partly because midwestern grain prices remained low. For a few farmers, 1987 was one of the best years since the 1970s.

Then came summer 1988. As the year began, agricultural economists were already forecasting a tight year in the dairy business, with high operating costs and a further drop in milk prices. Then came the drought of 1988 and the heat, which lowered milk production and raised the cost of feed grains purchased from the Midwest. But, as is inherently the case in agriculture, one year's drought may be followed by the next year's deluge: The spring of 1989 brought so much rain that in some areas farmers could not get their corn planted. By the end of 1989, the good news was that milk prices had made a substantial gain. Like the weather, though, milk prices are apt to change.

It is widely predicted by local farm and Extension people, as well as by local auctioneers, veterinarians, and equipment dealers, that farm attrition will resume. More farms are expected to go out in the next few years, some of them farms that just barely hung on through the years of the farm crisis, some of them farms that were propped up by off-farm income, or given a temporary reprieve by a moratorium on Farmers' Home Administration foreclosures. Even some of the financially healthy farms are likely to go out in the near future as many of the problems that make farming difficult in this area are getting worse now because of changes in the regional and local economies. Almost universally in all three counties, farmers report increasing difficulty getting and keeping good labor, a problem that will only grow worse, spurred by the major decrease in local unemployment rates in all of these areas. Rising property assessments and tax rates, despite inclusion in special agricultural districts, threaten some farms. Increased costs for energy and other farm inputs add more stress. And of course old age, failing health, lack of a willing successor in the family, and the inevitable barn fires are closing out some operations and will continue to do so.

Thus, there may be a second wave of farm exits, less dramatic, but inexorable. The ultimate disposition of their lands, whether for dairying or some other kind of farming, for recreation development, or just for turning into brush and forest, will have a considerable effect on the physical landscape and the agricultural complexion of the county. Like aftershocks of an earthquake, these later farm failures shake local communities, reminding them again of their vulnerability to economic forces beyond their control, and of the fragility of their agrarian identity.

CHAPTER THREE

Community Impacts:
The Special Significance
of Dairy Farm Losses

The years of high-level farm stress and the loss of a large number of dairy farms affected communities as well as individual farm families. The community-level impacts included not only economic effects but social and cultural effects as well. Some impacts were apparent early but were relatively short-lived; others lagged considerably behind the farm crisis itself but were longer-lasting and significant.

> One farmer, who is also a town supervisor, responded to my probe as follows: "It's hard to record the effect of farms going out on our community. The government won't be able to measure the effect statistically. All the government can do is count the numbers of farms that go out—and even that they don't do too well. But this doesn't tell the whole story. There are eight farms that went out in this township this year—and the year's not over yet. But the effect of that on the community will be delayed."

Using the same three counties in upstate New York where farm research was conducted, this chapter explores aggregate-level effects that local farm problems had on the economic, social, and cultural well-being of rural communities.

IMPACTS OF THE FARM CRISIS
ON COMMUNITY ECONOMIES

Officially, agriculture is listed as the state's number-one industry; and over half of the agriculture production (56 percent) is in dairy products. The remaining commodities include a broad mixture: Roughly 15 percent is in other livestock and products (including cattle, eggs, hogs, poultry, and sheep), and then under 10 percent each in vegetable crops, field crops, fruit crops, and greenhouse and nursery crops. On the state level the dairy industry remains important and strong, but on the local or county level there is considerable variation. The long-term trend, hastened by the farm crisis and likely to continue in the future, has been that dairy farming is becoming more concentrated within a few regions of the state and, within those regions, becoming increasingly concentrated in fewer and larger farms. The contrasts between counties are quite dramatic: Allegany, ranking about twenty-fifth out of fifty counties producing milk, borders on Wyoming, the state's second-highest milk-producing county, where nearly three times as much milk is produced on almost exactly the same number of farms. In the three counties where farm research was conducted, there was little slippage in total milk production levels or in each county's share of the state's dairy production.

Economic impacts of the farm crisis were cushioned in New York by the state's diverse rural economy, which absorbed farm closings more readily than was the case in the highly agricultural portions of the Corn Belt and Great Plains, where more that 200 counties depend on farming and ranching for nearly half of all earnings (Petrulis and Green 1986, p. 205). In rural New York the farm crisis had a more self-contained economic impact because agriculture plays a considerably smaller role in employment, business, and land use.

The employment role of agriculture in New York is relatively minor: Only 5 percent of the work force is regularly employed in agriculture (Eberts 1984, p. 54). The highest county levels of agricultural employment stand at 16.6 percent and 13.1 percent, but in most of the state's forty-four rural counties, the percentage is under 10. In the three counties where the farm crisis was studied, 1980 figures showed a labor force in primary industries (mostly agriculture) of 6.3 percent in Allegany, 7.2 percent in Chenango, and 9.6 percent in Delaware (Eberts 1984, pp. 387, 391, and 395). The typical farm in these counties has only one or at most two year-round employees, and very few farms still employ three or four people. Thus, the effect of the farm crisis on a county's overall unemployment rate would be quite minimal, even when 7 percent of its farms went out in a single year.

Certain localities and certain people, however, did suffer employment dislocation during the farm crisis. In townships where agriculture employs more than 20 percent of the work force, employment effects were particularly serious. The most vulnerable people in these places were farmhands, men who have traditionally spent a lifetime circulating from one farm to another as herdsmen or general farm laborers. Their positions became even less secure in the 1980s, as family farms tried to get by without the hired man or went out of business entirely. A few larger farms that went under displaced several employees. During the farm crisis years, some hired men and their families moved more frequently among a diminishing number of farm labor jobs. Those who lost jobs lost their housing, too, as well as such other noncash benefits as milk, firewood, and the use of a farm truck. Their lack of other skills made these "dairy migrants" difficult to place in nonfarm jobs without considerable job-training and job-seeking assistance.

Dislocation of farm women was also more serious than farm employment statistics indicate. Farm wives who work full time on the farm as part of informal family arrangements are not counted as "employed" on the farm, so when their farms were sold, these women were not officially counted as casualties of the farm crisis. But in fact, if not in statistics, there were numerous dislocated workers among farm women.

Although regular employment in agriculture is quite limited, in some areas there is additional seasonal agricultural work, using both local labor and migrant laborers who come in from elsewhere for harvesting apples, grapes, beans, and other vegetables. In this migrant labor there is now a trend away from local and out-of-state labor to foreign labor. For example, in Franklin County in summer 1988, two large former dairy farms that are now growing spinach and broccoli offered field labor jobs at $3.85 an hour for weeding, tending, and picking. By summer 1989, these farms were hiring Haitian migrant labor. Elsewhere in the state, apple growers have supplemented or replaced traditional Florida pickers with foreign laborers.

The effect of the farm crisis on agriculture-related businesses in these counties was mixed but overall not severe or long-lasting. Farm implement dealers and feed mills suffered the greatest attrition, but even these businesses were affected more by long-term economic and demographic changes than by the farm crisis itself. In one county, a 1987 Extension survey showed that despite some loss and consolidation, local agribusiness as a whole was still quite strong. Many agriculture-related business firms compensated for losses in farm business by making gains in serving or selling to the nonfarm sector. Suppliers of agricultural commodities adapted to new consumers by downsizing their products or services. A firm's name may change from "farm supply" to "farm and garden supplies," a transformation demonstrated by the merchandise on display in front of the building: Garden tractors may now outnumber and outsell farm tractors by at least four to one. At the county fairs, too, the displays of "rural-living equipment" from log splitters to lawn mowers, from wood stoves to water softeners, have grown faster than agricultural machinery displays. "Weekend farmers" sporting clean, new John Deere hats may inspect and climb on the big green tractors at the fair, but they don't buy. Even this shift, however, has not been entirely unhealthy for implement dealers if they could move into other market niches or otherwise diversify.

> The president of a large, independent regional feed and supplies dealer expressed optimism: "Recreational farming," as he termed it, now constitutes the fastest-growing part of his business in number of customers and in profits, if not in volume. He is erecting a new retail store to cope with the large increase in pet care products, lawn and garden items, and hardware.

> In another community, a lumber and hardware dealer now sells mostly to homeowners and contractors, not to farmers because, as he says, "There aren't many farmers, and the farmers still in business are not building now anyway." His newest specialty line is precut logs for log cabins for the recreational- or vacation-home market

Employment in farm-related businesses and services has decreased or remained stagnant. In the past, men who have given up farming, women who have taken off-farm jobs, and sons who chose not to take over a family farm have gravitated to jobs connected to the agricultural sector, including sales and services to farms, such as selling farm implements or insurance, or giving technical advice to other farmers as an employee of Extension or some other agricultural agency. Now, however, the pool of farm-related jobs is shrinking as a result of farm consolidation, loss of farms, and the straitened circumstances of remaining farmers, who buy less insurance and purchase fewer new implements. At the same time, more farm men and women are seeking off-farm jobs, so there is more competition for a reduced number of farm-related jobs.

The effect of farm loss on the financial and other professional services used by farmers, such as lawyers, bankers, and accountants, appears to have been rather minimal in the three counties, as these specialists serve a large and varied clientele, of which farmers make up only a small fraction. Furthermore, even if the number of farm clients has declined, the amount of business generated by each remaining farm has increased in recent years of complex farm finance and increasing farm size.

Land-use patterns, land prices, and property taxes have been affected differently in different counties. Although agriculture still remains the primary active use of the land in much of rural New York, and farmland still constitutes the majority of the property-tax base in many counties, both land-use and land-taxation patterns are changing rapidly. However, this is a complex phenomenon involving not only the farm crisis but, more importantly, new markets for rural land, especially for residential and recreational uses.

In sum, the economic impact of the farm crisis in New York was diffused in a diversified economy. At the state level, the rather limited effects of farm losses were absorbed by a diversified economy that was benefiting from urban recovery after the recession of the early 1980s. In counties that were suffering economic trouble at the time of the farm crisis, it was not farm losses that put them on shaky ground but manufacturing losses, factory closings sending local unemployment figures into the high teens.

SOCIAL IMPACTS OF FARM FINANCIAL PROBLEMS

In the social sphere, community-level impacts of the farm crisis may have been greater than in the economic, though again mixed and not entirely negative. The social impacts were quite subtle, as indicated by one farm wife.

"Our closest neighbor just sold his cows. I look over at night now and I see no lights in my neighbor's barn. I like my farming neighbors, and I feel diminished as they go out. Maybe that's just a woman's emotional feeling. But we have had so many shared struggles and shared joys. There's a sadness now. It seems like our whole neighborhood's going out of farming. It changes the character of our neighborhood."

Impacts on Formal Social Organization

During the difficult years of 1985 through 1987, some of the formal social groups and organizations in these rural communities were seriously affected by the stresses on local farmers. Traditionally, members of farm families have been active in community social organizations of all types, in local governing bodies, in local churches, and especially in the many community organizations that are farm based—Grange, Extension, Farm Bureau, the Holstein Club, the milk cooperative, and the local boards of governmental agricultural committees, such as Farmers' Home Administration, to mention just a few. The sheer number of farm-based organizations is itself indication of the importance of farming in the social life of the community. In these difficult years, participation by farm families decreased somewhat because they lacked the time, money, and energy, or because they didn't want to reveal their farm problems to others. Young farm couples, among those most affected by the cost-price squeeze, were unable to join the groups that their parents' generation had always participated in, a withdrawal that was troubling to both generations.

"The Farm Bureau and Grange used to be very active. They're down to just a few people now, mostly older people. If we lose these organizations, we lose our social life in this community. And we lose farm power in the county, too. Those organizations used to be pretty influential around here."

"The young farm wives don't come to Extension meetings any more: They can't afford a babysitter. Or they're working so hard on the farm since they let the hired man go, they simply don't have the time to do committee work or to volunteer for us. Or they're working off the farm, and still trying to put in some time on the farm too—and they're simply too tired to go to programs and meetings."

"My husband was in the fire department, but he's not anymore. We used to be in two or three farm organizations, like Farm Bureau and the milk co-op. But we're just too busy and too tired of rushing to get there. You're not feeling good about yourself because your own operation is not doing well. So you isolate yourself—even though that's probably just what you shouldn't do. You avoid groups so that you don't have to feel bad about yourself. If you do go to a meeting, you don't open your mouth—and everyone else is bragging about their milk production or how tall their corn is. But why go if you can't open your mouth? So next time you don't go."

The stress on farms and withdrawal of some families from farming had noticeable short-term effects on farm-based organizations for youth, but these organizations responded creatively to keep youngsters involved and to surmount the growing difficulty of enlisting farm parents as volunteers to run youth groups.

The 4-H dairy clubs lost members, in one county sliding from 125 to 75 youngsters in the Holstein Junior Club in just four years, with the biggest drop from 1986 to 1988. The proportion of total 4-H members in dairy groups declined markedly. Numbers of dairy exhibitors in the county fairs also declined. However, with state Extension encouragement, local 4-H programs are adjusting to new community situations and needs, new clientele, and new pressures by modifying and consolidating dairy programs and by diversifying overall programming to appeal to a wider range of interests in the community. In some counties, 4-H is now doing more of its youth work in already existing settings and groups, such as classrooms and library story hours, and on a one-time-only basis rather than in sustained, regular meetings. Family-oriented projects that don't require a club are also becoming more standard.

In a similar way, Future Farmers of America (FFA), nationally as well as at the local level, is now focusing its appeal and activities on youth who are probably not future farmers at all, or even future operators of agriculture-related businesses. Instead of farm animals and tractors, the emphasis now is on public speaking, leadership training, and computer skills. As the teenage president of one of New York's FFA districts insisted, "It's not just farming."

Inevitably, changes in local agribusiness have affected the formal organizational life of the community, but this is not specifically a result of the farm crisis. The feed mills and farm stores have usually been stalwart contributors to local agricultural clubs, organizations, and activities such as Extension, 4-H, and FAA, as well as churches and Little League teams. When one such firm closes, other firms or branches elsewhere in the region may be able to provide adequately for local feed or supply needs, but they do not fill the vacuum in terms of local community roles, especially the local leadership roles that had been filled by owners and managers of local firms. Bank mergers may have similar leadership impacts by limiting discretion of local branch banks to make public-service contributions of time, talent, and money.

On balance, though, it appears that the formal social sector in three counties where dairy farms were under stress or failing was not seriously threatened by the farm crisis. The impact of farm problems was limited, even self-limiting, rather than major and self-propelling. Formal social institutions have been modified in their operation or their appeal, to retain members and even gain new replacements to make up for losses. Some of these organizations have survived by becoming less dairy-oriented. Even the New York State Grange, which dwindled to 28,000 members in 1988, from 143,000 in 1951, now formally states that it is "no longer just for farmers," but "dedicated to preservation of rural lifestyle and environment" (*Rural Futures*, February 1989, p. 5).

Impacts on Informal Social Interactions

The informal social interaction patterns that weave farm people together in that subset of the rural community referred to as "the farm community" were more painfully affected by the economic strain on local farms. But like the formal agriculture-related organizations, informal social patterns appear to have survived.

Because many agriculture-related businesses serve important functions in social interaction and information exchange among farmers, when these economic institutions fail or are transformed to serve other clientele, the informal social life of farmers is also affected. The feed store, for example, has traditionally served as a gathering place for local farmers, a social center in which farmers exchange information and ideas. Here farm people relate their experience with and evaluation of new feeds, pesticides, or techniques, sharing information and comparing results. As a feed store converts from serving "real farmers" to serving the more lucrative trade of homeowners and vacationers, it leaves one less gathering place for farm people. In some cases, a village coffee shop may take up the slack, becoming a daily gathering place for farmers at about the time they finish morning chores.

Much farm-to-farm socializing takes place at crop demonstration days, auctions, cattle shows, in formal meetings of farm organizations, and in loose "clubs" of farm people. Most of the farm groups have been able to survive the loss of some members and integrate new people who have recently entered farming locally. But some groups suffered, especially during the tense summer of 1986, in the period of the federal herd buyout, as some farm operators felt edgy and were wary of having others know their business and their bids.

One group's informal evening "meeting" began in the living room of that month's host family as four couples drifted in, the men's hair still wet from their post-milking shower and with much joshing about the unaccustomed cleanness of the men's clothing. Informal conversation went on a couple of hours, mostly about crops, about how the cows were doing, and about other farmers: "Did you see the junk hay they baled over at the four-corners?" Mixed in were reports of local happenings, rumors of political doings in the county seat, and conversation about schools, taxes, and new neighbors. Later, everyone moved into the dining room for coffee and dessert, many selections of hearty fare, until they broke up shortly before midnight.

One informal Young Farmers' Group that had originally started under the Farm Bureau and then taken off on its own, had only four families out of its original fifteen still in dairy farming. As a key member reported, "three out of those four, including us, are highly stressed." During the difficult spring of 1986, while members had been making and implementing their painful decisions to get out of farming, the topics of conversation when the group met had changed from corn crops and calving to school programs and college bills—anything to avoid talking about their farms. That summer the group never managed to get together at all.

THE DEEPER IMPACTS:
EFFECTS ON RURAL IDENTITY

Because New York's rural communities have diversified economies and social and institutional structures based less on agriculture than on other activities, one might then dismiss the farm problems as affecting only individual farm families, only a small minority of the population, but not the overall rural community. Certainly, in comparison to the stark realities of rural ghost towns in the Midwest, the economic and social effects of the dairy farm crisis on rural communities in New York appeared to be relatively small and somewhat muted. And yet, in the three counties discussed here, as well as most of the rest of the dozen counties in which research was conducted, the farm problem was very much on many people's minds. People talked of the farm crisis; people knew of farms that had recently gone out and were disturbed about what they perceived happening to and on farms. More than that, many people in these rural areas felt that the crisis that was happening *on* local farms was also happening *to* local communities. In deeper, more subtle ways, the farm crisis for these rural communities represented a cultural crisis, a crisis of rural identity.

Community Self-Perception:
"Agriculture Is Number One Here—Or Is It?"

"This is farming country."

"This is dairy country."

"Agriculture is our backbone."

These phrases came up over and over again in interviews with a wide cross-section of farm and nonfarm rural people. The statements were made emphatically, usually at the start of an interview and usually in response to my broad question of "Tell me about your community" (or "Tell me about this county"). But most who used such phrases were not at all specific about what they meant by the claim. After a while, I began to ask, "What do you mean?" "In what way is agriculture number one here?" "Could you talk about that?"

My prompting for specificity usually provoked a long silence, stroking the beard or running fingers through the hair, a shift in sitting position, reflecting not so much physical discomfort as mental discomfort about having to explain an assumption that everyone (with the exception of this probing anthropologist) takes for granted. After a bit of thinking, the answer most people gave was "Well, now that you ask, I guess I don't really know."

The president of a large family-owned feed and seed business seemed somewhat taken aback at first, then attempted to put his thoughts into words. "I use the phrase 'Agriculture is number one in this county' all the time," he admitted. "But I do have trouble with it. I don't really know *what* it means. Is it the value of products? Well, the local agricultural industry turns over $250 million annually—that's agricultural products and money generated in the community through farm purchases of other goods and services. But the factory in town produces at least that much in products—and it pays hundreds of employees as well. Certainly most residents of this county don't work on farms—or even in farm-related businesses. So how *is* agriculture really number one? I don't really know."

A county tax officer said emphatically, "Agriculture is *not* number one in this county. But many people still believe it is, even though that hasn't been true for years."

"Agriculture is number one here" is simply an undefined, unquestioned article of faith, an assumption that most people feel should not be questioned and needs no discussion. In fact, the uneasiness with my questions and the difficulty in providing a specific answer to my probes revealed the changing role of agriculture in rural communities. If many people were unclear on what role agriculture really does play in their locality, they seemed certain that the role has been diminishing gradually over the decades but much faster in recent years. However, what they talked about was not the economic impact of farm loss but the effect on "farming communities," the change from a farming community to a nonfarm community, a long-term change that had recently speeded up.

"Years ago, every farm in this township was operating. Gradually some of the old farms went out, so there were only a few left. Suddenly, the rest of them are going fast. Now, along this road between our place and the town line, there's not one farm shipping milk. At this point, I'd have to say we have become a nonfarm community."

"My family may be the last family to farm here. And if we go out, that's the end. Of course, there will still be people living around here. We'll stay. And people are coming in and buying up old farmhouses, fixing them up so they look nice, staying in them summers and weekends or even year-round. But those people don't really farm. They won't be able to keep the rural areas the same because the backbone of the community is gone; the family farm is gone."

A farm woman, using the same metaphor, said, "Agriculture is the backbone of this county. Now it's being cut out. It's a great loss. When you take away the *farming*, even though there are people still *living* there, it's not the same."

The Cultural Importance of Farming

In these three counties, research revealed that the most significant impact of farm losses—but the hardest to measure—has come in the form of an assault on community identity and self-image. Anxiety about the farm crisis was rooted in the ideational or cultural role of dairying as central to the definition of "who we are." "Agriculture is number one here" is, above all, a cultural belief rather than an economic statement.

Residents of these rural counties, including people with no firsthand contact with commercial farming, expressed real concern about the rapid loss of farms; the difficulty facing farmers was a topic of ready conversation. There was widespread local awareness of farm-number counts and although the figures people mentioned may not have been precise or accurate, residents talked readily of the numbers of farm sales, auctions, and bankruptcies. The declining farm count served in people's minds as an index of the farm crisis, a measure of both the problem and the local anxiety level. Importantly, though, concern was expressed not only for the individuals and families who were having difficulty but also for the *collective* problem of loss of active farms in the community: People were concerned about loss of farming itself, as central to local life. What they were sensing, though few put it into these words, was the loss of farming in its sociocultural role, as the basis of local identity.

Undergirding the cultural importance of agriculture in defining the community—and the severity of the assault on community self-image as farms rapidly went out—is that the farms and farmers in a community include not only commercial farms but also many "noncommercial" farms: backyard farms, part-time farms, or retirement farms, and the many small, marginal farms where older people still keep a small herd and a few beef cattle. As close as it can be reckoned at the start of this decade, only about 4 or 5 percent of residents in these three counties lived on commercial farms (officially defined as generating over $40,000 in income annually), but for every two commercial farms there were at least three or four small farms that did not regularly sell much of anything, that may not have made much money or may have consistently lost money. Thus, many people in each county were—and remain today, even after the difficult years of the mid-1980s—self-proclaimed "farmers," by sentiment if not by income or government designation. Many other residents not in farming at all had relatives, neighbors, or friends in farming. It is the number of people with an attachment to farming, not simply the number of commercial dairy establishments or the dollar value of their farm products, that generates the agrarian mind-set of these communities.

The cultural importance of farming has spatial and temporal dimensions. Farms are part of the cognitive landscape as well as the physical landscape. The most common local geographical referents and landmarks are farms and farm buildings. People typically give road directions in terms of farms: "Go down the tar road about a mile till you see the big white barn with the two blue silos. Then take the dirt road on your right up a steep hill to our farm. You'll see the red barn just beside the road." Farming activities also mark the times of day and seasons of the year. Rainy days during haying time or lack of rainfall when the corn should be germinating are mentioned with anxiety and concern by many residents who are not themselves in farming; people simply know what these seasons are and what activities and conditions they imply. Even the daily round is something that the community takes for granted: The need for a farmer to "get home in time for milking" is recognized throughout the community. The rituals and ceremonies of the annual calendar, for some climaxed in the local agricultural fair, are known countywide.

Why the Farm Crisis Loomed So Large in Local Perceptions

On the regional level, for the Northeast as a whole, researchers have found no evidence to support the notion that there has been "any dramatic relative or absolute deterioration of the socioeconomic well-being of the rural population that might be attributable to adverse impacts of farm structural change on rural communities" (Buttel et al. 1988, p. 212). Indeed, research in three counties has demonstrated that neither the local economies nor the local social organization sustained much permanent damage as a result of the farm crisis. Nonetheless, because of the cultural importance of farming, the farm crisis created a great deal of local anxiety and has had some longer-term effects in terms of loss of rural and community identity.

One cause of heightened anxiety was that local farm problems were becoming evident just after a peak of national media concentration and public concern about the farm crisis in the Midwest. The collective mind already had the images and vocabulary of farm families suffering the crisis, of suicides and broken marriages, of bankers and other farm lenders foreclosing against helpless farmers. Into this media-formed awareness of a distant problem suddenly there came the close-to-home realities of local dairy farms in trouble, of pastures sprouting a new crop of "For Sale" signs, of local newspaper columns filled with ads for farm auctions and machinery sales. And it all appeared to happen so fast. In fact, the loss of farms was especially noticed because there had been a slowdown of exits from farming all through the 1970s, making the speedup of farm exits in the 1980s seem even greater than it actually was.

A thoughtful farmer commented, "All this has been going on a long time, really. But it's scary now because it is happening so fast, too fast for economic and social adjustments. For the first time in this community, we aren't sure what kind of a future we're going to have here."

Local concern with the farm crisis was also heightened by an effect of scale. In the past, when there were over 800 commercial farms in a county, the loss of ten farms was not a major shock. But as the farm count in a county sank to 500 in 1980 and down below 350 by 1988, if ten of the remaining farms go out in the next year, the impact is considerably greater, for it is ten removed from a smaller total. The loss of each farm now may leave a bigger hole in the local farm picture. Furthermore, some of the farms that went out in the mid-1980s represented not just a single farm, but the combination of several previously separate small farms. So a farm loss in the 1980s might really represent the loss of three or four farms in terms of acreage, number of cows, milk production, farm buildings on the landscape, and employment possibilities. And many of the farm losses of the 1980s are likely to be irrevocable, as not all farms that go out nowadays are sold or rented to another person who will continue to operate a farm there. When a farmer goes out of business now, the land might be sold to a developer to subdivide for fifty vacation homes—thus resulting in a much more significant change than simply turnover of farm ownership.

In Chenango County, of the twenty-one farms that went out of business in the first half of 1988, only three had dairy operations on them in 1989.

Local perception of the farm problem *as crisis* was also heightened because the pattern of farms that were in financial trouble contradicted past experience and current expectations. It was bewildering to find that the farm in most serious trouble now was not the old out-of-date, marginal-soil hill farm operated by a couple in their seventies whose sons had long since moved away, but rather the modern operation, perhaps on good soils in the river valley, owned and run by a good farmer, an educated farmer, a young man still in his prime. (Similarly, in the midwestern crisis, the crop farmers who went under were predominantly among the more educated, more modern, more highly capitalized younger farmers of the region. Murdock and Leistritz 1988, Otto 1985a.) The shock of "a good farmer" going out is a deep one because it violates local assumptions about who "fails" in farming and who is expected to do well. This inversion of the collective understanding of "the way things are supposed to be" made the farm crisis more frightening.

Farm losses also loomed large in local perception because they are so visible. Farms, farm operators, and farm families are visible in the sense of cows in the fields, tractors on the hillsides, and human activity around the roadside barns. When activity ceases, other people notice. Farm exits are also visible socially in that many farm family members are respected members of the community, active in community affairs, and part of the community identity as "an agricultural county." Community residents, both farm people and nonfarm people, know them and notice what happens to them. Diminution in the number of farming families, even if the total milk output and sales receipts in the county remain stable, is perceived locally as diminution of "the farm community." Because of these perceptions, a period that economists have labeled only as "agricultural restructuring" or a "farm problem" was interpreted locally as "the farm crisis."

Perhaps more than anything else, the farm crisis loomed large in local minds because it was occurring at the same time many other major economic, demographic, and institutional changes were sweeping through rural communities. There was a greater penetration of changes from outside, from the urban areas and the society as a whole, but the farm crisis was the most easily verbalized of the changes. It was simply easier for local people to think about and talk about "the farm crisis" than to define or discuss other broad-scale changes. To some extent, "the farm crisis" became the symbol of what was happening, the symptom of what was wrong, and, in some minds, the cause of all the other perceived changes in rural communities. Ironically, perhaps, in this process the residents of rural areas differed little from the general American public in the belief that the problem in rural America was the farm problem, and that "doing something about the farm problem" would fix rural America. Blaming the farm crisis for all the changes and problems people perceived, however, was a faulty diagnosis; and a faulty diagnosis will surely give rise to faulty prescriptions for what to do to help rural communities survive.

To understand what is happening in and to rural communities in the present time, then, it is necessary to understand the wide range of other changes, in addition to agricultural change and farm loss, that are occurring at the same time. A good starting point, closely linked to agricultural change, is change in the nonfarm rural economy.

PART TWO

Shifting
Nonfarm Economies

CHAPTER FOUR
Paradox in Rural Economies: Vigor and Vulnerability

The farm crisis, of course, did not happen in an economic vacuum; it occurred within and as part of a larger context of changing rural and national economies. In fact the nonfarm sector of rural economies was in greater flux in the 1980s, and in deeper difficulty, than was the agricultural sector. The nonfarm economy of rural New York, with its tight connection to regional urban centers and hence to the globalized national economy, was experiencing significant changes that reverberated through small communities. The focus in this chapter and the next is on the nonfarm economic trends that affected rural communities and on problems these changes caused on the local level.

The nonagricultural sector of rural economies in New York and the Northeast was buffeted by the early 1980s recession but has made substantial improvement since then. By most indicators recovery has been stronger in the rural Northeast than in the urban Northeast or the remaining rural areas of the nation (Deavers 1988, p. 1). But this recovery, which some state officials exuberantly referred to as "resurgence," also contained troublesome weaknesses that showed up more as time passed. And recovery was uneven, with certain populations and localities definitely left behind. The tenuous economic position of some localities, however, was obscured by aggregate figures showing that overall each county or state in the region was better off in the late 1980s than earlier in the decade.

In order to explore aspects of the rural nonfarm economy more fully, the geographic scope of research was expanded beyond the original three core research counties where the farm crisis was studied to include Franklin County in the northern Adirondacks as a fourth core research county and, to a lesser extent, three of its neighbors, Clinton and Essex counties in the northeastern tip of the state and St. Lawrence to the west of Franklin (see Map 1.2). Vignettes of these North Country counties illustrate the paradox of vigor and vulnerability.

A CASE ILLUSTRATION: CHANGES AND CONTRADICTIONS IN THE NORTH COUNTRY

Brief Recent History of a Depressed Rural Region

The North Country, the northern tip of the state that includes and surrounds the Adirondacks, is an area widely known for both its mountainous beauty and its depressed economy. Counties in the North Country have perennially been at or near the top of most indicators of economic distress in rural New York, often having the highest unemployment and poverty rates in the entire state. The region's desperate economic position was catapulted into national attention at the Democratic National Convention in San Francisco in 1984, when Governor Mario Cuomo made a nominating speech in which he called attention to "the abject poor of Essex County in New York." Too mountainous for much agriculture, Essex County had lost its core industry, iron mining, in the early 1970s. In one township, "a community of over 5,000 population lost its livelihood. Primary jobs were lost by the closing of the mines, and secondary jobs in the retail and service sectors were lost as businesses failed" (Essex County 1988). After unemployment benefits ran out, there was simply no way to make money in the stagnant local economy, and no place to go: In 1975 transfer payments supplied nearly a quarter of personal income in the county. At about the same time, several communities in the county lost paper mills that had been important in the local economy. Because these mills were small, obsolete, or environmentally unsound, some were closed or were purchased by larger firms and then later closed. Essex County experienced a minor economic boom in connection with the 1980 Winter Olympics in Lake Placid, but after that came a bust and more discouragement. During the recession periods of the early 1980s, month after month the unemployment figures documented the poor performance of the local economy.

Other counties of the North Country, similarly depressed for many years, fared no better than Essex in the early 1980s and were slow to improve after that. In Franklin County, the situation still remained bleak after the rest of the state had already moved into recovery. High unemployment and poverty figures continued, seasonally exacerbated by the North Country wintertime unemployment, which is only slightly mitigated in winter resort towns. As late as autumn 1986, the picture still looked grim. Local figures that fall reported that the labor force of over 21,000 in September shrank by 800 in October and another 300 in November, a 5 percent drop in two months, even before winter set in. The opening of 300 new jobs in services and trade had been more than offset by the closing of one of the few factories that had employed over 200 workers and the closing of several small manufacturing firms. Other plants were expecting phase-downs. The county's jobless rate notched up from second highest in the state, at 9.2 percent, to highest, 11.9 percent.

> "Franklin County *defines* itself as one of the leaders of the state in poverty and unemployment," said a county development leader. "This is part of the county's image of itself. And the numbers support the image."

Residents of these counties carried on with their time-honored "make-do" strategies of getting by as best they could, combining a variety of informal economic strategies for supplementing employment income and procuring goods and services on a noncash basis. But the continued gloomy economic reports from the North Country, long after other areas of the state were recovering from the recession, caused outsiders to wonder whether the time had come to give up on the region, for local people to leave, and for the rest of the state to abandon any thought of economic recovery in the north. Then gradually, slowly, and quietly the North Country, too, began to turn around economically.

"A Whole New Mood of Optimism" Sweeps the North Country

By summer 1988 the North Country was in the midst of a major economic turnaround and was exuding an unprecedented optimism. In St. Lawrence County, another new state prison was opening up. In neighboring Clinton County, the city of Plattsburgh seemed a veritable construction site, with expensive motels and shopping malls expanding right out into the open country. In Essex County there was jubilation that their proposal for an "economic development zone (EDZ)" had been funded by the state, one of the few rural proposals to win funding. (Plattsburgh in Clinton also hooked an EDZ that year, but its proposal was entirely for an urbanized area.) The Essex proposal included ambitious plans for a broad range of infrastructure and economic development, centering in the very township so hard hit by the loss of iron mines. The general upswing in the North Country was succinctly captured by the commissioner of social services in one county. Citing the steady decline in welfare caseloads since 1985 and the greatly improved employment picture, he talked not just of the statistics but also of an attitude change in the county: "It's a whole new mood of optimism."

As if to add icing to the cake, a new "comprehensive strategic plan for economic development in the North Country" had just been released by the state Urban Development Corporation, and an entity entitled Development Authority of the North Country (DANC) was created. Broad goals were set up: to improve job opportunities; to attract and retain young, educated people; to diversify the region's economic base; and—withall—to "preserve the unique North Country physical environment and quality of life" (New York State Department of Economic Development 1988, p. 7). A master plan included proposals to accomplish these goals, and outlined initiatives that "will help spur new opportunities and resurgence in the North Country."

In this economic upsurge, no northern county seemed to have come up farther and faster than Franklin County, although as one local official remarked, "For us, there was nowhere to go but up."

In Franklin County in summer 1988, all economic indicators looked positive, and local spirits were up; there was a bustle of local activity, a good deal of construction, and a confidence about the future. Unemployment statistics had been marching quite steadily downward since 1986. In November 1987 the work force was expanding, and unemployment had reached 7.5 percent, "the lowest it has been for that month during the fourteen years that local unemployment records have been kept." New jobs were opening up and few were being closed out. In the preceding twelve months, 1,400 new jobs had been created, including 400 in manufacturing, 300 in service and government, and 100 in construction and trade. Headlines in local papers promised "Brighter Franklin winter jobs picture expected" and exclaimed over the double success of reduction in welfare rolls and unemployment rates. True, there were still seasonal problems: Unemployment returned to 11.5 percent in January 1988. But more new firms were opening up, a major employer was shortening its usual Christmas inventory shutdown, one clothing manufacturing company that had shut down in 1987 was being reorganized and revived, and new construction projects, including a hospital addition, county offices, and housing, were bringing some people back to work early from winter slow periods.

After the winter slack period, spring 1988 unemployment quickly went back down to single-digit numbers, 8.9 percent for March and down to 6.2 percent in April. In this new job situation, new training programs, conducted cooperatively by state and local agencies and employers, helped put to work people who might otherwise have been "unemployable," thus further reducing the welfare rolls as these newly trained workers picked up their first jobs. Capping it all and fueling the optimism was the dynamism of the county's "growth industry," the state prisons. One correctional facility had already opened, taking up some of the slack of people out of work; a second was under construction and due to open soon and would actually add to local jobs with a variety of employment opportunities. Predictions were that as small businesses continued to expand and the prison added new jobs, the effect would reach all the way down to people currently on public assistance, who would move into the jobs vacated by people who got better jobs in the expanding economy. Everyone on the economic ladder would move up at least one rung. In July 1988 the unemployment figures for May were released: an almost unbelievable 5.8 percent figure, heralded in local reports with boldface print and exclamation points. County officials and economic development enthusiasts exuded satisfaction.

With all these signs of economic turnaround and community confidence, it seemed that perhaps, at long last, the North Country's age-old problem of poverty might also, finally, have been turned around. Perhaps the rising economy of the North Country was lifting the entire population.

A Look at the Down Side

Further research in these counties in that exuberant summer of economic recovery revealed some contradictions and some concerns. Digging deeper into local material and broadening the range of people interviewed led to some startlingly different impressions of what was going on.

Soon after the early, optimistic interviews, I had an opportunity to probe the other side of the picture in a group discussion. I had been asked to lead a four-county workshop for human service workers, including people from Cooperative Extension's Expanded Food and Nutrition Education Program for low-income families (EFNEP), from WIC (the federal Supplemental Nutritional Program for Women, Infants, and Children), and from programs assisting pregnant and parenting teens. I began the session by recounting to the assembled group the latest facts and figures of the North Country economy, telling of the confidence and optimism that I'd found in the entire region during recent research. I talked of new construction, of grants, of new manufacturing firms, of low unemployment and reduced welfare rolls, of more housing starts, and all the other positive economic indicators, plus the generally positive tone I'd picked up in so many interviews. As I finished recounting these positive findings, I asked the assembled group for response and discussion. They let me have it!

Around the table, counteracting comments erupted vociferously. These local human service workers, all of whom were women, had for years been spending their energies and their time—much more time than they'd been paid for in most cases—working directly with the low-income population of their counties. These workers were seeing a totally different side of North Country life. With a good deal of feeling, backed up by many close observations, they described a much less rosy picture: "Those people who gave you the glowing picture, are they ever out in the field?" "It depends on who is supplying the statistics. Some people sit in their offices and look at the numbers. We spend our time out there working directly with people." "Those who doubt there is poverty here any more should come out and see where we are working."

Their dissent from the rosy picture tumbled along at a fast pace, with nearly everyone adding her own individual perception, her observations in her own community. "The construction jobs and the prison jobs are not going to the people we work with." "There's a lot of people not on the unemployment lists who aren't even counted." "Many of the families we work with don't get counted for unemployment any more: Some have part-time jobs; some are beyond eligibility for unemployment benefits and have given up trying to get jobs." "Many of those so-called new jobs are just people being hired back. And if you didn't have the job in the first place, you won't get it now." "There's hunger now, and the social programs are running out of funds. The food pantries are running out because so many people have come—*in summer*." "Women are *wearing* their lack of nutrition—you can see it. We're seeing more kids in summer recreation who have no breakfast and who seem in bad shape." "People are falling through the cracks, making just above eligibility guidelines, mostly on part-time jobs. Rents are skyrocketing, and it's hard to find a place if you have two kids. Many places are in terrible condition. Public housing does have a sliding scale of rents, but there's not enough of it and there's a huge waiting list." "The wage scale is still so low that a woman with a child or two can hardly afford to work. We had a woman on our clerical staff in the office: By the time she paid child care, she had nothing left but $50 take-home per week—she left her job and went back on public assistance."

These observations by local human service workers were real, firsthand, and disturbing. They indicate that there may be a wide and perhaps growing divergence between some communities riding a wave of economic improvement and others still back in the depths of economic problems; between some people who are becoming more affluent and others who are having an increasingly hard time climbing up to or staying above the poverty line. Despite the positive indicators, both here in the North Country and throughout rural New York, among the bolstering signs of recovery there were also some serious problems.

> As one county planner put it, "By one set of data, things are getting better. By another set of data, things are getting worse. It does seem like economic conditions are getting better: Land values have moved back up from their earlier depressed levels; there are fewer vacant stores and more new businesses; things are getting spruced up; there is more activity; houses are selling quicker. But, yes, there are other indicators that in some other respects things may be getting worse—at least for some people."

CHANGING COMPONENTS OF NEW YORK'S RURAL ECONOMIES

The complex and diversified nature of this state's rural economy makes it difficult (particularly for a noneconomist) to generalize, but at the local level the most striking characteristic of the rural county economies in this time was change. Recent and projected changes, involving the shift from goods to services and the driving force of international competition, are of such major proportions as to warrant being termed "a transformation" (Bouvier and Briggs 1988, p. 49). Reflecting national economic trends, each sector in the economies of these rural counties was itself undergoing change, and, at the same time, the relative role of each sector in the overall county economy was changing, too. To indicate what these changes look like on the local level, and to elucidate some of the underlying causes of the paradox of vigor and vulnerability, we look briefly at four sectors of local economic activity. (See Appendix Two for a summary of economic data from the four core counties.)

Lumbering, Mining, and Other Extractive Industries

No area in rural New York is presently dependent on resource extraction such as lumbering or mining as its major economic base, but these activities may compose an important part of a mixed local economy. Lumbering tends to be a sideline activity in many regions; in the North Country it is a primary, though seasonal, occupation for many men during at least some periods of their lives and is also important socio-culturally, as part of "the way of life here." In recent decades, lumbering has slumped. Many lumber and pulp mills have closed down, more raw logs are being shipped out of the area (to Canada) for being made into lumber or paper, and new regulations, including weight limits on hauling logs on public roads and environmental restrictions on forestry practices and mill effluents, have also diminished this industry locally. As in northern Michigan, commercialization of logging and the growing use of very expensive high-tech machinery have changed logging from a farmer's seasonal activity accomplished with animals or machinery already available and idle, to a corporate venture with tremendous capitalization— that has squeezed out local small-scale logging (Rieger and Schwarzweller 1988). Additionally, the rising pace of second-home development has withdrawn some forested land from use for lumbering. Another forest product activity in certain areas is maple syrup, but although the seasonal income from syruping is important at the level of the household, it does not constitute a significant share of any local economy.

Oil and gas extraction has, in the past, been important in the western part of the Southern Tier, including Allegany County, a legacy remembered in an oil museum and many oil-related place names, such as Petrolla, and Wellsville. Oil extraction had been a booming industry back in the 1930s, the genesis of much of the "old wealth," and the origin of some of the machine-manufacturing firms still in business today. The oil industry diminished considerably over the decades, revived slightly in the mid-1970s, and still makes a contribution to the local economy, providing household fuel and a source of cash for some rural families.

Mining has been important in certain regions, especially the North Country, but it, too, had already been greatly reduced by 1980. The loss of iron mining in Essex County in the mid-1970s has had serious long-run consequences. Also in Essex County, in a remote mountain area, one of the world's largest titanium mines, which once had a whole village of mining families at the edge of the pit, has for decades been scaling down toward closure by the end of the 1980s. In St. Lawrence County, loss of iron, zinc, and talc operations caused employment dislocations. Elsewhere around the state rock quarrying and sand and gravel operations provide some jobs, although land development in some areas is reducing quarry access.

Manufacturing

In the rural parts of the state as a whole, manufacturing has traditionally been a mainstay of the local economy, generally employing around 25 percent of the county work force. Rural manufacturing held fairly steady in the 1970s and through the first half of the 1980s, even while nationally and in the state's urban areas, manufacturing employment declined significantly (Bouvier and Briggs 1988, p. 50).

In 1980, manufacturing employed just over one-third of the work force (34 percent) in Chenango County, making this officially a "manufacturing de-pendent" rural county (the cutoff for this designation is 30 percent), and just over one-fourth in Allegany and Delaware (26 and 27 percent, respectively). In Franklin County in the North Country, however, only 17 percent of 1980 jobs were in manufacturing (Eberts 1984, pp. 386–405).

Manufacturing plants in the rural counties of New York vary widely in size, products, production processes, and management approaches. In the counties included in this study, it is mostly "light industry" including chemicals, pharmaceuticals, industrial machinery from aerospace components to turbines, ignition systems, clothing, shoes, health care products, calendars, cutlery, building materials, and cheese and other dairy products. Activities include plastic injection molding, skilled machine-work, metal fabrication, and a variety of sewing and assembly work, as well as equipment handling and merchandise warehouse work. The very smallest plants, of which there are many, are often family operations employing only a dozen or so people.

One example is a small foundry that makes metal patterns (forms) to be used for molding plastic blister packs for retail merchandise. It is a family business, started by the father, now run by two sons; many of the dozen skilled men it employs are relatives. Another example, in the same county, is a new firm that makes specialty tourist and seasonal gift items. It was started by a woman with a few workers in her home and then expanded into a vacant commercial building in town, with a larger, entirely female work force.

The backbone of local manufacturing in most of these counties is made up of small plants employing between twenty and 100, such as a log-home manufacturing firm, owned and operated by a local man whose family has long owned and operated a building-supply business. Mid-sized plants of a few hundred employees are less common, with some rural counties having as many as fifteen such plants and others only a half dozen. Only a very few plants in these rural counties employ over 1,000 workers.

Allegany has two large plants that together compose the bulk of its manufacturing employment; Delaware has two, located in a corner of the county and serving a three-county employment area. Chenango, where manufacturing constitutes a greater share of county employment, has approximately seventy manufacturing firms, including two large ones and a few between 500 and 1,000. Franklin County, in the North Country, has no large plants and only two mid-sized ones.

Service and Retail Trade

The service sector, including both professional and wholesale and retail trade jobs, has traditionally been the largest employment sector in these rural counties, amounting to over 60 percent in all rural counties of New York in 1970 (Buttel et al. 1988, p. 211). Statewide, growth in nonmanufacturing employment in the 1960 to 1980 period "greatly exceeded the job losses in manufacturing" (Bouvier and Briggs 1988, p. 50). By 1980 service employment in the counties included in this study ranged from 59 percent in Chenango to 77 percent in Franklin (Eberts

1984, pp. 386–405). However, further growth of the service sector and its share of total employment may be limited by the small size of the local population. It is generally the case that for rural communities with small populations, "their disadvantage in a service economy is even greater" than in a manufacturing-based economy (Flora and Flora 1988, p. 6). Although rural New York is not losing population at anywhere near the 1980s loss rate experienced in many midwestern counties, the small population may be a factor that limits further development of the local service economy. In some rural areas of New York, higher population density in any form seems unlikely, whereas in other areas a higher density of population will come only in the form of prison inmates and residents of long-term health care facilities, such as nursing homes and facilities for the developmentally disabled. Such institutionalized populations already provide a significant share of local service-sector jobs. Franklin County has both types of facilities, and they are prized as stable employers.

In the more rural counties, the service sector is heavily weighted toward the low-paying end and toward insecure retail and tourism jobs rather than the professional service jobs. The better service-sector jobs in many rural communities are with the school districts, hospitals (if they exist locally), and also local governments. These jobs may be sought after as being more secure than entrepreneurial endeavors or even manufacturing and because they provide desirable health and retirement benefits.

In the last two decades, rural communities in New York have experienced the same gradual and profound restructuring of retail trade that has occurred all across rural America: the substitution of major regional and national chains for local, main-street businesses. With their greater variety and cheaper goods, the shopping malls near the larger towns have become the preferred place for people from small towns and rural countryside to shop for food, children's clothes, household necessities, and entertainment products. Residents find that the convenience of being able to accomplish many purchases on the same trip or of being able to shop near the larger town to which they daily drive for work are attractions that the smaller retail stores of the villages simply cannot meet. This phenomenon has been studied more extensively in the rural Midwest, for example, in Iowa, where regional malls were overwhelming small-town, main-street businesses, including grocery stores (Borich et al. 1985, Stone and McConnon 1982). Researchers in rural Kansas found that the large chains "are able to use their size to advertise extremely effectively, and perhaps more importantly, they use part-time labor more effectively" (Flora and Flora 1988, p. 7). In the rural counties of New York State, shopping malls have indeed become significant employers, drawing workers from throughout the county to malls near the largest village, or to a small city in an adjacent county. The malls specialize in entry-level, low-paid, and part-time workers: teens, senior citizens, and many mothers of young children.

Reflecting this growth of suburban malls, but also tied to rural exodus and to the fact that many residents of small communities commute out to work, the number of vacant stores in small villages in rural New York has increased over recent years, though this loss is neither universal nor irreversible. Some new services and retailers have entered some vacant buildings, and new products, such as home videotapes for renting, have spawned some new retail outlets. Laundromats continue to hold strong in small towns, and the ubiquitous convenience stores providing gas, snack foods, groceries, beer, video rentals, and miscellaneous items also provide a few local jobs.

Especially in the North Country, tourism plays an important role in the overall local economy, and employment in hotel and restaurant work is significant. As in other rural resort spots around the nation, however, tourism tends to be low wage, minimal benefit, part time, and quite seasonal (Smith 1989). In the Adirondacks, there is a relatively short summer high season and a shorter winter season, with many months of dormancy in between. Jobs in resort facilities have traditionally been at entry level and have been filled mostly by women with few other job skills or opportunities, and workers have been paid accordingly. Recently, however, the improved employment picture in counties such as Franklin has made it difficult for resort employers to attract their customary labor force. Consequently, they have had to dip farther into the teenage and senior-citizen brackets, to bus workers in from farther away, and to begin offering higher wages.

Land Development

Land development has played an increasing role in some areas of rural New York, a result of push factors in urban areas, attractions of rural areas, and an excellent road network, including both interstate and state highways. Where adjacency and scenic amenities are combined, the 1980s produced high levels of land transactions, many purchases by nonresidents, steep increases in land values, and an influx of second-home vacationers and retirement people and some year-round residents. Although the land and construction boom had cooled off throughout the Northeast by 1990, its effects at the local level remain significant.

Delaware County, three hours or less from the New York–New Jersey metropolitan area, experienced a tremendous increase in nonresident property ownership—such that nearly 40 percent of all land parcels in the county now belong to nonresidents and about 54 percent of landowners are nonresident, with one township registering over 73 percent of its landowners as nonresident. Prices for rural land have climbed rapidly, even as farms were going out of business because of financial upheavals in dairying. Almost any farmer could raise cash by selling off a 5-acre piece of woodlot—or by selling the whole farm to a speculator or developer.

The development boom has boosted the price of local housing and added to local tax revenues, but it has also increased municipal service expenses. Its contribution to local employment, retail sales, and income has not been well documented. The influx has generated jobs in construction and a seasonal increase in retail sales and other service jobs, as well as part-time supplementary jobs in lawn and garden care and property patrolling for absentee owners. Retail sales have increased, but only in certain rather narrow categories: Weekenders may buy some groceries and gas, leisure items and souvenirs, but rarely purchase big-ticket items, such as cars or appliances—and, again, documentation is scarce.

Although land development may pump outside resources into a community, bringing on a construction and real estate boom, it also ties rural economies even closer to the fortunes of urban economies. The advantages may accrue mostly in times of urban prosperity, thus leaving the rural area especially vulnerable to urban economic downturns—a situation that was causing some anxiety by 1990. It is also true that land development of the vacation or retirement type may help outsiders more than local people.

RURAL ECONOMIC INDICATORS: A MIXED PICTURE

The "Generally Poor Rural Performance"

During much of the 1970s, fueled by the farm boom and the oil boom and by a new population migration pattern favoring rural areas over metropolitan, the economy of rural America had been especially robust. Following that, however, it sagged. "Measured by employment change, the poor performance of the rural economy in comparison with the metro economy during this decade is striking" (Deavers 1988, p. 1). For the news media and the public, the farm crisis was the most prominent and visible sign of difficulty in the nation's rural economy, but a greater cause of rural economic stagnation lay in downsizing of the manufacturing sector and in a further shift from manufacturing to service-sector employment, in other words, in the "restructuring of the labor force."

Although the rural Northeast has slightly outperformed the urban Northeast in employment in the late 1980s and outperformed other rural areas of the nation throughout the decade, the really significant trend is that most of the increase in employment in this decade has been low-wage employment, so that an increase in the number of jobs, often assumed to be an indicator of economic growth, does not necessarily mean a more adequately employed population. This shortcoming of the restructuring of the labor force in the 1980s obviously applies to urban jobs as well as rural jobs (Bonanno 1988, pp. 9–10; Tomaskovic-Devey 1990) but may have special salience in rural America, where better employment options for local workers are scarce. Economic analysts concluded that the effects of the recessions of the early 1980s were deeper and longer lasting in rural America (Deavers 1989a). The fragile and incomplete economic recovery is especially apparent at the local level, and despite wide variation among the research sites, some generalizations are clear. (See Appendix Two for economic data.)

Unemployment

Unemployment rates in rural counties of New York have historically been considerably higher than the state average. In 1980, unemployment rates in the counties included in this study were in the range of 7 to 12 percent, and then increased substantially during the recession, ranging from 10 to 20 percent. They started to recede in 1985 and 1986, with official unemployment rates in New York's rural counties tumbling to historic new lows by 1988. In that year, Chenango County's unemployment hit its all-time low of 3.7 percent; other counties were somewhere around 4 to 6.5 percent. However, unemployment began rising again in 1989.

In Allegany County, where manufacturing had previously been a comparatively large and stable source of employment, the unemployment rate fluctuated a great deal in the 1980s. Unemployment stood at 9.5 percent in 1980, rose to 11.7 percent because of major labor force reduction at the county's two large factories, then worked back down to a record low of 4.4 percent late in 1988, but climbed slightly through much of 1989. Even if the number of jobs was growing—indeed, setting a new record in autumn 1989 for the highest number of jobs ever counted in the county—at the same time the number of people seeking jobs was also increasing, so that the unemployment rate actually went up, although the number of registered unemployed people remained constant.

The magnitude of actual unemployment may be considerably higher than the official unemployment figures indicate: Undercount of unemployment is regarded as especially large in rural areas because they "contain disproportionately large numbers of both discouraged workers and involuntary part-time workers" (Shapiro 1989, p. 29). And unemployment among young adults remains high.

This undercount showed up on the local level, for example, in Allegany County in summer 1987, when there were 1,400 people officially counted as unemployed in the county, but at the very same time, the Private Industry Council showed 2,300 people on its computer records as wanting employment.

In Chenango County, where unemployment had come down to 7.4 percent in July 1985, the sixteen- to nineteen-year-old cohort registered an unemployment rate of 17.8 percent, (19 percent for females, 16.4 for males). In the twenty- to twenty-four-year-old cohort, unemployment was 11.7 percent (13.3 percent for males and 10.1 percent for females) (Norwich, Chenango County 1986, p. 49).

Income Levels

Rural New York has perennially had a low per capita income, relative to the rural parts of many other states and relative to the more urban parts of New York. In the rural counties of the state in 1986, the average annual labor and proprietors' earnings for a full-time worker was $17,569, which put New York in twenty-sixth place in the nation. The ratio of nonmetropolitan earnings to metropolitan earnings in New York in that year was .58, which put the state in a tie with Michigan for the highest rural-urban earnings differential in the nation (Horowitz and Dunn 1989, pp. 12–13).

> In Allegany County, per capita income in 1985 ranked the lowest of any county in the entire state, amounting to just 62 percent of the state per capita income figure. In absolute dollars, this meant that in that year, income in Allegany County reached approximately what the state level was back in 1979 (adjusted for inflation).

In the recent decade, income levels in rural counties as a group have increased more slowly than metropolitan incomes (Eberts and Khawaja 1988, pp. 9–11). Although the per capita income for the entire state showed a 1979 to 1985 increase (in adjusted dollars) of 5.6 percent, the three counties of the westernmost Southern Tier, all of them rural counties, went down. Allegany fell 2 percent, and its western neighbor, Cattaraugus, fell 2.9 percent. Thus, in a five-year period from 1981 to 1986, the "already staggering income gap" between the New York City metropolitan area and the state's most rural counties became even wider (Eberts and Khawaja 1988, p. 11).

VULNERABILITY OF RURAL MANUFACTURING

Because many rural counties are dependent on manufacturing for a quarter to a third of their employment, they are vulnerable to tighter competition in national and international markets and to new trends in corporate management style. Since 1980 the counties under study have shown a somewhat unsteady manufacturing employment, with a significant drop in manufacturing jobs starting about 1983, when some key manufacturing plants closed. Recent rehirings and even job creations or expansions in the manufacturing sector have been greatly welcomed but perceived with caution locally as possibly only temporary and also as offering lower pay than the jobs they replaced. Many local people express an insecure feeling about the continued health of the manufacturing sector and of their continued dependence on it.

> Allegany County was particularly hard hit by labor-force reductions used as a management strategy to lower production costs and meet foreign competition. Two large plants account for the bulk of manufacturing employment locally, a concentration that the county's economic development director described

as "a poorly diversified manufacturing base, dependent on a few firms which are impacted by cyclical and uncontrollable markets." Employment in the two plants together peaked in the mid-1960s around 2,500 workers, tapered off gradually, and then was cut steeply in 1983–1984, to about half of that. Since then, these companies have been adding back gradually, reaching up to about 1,700 in 1988. The turnaround reflects merger and expansion decisions made by outside management in favor of the facilities in Allegany County, and reflects the effort put forth by a dynamic coalition of local economic and governmental leaders and agency people, combined with the attractiveness of an available labor supply of skilled machinists.

Loss of Local Ownership, Control, and Management

Another major national economic trend with increasing—and increasingly negative—effects on rural economies, is the loss of control by rural communities over their own manufacturing firms. Rural counties in New York, compared to metropolitan regions, have experienced a disproportionate loss of control over the firms and the mix of firms that compose a major segment of their economic base. Locational decisions and plant expansions, as well as plant-reduction or plant-closing decisions, are made "by the criteria of metropolitan people, institutions, and communities rather than the leadership and criteria of local communities and control" (Eberts 1984, p. 65). In some cases the absorption of an ailing local firm into a larger corporation resulted in a sufficient infusion of capital or reorientation of marketing to bolster a local plant. But in many communities in rural New York, the long-term result, eventually, seems to be in the other direction: the eventual shutdown of the local plant. When this happens in rural communities, there may be few substitute employment opportunities available locally, and displaced workers may have to commute longer distances or move away to find adequate and appropriate jobs.

The term "local management" may now be somewhat of a misnomer in rural manufacturing firms, as management personnel are "local" only in that they administer the local plant, not in the sense of being of or connected to the local community.

A community leader explained, "You can't get managers who come from elsewhere and plan to leave soon to become involved in the community. In fact, many choose not to live in our community where the plant is located; they live in so-called better communities outside the county. And they know, as everybody else knows, that they'll be moving."

The president of a small, local, family-based firm pointed out that not a single person from the management of the large factory in the village is a member of the local Rotary Club. "As we've lost local industry and lost local ownership of the industry that remains, in both cases, we've lost local leadership. Managers come to this plant from elsewhere, and they don't want to live in this village. They don't want to get involved in local activities."

Although the old-fashioned, paternalistic relationship of employer and employee that obtained in many locally owned manufacturing firms in the past may have hidden a number of abuses, it did have some advantages for local workers, not the least of which was a feeling that management and workers had a shared fate. In many cases, workers felt an attachment to "their" plant, a security about it as a lifelong employer and a loyalty bordering on defensiveness. In many communities, the mutual interests of management and workers was remembered by residents who grew up locally in the 1960s and 1970s. If, as radicalized youngsters, they had made critical comments about the local factory, they were quickly silenced by parents with ready reminders: "Where do you think your food has come from all these years?" or "Watch what you say. It's the mill that is putting food on the table and your brother through college."

Under the old system, there was a feeling, partly reality, partly myth, that "everybody" connected to the local firm was pleased to be where he or she was and that the local factory both contributed to and partook of a local quality of life that everyone rated very highly. In the changed corporate climate of mergers, buyouts, and internationalization, however, local people have suddenly learned that the local quality of life can no longer, by itself, hold or attract jobs. Small communities in rural areas now realize that lovely scenery, good deer hunting, good schools, and a low crime rate will be insufficient either to save the jobs they have or to attract new jobs. As the economic development director in the county that just lost its fourth-ranked employer said, "The loss of this company is a psychological blow to us. Now for the first time an industry has said to us, in effect, 'Yes, you have all of these good things, a nice place to live and all that—but we're going for the $1.25 wages. Good-bye.' "

One of the minor but irritating problems for local people in corporate mergers and buyouts involving their local factories is that each new corporate owner changes the name of the newly acquired plant, and people become confused about what to call the factory that is the backbone of their community economy.

> The new ownership of a major plant in one village had provided a new name for the plant, but many residents could hardly pronounce the new name and had trouble remembering it. In referring to the plant, residents would often go through two previous names, then tentatively say the current new name, often with a modifier following: "or whatever its name is." There appeared to be a psychological block against learning the name, an attempt at denial of the new and unpredictable economic reality. The name change was symbolic on the part of the parent company, and in the local community the symbolism was noticed. People's trouble in learning a new name revealed a heightened sense of their own vulnerability.

Although the point may seem trivial, in a period of economic stress and rapid change in many aspects of community life, a change in the name of a community's primary employer may be quite significant. The loss of an old familiar factory name and the substitution of a new name, perhaps a technical or foreign name that is quite unfamiliar, symbolizes the change from a community with a "local" economy to one with an externally controlled economy. Furthermore, the former name of a local company may be significant socioculturally, for it is part of the identity and history of the community. Many firms in rural communities were named after a founding father, a man who had started the firm, made his money, turned the management over to sons and grandsons, and donated part of his fortune to the town. The family, socially prominent and public-spirited in their time, may have left behind a local legacy of history, architecture, and philanthropy: Its name may be engraved on the entrance to the town ballfield, park, or library; streets and scholarships for high school students may bear the family name. The factory may have continued to carry the family name even after the first merger or two. But, suddenly, the firm has a new, more remote owner and, to go with it, a new name. From the perspective of local people who have always identified with "our company," the corporate name change can be a blow to the identity of the community and its workers.

Places of Vigor and Places of Vulnerability

Even though rural America has in general lagged behind the national pace in recovering from the recession of the early 1980s, some places have fared better than others. Rural areas that have done best include those with a diversified economy that is not heavily dependent on either agriculture, mining, or manufacturing and those adjacent to metropolitan areas. In areas where geographical proximity puts residents within commuting distance of stronger urban economies, rural communities have been able to attract "footloose industries" (for local employment), professional people who can work at home (bolstering the housing market and adding to property-tax revenues), and retirees and recreationers (adding to local service-sector employment).

Economic vigor and vulnerability are not evenly or randomly distributed, however. The comparative advantage for the future is tilted in favor of the areas that are already in the best shape economically; some communities have better prospects than others for retaining manufacturing plants or gaining good service jobs. Larger towns with more business activity, more economic diversity, and less poverty may gain enough jobs to balance those lost, at least in number of slots, if not in terms of job quality. The smaller, poorer, more remote communities will not lose many jobs because scarcely any jobs exist now, but they are unlikely to gain any jobs either, and so to the extent that their residents are employed, they will be out-commuters. In the "smokestack-chasing" strategies of the early and mid-1980s, some communities simply were unable to compete effectively in the race to acquire new industries.

Gradually, this strategy of intercommunity competition turned out to have drawbacks, even for the "winners," in terms of unduly high costs in infrastructure investments and tax abatements. It has been replaced by a new approach called "grow your own," which concentrates more on helping local people to start up their own enterprises and assisting already existing firms to expand and grow. Even in this less competitive, local-entrepreneurial approach, the advantage will likely go to those already out in front, but the dynamism and vision of local leadership may play a bigger and more effective role in shaping community economic growth.

The rural paradox of vigor and vulnerability will continue to differentiate among communities, as one community's economic growth may be matched by another community's economic stagnation. Divergence between dynamic centers and stagnating peripheries reflects not only present realities but future trajectories. It reflects in miniature the divergence between metropolitan and rural America.

CHAPTER FIVE

Plant Closings
and Substitute Jobs:
Labor Force for Sale

Suddenly, all those economic trends like mergers, offshore employment, and loss of local manufacturing, all those things we've read about, have now come to our county.
—An economic development director in a rural county

In rural New York, locals say, national trends arrive late. In the mid-1980s many residents had only a secondhand, media-based familiarity with the national and international market forces that were bringing about a major restructuring of manufacturing. Factory closings were something rural residents knew about only dimly, something that was happening elsewhere.

Suddenly, however, the sense of isolated security is no longer tenable: National trends have become local realities. Inescapably, rural people have become aware that the driving force of international competition is shaping management decisions that affect their own communities. Workers in local manufacturing plants in rural New York, especially plants taken over by outside ownership, are increasingly aware of their own vulnerability. Suddenly corporate buyouts resulting in name changes for the familiar local plants became significant events in local lives. The major impact of plant reductions and closings, of course, falls most heavily on the workers who lose not only jobs but also the security of their economic future. But communities also suffer, both economically and socially, in terms of the short-term strain of responding to employment loss and in the long-range, overall vitality of the community.

Economically, the loss of factories has had a much more pervasive and deeper impact on the economies of rural communities in the last decade than has the loss of farms. The downsizing and loss of rural manufacturing facilities have been responsible for much greater losses in employment, retail trade, and real estate values and have produced a much greater strain on the community service capacity. Unlike farm losses, factory closings have their biggest effects in the economic sphere. And unlike the farm situation, where the demise of a few farms may be balanced by the expansion of those remaining, when a rural factory cuts back or closes down, other plants in the community, subject to the same forces of international competition and external ownership, may not be in a position to expand, even though extra trained labor may be available. Even where a factory closing was followed by an opening of another manufacturing firm, laid-off workers who found new factory jobs suffered a substantial cut in pay not only because they were starting over, shorn of the seniority and raises they'd earned over the years and with little bargaining power in an employers' market, but also because the entire pay scale in the new manufacturing jobs may be significantly lower than in the old firms. From management's point of view, cutting labor costs has been the essential strategy for meeting foreign competition; the high wages that rural factories had been paying was what they sought to escape in moving overseas. The few plants that now move into rural areas from, or instead of, urban locations have done so because they anticipate lower operating costs, particularly labor costs. Displaced rural workers have thus been over a barrel in that they have had to accept the new, lower pay scales or go without jobs. Rural community leaders too, have been caught in a tight situation, in that they have had to accept—indeed, to entice—new, smaller manufacturing firms with reduced wage rates and inadequate benefit packages because, for both the worker and the rural community, there was nothing else available. Retaining or attracting the better-paying, stable manufacturing firms is, for many rural communities, no longer an option.

The great transformation in manufacturing employment in rural communities is hardly different in nature from what has been happening in major urban areas of the nation. But at least in the case of New York, its consequences are quite different because rural counties and upstate metropolitan counties had been more dependent on manufacturing than the New York City metropolitan area and were less able to compensate for manufacturing job losses by moving into the service sector. The consequences have also been more serious in rural areas because of a scale factor: The loss of a few mid-sized plants in a county of 50,000 people, or of just one plant in a community of 1,500, packs a much stronger wallop on workers and community than the same closures would in a metropolitan area.

This chapter will concentrate on a few specific examples of plant closings. The cases illustrate the range of situations, plant sizes, production fields, and work forces, but the focus is on the impact on workers, their families, and their communities.

CASE STUDIES OF PLANT CLOSINGS

To understand the full impact of rural plant closings, it is necessary to realize that many small communities were losing not just one plant but several in quick succession, as part of a general downsizing of manufacturing in the Northeast and in response to boardroom maneuvering in distant corporate headquarters. When any nearby factory announced a cutback or closed down, it sent a case of employment jitters reverberating through communities, as people worried whether other companies, also owned and directed by outsiders in other cities, would make similar decisions. Some communities were suffering a whole series of plant closings on top of already serious long-term unemployment and poverty problems.

> In one central New York county, there have been cutbacks, succession of firms by other firms, and closings. A garment-manufacturing firm in the county seat, employing 100 or more entry-level women, went out in 1987. Its vacated space in the small downtown building was later filled by another garment firm, and when that also left, an assembly plant for small household appliances moved in. Ten miles up the highway, in a village of 1,500 residents, stands a factory building that had closed down in 1983, throwing 200 workers out of jobs; it still stood vacant in 1989. A few blocks away, a factory that was the county's fourth-largest employer suddenly shut down in spring 1989. A year later, the building remained empty.

A County's Fourth-Largest Employer Moves to Mexico

In December 1988 the management of a factory making hospital and health care products announced to each of the three shifts that the plant would close down by June. With Christmas coming and property taxes due in January, workers were stunned and upset. Layoffs would begin in February and would be staggered through the spring. Every employee was guaranteed two weeks' notice, but no employee knew if she would be in the earliest batch or among the last to go.

> "I was totally surprised, in shock. The thought of all those bills to pay and no way to pay them—I couldn't sleep nights. We fought a lot, sometimes over stupid things like whether to get three pounds of hamburger when it was on sale, or only two."

It was a difficult spring for the approximately 500 employees, almost all of them women and many of whom had been working at the plant for years. Of the plant's work force, 155 employees lived in this valley village, a place of about 600 families, so that job loss directly affected a quarter of village families. The ripple effect spread throughout the adjoining hilly countryside: Plant workers lived in fifty-five communities in eleven surrounding counties, including some very small and poor communities with little other employment available nearby.

As phased layoffs took place during the spring of 1989, a large sign was erected on the lawn in front of this main-street factory proclaiming a message that captured and epitomized the change in rural manufacturing in this decade: the irony of good facilities and good workers, but no work.

> "FOR SALE OR LEASE: PRIME MANUFACTURING FACILITY; EXCELLENT WORKFORCE AVAILABLE."

A generation and more ago, this building was occupied by a locally owned

knitting mill making mittens. Ironically, the man who is currently helping to place workers in training or new jobs had been "born into that mill," as both his father and mother worked there. Over subsequent years, the building had been purchased by outside owners and its name and product line changed, though many of the workers stayed on. The latest change in ownership, management, name and products was in 1982, when the plant was included as part of a division of a firm headquartered in St. Louis, which, in turn, is owned by a parent corporation based in New York City. Once again, many workers stayed on. In recent years, the local plant has been making a variety of plastic medical devices, such as breathing assistance devices, syringes, and catheters for hospital and home use.

The reasons for the shutdown were given to the press as consolidation taken to "reduce the overhead costs and maintain a competitive position in the marketplace." The operations would be transferred to "other existing manufacturing facilities," which turned out to be in Mexico. The crucial factor was cheap labor: Instead of an average of $8 an hour here, plus benefits, the company could pay $1.25 across the border, without benefits. According to a local economic development official, "It wasn't a matter of discussion or bargaining with the employees. There was no way that the workers here could have given up enough pay to keep the jobs here."

The news was hard to believe. The plant looked busy, with three shifts operating around the clock, as required in injection molding. In fact help-wanted ads were still running in the local paper to add temporary staff to meet the plant's orders; and approximately forty temps had just been hired. Management-labor relations in this non-unionized plant had been fairly smooth. Employees had earned a reputation for being "good workers" and took pride in working here. "The company was good to them and they to it."

The workers spanned skill levels, educational backgrounds, and wage levels. For many, the plant was the only place they had ever worked. The majority of positions were in assembly, not highly skilled, paying $7.30 an hour, and in machine operating, semiskilled, at $7.50 to nearly $8 an hour. Some skilled machine-operators and clerical workers were receiving $9 to $12 an hour. In one of the few cases of a husband and wife both employed here, the couple had come here together without finishing high school, he as a mechanic and she as an assembler, and worked up in wages over the years to a point where together they were earning about $50,000 annually.

The pride and good feeling that had permeated this work force, and workers' satisfaction with a good work environment contributed to the bad feeling people subsequently had about the company: They had lost not only a job but a good job in a good work environment. As the reality of pink slips and "last day" bore down on workers, their pain and panic was translated into anger at the company. And as they began the job search in the start of summer 1989, they suddenly realized that the job situation outside the plant was not very good. The county's major manufacturing employer, located in the county seat, was definitely not hiring. Most of the jobs advertised in the four cities within a forty-minute to one-hour commute would not pay enough to offset extra costs in transportation and child care. Moreover, a major plant in one of these cities had just announced a termination of several hundred workers.

By the time work had nearly ceased at the plant, 365 workers had registered with the job assistance program sponsored by the Private Industry Council, but of these only twenty had found jobs. A rundown of the employees (by position, not name) and the jobs these twenty found revealed that only about six were making as much as they had made previously, with one making more. Most were working full time but earning considerably less, many about $5 an hour, compared to the $7.30 or so they had been earning. Their new jobs varied from inventory clerking to department-store work, to assembly-line work and sewing-machine operating, to receptionist and warehouse work. Some were commuting up to 50 miles farther away. A dozen were in on-the-job-training (OJT) contracts at a new firm that had just moved into a building vacated by another plant that had left. Another eight were in other OJT programs, in which employers are reimbursed for up to 40 percent of wages during the training period.

One displaced line worker, a few months later, was working third shift at the new household-appliance assembly plant in the county seat. She had liked her previous job at the medical products plant, the line of work, the people, and the work environment. But she is unhappy with her present job for several reasons: the night hours, some dangerous work operations, shift co-workers she doesn't trust, and especially the pay cut: $2.50 an hour less. One of her friends from the closed factory also took a job at this small plant—and quit after three days.

Education was seen by many of the terminated employees as necessary to getting a decent job. About fifty employees enrolled in a set of classes sponsored with state funding by the local BOCES (Board of Cooperative Educational Services), involving classroom retraining for various occupations such as data processing and food service. These courses were seen as particularly important by women who were single mothers, who saw the handicap of inadequate education as seriously limiting their options. About 20 percent (roughly 100) of the terminated workers lacked a high school diploma, and many of these had other life factors that might limit job prospects.

A Major Employer in a Remote Area Moves out of State

In the rural northeastern tip of the state, against the Canadian border, a foundry that had employed over 500 people was closed down by the out-of-state parent company. Although the local foundry was not doing very well, it had been doing better than the company's other subsidiaries. Employees had participated in ideas to cut production cost, and even though half of the workers were union members, there had not been a strike in over a decade. The plant had been operating for a century and a quarter, controlled locally until recent years. Some of the workers had been with the plant for twenty to thirty years, and many were earning a solid $10 to $12 an hour. They were established family men, living modestly but comfortably, and with financial commitments that weighed heavily on them when they lost their jobs. The announcement of closing came in October 1986; final shutdown came in January 1987, when the operation was moved to Ohio. A year and a half later, in July 1988, some of those laid off were still looking for work, and many were still in the temporary, lower-pay substitute jobs they took as their unemployment benefits, union benefits, and severance pay had run out.

Some people took stopgap jobs of various sorts, some involving night shifts or Saturdays, which, added to the longer daily commute, was causing stress in families. Some of the highly skilled machinists, such as lathe and drill press operators, picked up other kinds of jobs in growing Plattsburgh, and some took foundry jobs across Lake Champlain in Vermont, at more than an hour's commute and where housing costs are too high for people to contemplate moving. Most of the jobs people found were at considerably lower wages and less skill than their former jobs. Some men initially decided that a $4-an-hour job simply wouldn't do and decided to wait until better jobs might become available rather than jeopardize unemployment and union benefits. But as their saving accounts also dwindled over the year, they were forced to take whatever they could get.

Older men, aged forty-five to sixty, had the greatest trouble finding jobs, and most were still without work or satisfactory work a year and a half later. Many of these men did not have a high school diploma, as that had not been needed to get a job at this plant when they started; and while at the plant the lack of a high school diploma had not prevented them from moving gradually upward to comfortable wages. Some who were fifty-five or over took retirement with only half their benefits. Education was a route pursued by only a few: To do so would require having a fully employed spouse whose jobs provided adequate wages and family health benefits. Most families have continued to live in their hometowns because they can't afford to buy a house wherever they might get a job. Some homeowners had negotiated an agreement with the local bank whereby they were just paying interest on the mortgage, not paying on principal. Most former plant workers lost their medical benefits, as few were able to afford the $194 per month to keep insurance through the company.

After shutdown, the building was sold to a Canadian firm and was divided up into space for several small businesses. A few, small, garment- and toy-manufacturing firms had started up, especially Canadian firms, with a pay scale reported to be slightly higher than in comparable small U.S. firms. Together the firms in the building employ about eighty people, many of whom receive near-minimum wages and some of whom were hired only for six-month stints, thereby never gaining health benefits.

This plant closing had a domino effect in this peripheral and perennially poor area where foundry employees had been among the best-paid local workers. In the township alone, 133 families were directly affected, and in some families both the husband and wife lost jobs. Local businesses were hurt: For example, the bowling alley was having a hard time because people could no longer afford to bowl. By 1988 some families were seriously reducing their expenditures. Some were cutting food budgets in order to meet other obligations—and because the local school district had no lunch program at all, no free or reduced-price lunches were available. The village mayor had succeeded in passing a 10 percent cut in property taxes, and even the "hold-the-line" school budget barely squeaked by the voters.

To help families that could not get help from agencies, townspeople established a special fund that could be used to help make a house payment, to pay insurance premiums, to pay off a deferred car payment to avoid losing the car, or, in one case, to pay transportation for moving to Maine. A local committee organized the fund-raising and made decisions on allocating the money. There were bake sales, auctions, and school-based fund-raisers that involved the whole community. Maximum funding per family was set at $400, and seventeen families were helped.

COMMON THREADS AND IMPLICATIONS

Even in the Northeast, with its diversified rural economy and its high level of urbanization, major dislocations resulting from national and international forces in manufacturing are seriously affecting rural communities. As rural manufacturing firms become increasingly vulnerable to the new climate of business decisions that are made in distant places, the local quality-of-life factors, the amenities of small-town living, will no longer be able to hold or attract jobs.

Certain human problems resulting from downsizing or departure of factories are predictable, and certain groups of people are especially likely to be hurt in the process. The impact of a factory closing is different on different levels of employees. Although managers and highly skilled workers may be poised and ready to move, geographically or occupationally, to get in on the start of a new venture, assembly-line workers and lower-skill laborers are less able to make big leaps. This differential is clear just in terms of housing. Management people own housing that is readily marketable and has probably appreciated over the few years they have owned it; if the owner has trouble finding a buyer, the company will purchase it. On the other hand, assembly workers, who are more apt to be local people and to have been at the plant longer, may be tied financially and socially to the houses they own. A middle-aged line worker's house, with its low mortgage or mortgage-free ownership, represents a distinct advantage for keeping housing expenses down. Selling such a home in a small, economically pressed community—if it were possible to find a buyer—would not bring anywhere near what owners would have received before a factory shut-down or what they might need in down payment and mortgage payments for a house in a locality that has a strong enough economy to hold good job possibilities. Strong ties to family and friends, which sustain workers when they become unemployed, further compel these displaced workers not to leave, but to settle for whatever substitute employment they can get locally or to begin a life of commuting out farther to urbanized areas.

As the rural employment picture changes, the penalty for inadequate formal education is becoming much greater. Individuals presently losing their jobs because of plant closings had, until now, been able to bring home a good salary just because of their longevity at the plant and their adequate performance there. But their limited and dated education renders them barely able to compete now for decent jobs—or to perform satisfactorily if they should get such a job. This means that education, job retraining, new skills, and even college education, as well as basic literacy, adult education, and high school equivalency, are extremely important for adults who still have more than ten years ahead of them in the work force. As rural economies undergo further transformation, the quality of high school education of local youth also becomes more critical.

> When a cheese plant closed, putting 100 people out of work, the fifteen non–high school graduates had great difficulty finding replacement jobs. All but one were men, mostly in their forties and fifties. Only one found a regular job in the first three months after shutdown.
>
> An adult basic education coordinator in one county put it succinctly: "Even though unemployment rates are down, we no longer have the opportunity to place the unskilled person without a high school diploma, especially those who have had little job experience. And with the closing of plants that had high-paying jobs, older people with one skill and no education now can't get jobs—certainly not jobs at their former pay level. They'll have to have training for new jobs."

The pay scale of the manufacturing firms that close down will never again be duplicated, either in the remaining manufacturing or in the retail and other service jobs. Most terminated workers will be fortunate to make 75 percent of their previous earnings, unless through carefully selected education they get a very different kind of employment, or unless they migrate outside the area. The downsizing of manufacturing and restructuring of the labor force will inevitably translate into a tight financial situation in rural areas, both for individuals and for communities.

JOB CREATION: SHORTCHANGED BY NEW JOBS

New jobs are indeed being created in most of these rural communities. In fact, in many rural places job creation has held its own against job losses—in terms of numbers of jobs. For the Northeast as a whole, though not in other regions of rural America, "rural economies have slightly outperformed metro economies in terms of job creation" (Deavers 1988, p. 1). However, there's more to the job-loss–job-creation balance than just a numbers game. If for every job lost there is one job gained, the score may well *not* be evened up. The nature of the job, measured quantitatively in terms of wages and benefits and also measured somehow qualitatively in terms of employee and community satisfaction, is also part of the equation. In the present economy, the job that is lost and the one that is gained are generally not an even trade.

Three points about the new jobs nationwide are particularly significant for rural workers and rural communities First, wages have risen only slowly, despite the labor shortage in some regions (Uchitelle 1987). Of the jobs created in the 1980–1988 period, a large fraction are low paying: The Senate Budget Committee reported that half the newly created jobs in the period would keep a family of four below the poverty line, even if the worker was employed full time, year-round. Second, an increasing number of jobs do not pay health benefits, often because they are temporary or part time. The third point is that full-time jobs are not growing as fast as part-time jobs. For people who are involuntarily in part-time employment, the difficulty in covering household living expenses may force them to turn to government programs such as medicaid and partial welfare assistance (Levitan and Conway 1988).

Many of the jobs advertised in store windows and in classified ads in small-town newspapers are part time, and most are not adequate employment for the people who hold them. Even if a worker were to take *two* half-time, service-sector jobs, such as those at local fast-food restaurants or supermarkets, both together do not equal a single full-time job that was lost from the local manufacturing plant, as each of the part-time jobs offers lower hourly wages than the full-time job, neither offers benefits, and both may be temporary or insecure. The employment twist that appeared puzzling in the later years of the decade was that so many jobs were available just at a time when many jobs were being lost. That a labor shortage is claimed while workers are being laid off reflects the continued labor-force restructuring and change in regional manufacturing and reflects, too, the paradox of vigor and vulnerability.

In one case a factory publicly declared in June 1988 that it needed 100 or more additional workers: "We desperately need people," said the company's chief executive. Six months later there were a few layoffs, and nine months later nearly 100 workers were let go.

The shortfall in wages, benefits, and security between "old employment" and "new employment" is not uniquely a rural phenomenon, of course, as it is endemic in the national economy. However, it hits rural workers harder because the differential between the jobs they have lost and the substitutes they can find is especially large and because, again, there is a restricted pool of jobs for rural people. The implications of this disadvantageous trade-off for rural areas are reflected in the title of a recent report: *Laboring for Less: Working but Poor in Rural America* (Shapiro 1989). In rural areas even families with one or more members in the work force are more likely than urban families to fall below the poverty line (Shapiro 1989, p. xi), and the poverty rate among rural family members who work has increased in the period from 1979 to 1987, in the Northeast as well as in all other regions (Shapiro 1989, p. 18). Although not everyone losing a rural manufacturing job will fall below the poverty line or will remain below it more than briefly, for most of the displaced workers, the gap between the "modest but comfortable" standard of living they once had and their present circumstances is wide indeed, even though they may be working just as much and using the same skills. Another major implication is that, for rural areas in particular, the falling unemployment rates, so sought and so heralded, are not necessarily an indication that all is well on the local employment scene. People are indeed at work now, but they are working for less. This impoverization of the work force in part explains the apparent anomalies that the poverty rate has not dropped nearly as quickly in recent years as has the unemployment rate and that the growth in aggregate household income has not kept up with the growth in number of people employed.

RURAL EMPLOYMENT ISSUES FOR THE FUTURE

Mismatch Between Jobs and Potential Work Force

Another problem in the employment picture in rural communities is the mismatch between the new jobs that open up and the available local work force. Although there are now employers who want workers, and also potential workers who want jobs, the two do not fit together well. This mismatch is a major urban issue as well, for there, too, the backlog of past economic problems haunts the present. But its effects may be particularly significant in smaller communities. In some of the rural counties coming off of periods of high unemployment, there is a backlog of people who have had neither the formal education nor job training nor work experience to qualify for the jobs opening up. For these potential workers to become actual workers, for them to fill the labor-market demands of coming decades, careful, creative employment training programs, programs that do a great deal more than simply teach job skills, are needed, as are innovative ways of helping long-term unemployed people get into and stay in the labor force.

In the North Country, a state employment director goes out of his way to minimize or smooth over the mismatches, and particularly to help people surmount the difficulties of moving from welfare to work. An example was the case of one employer who came to the employment office wanting a part-time worker but unable to say whether he would be able to keep the worker past six months because of uncertainty over landing a big contract. The employment director worked with the Department of Social Services to arrange protection for the potential employee so that if the job did end in six months, his assistance case could be reopened quickly, without the usual waiting period. The protection was guaranteed, but in the end the employer did get the contract and was able to keep the worker on the payroll.

In Allegany County, a very active and comprehensive Employment and Training Center was put together by a consortium of local organizations, spearheaded by the local director of the Private Industry Council and including the county Department of Social Services, the state Employment Service, the two-county BOCES, and others, in an exemplary interaction that gets beyond the turf battles that so often prevent useful interagency cooperation. It is designed to be a "one-stop job service," that works with both employers and potential workers and specializes in finding and utilizing a variety of funds to conduct training programs for hard-to-place workers, such as long-term unemployed people and people on welfare. Many of these potential workers have several of the official "barriers to employment": lack of education, vocational training, job skills or work experience; poorly developed work-related behaviors and attitudes; poor job-seeking skills; serious transportation problems; single and teen parenthood; health problems and disabilities; and older age. Training programs focusing not on job skills per se, but on job-seeking skills, job-readiness, work habits, and basic life skills are regularly conducted by this consortium.

As of spring 1989, the Employment and Training Center in Allegany County could boast that more than 78 percent of its clients obtained unsubsidized employment (63 percent is the state's minimum standard for these programs). In the center's programs for youths between fourteen and twenty-one, 78 percent of clients had positive terminations (again, above the state minimum of 69 percent), either unsubsidized employment or returning to school full time. The costs of such training came to $2,635 per adult client and $1,941 per youth (well below the maximum costs the state allows: $4,921 per adult and $5,294 per youth).

The mismatch problem continues, however, and is too large for training programs alone to solve. In summer 1988, for example, many new job openings were being called in to this active local job-training and placement consortium: During one of my visits, six new jobs had been called in before 10 a.m. But most of the jobs opening up were not suitable for this long-term unemployed population, as they required high levels of specific skill and experiences.

> In Allegany County in early June 1988, over forty jobs were listed by the New York State Job Service as "currently available." One-fourth of the jobs were part time, including jobs as inventory clerk, house cleaner, sales clerk, cook and waitress, bartender, computer operator, switchboard operator (temporary), receptionist, janitor, deliverer, and lawn worker. Some of the thirty full-time positions, including jobs as mill worker, truck driver, auto painter, cashier, dairy-farm worker, and cook, required considerable experience. Others, such as jobs as welder and tractor-trailer driver, required both experience and extra certification. One auto-mechanic job demanded not only certification and an inspector's license, but possession of one's own tools. Still other full-time jobs required either two years or four years of college education, with some needing computer knowledge.

> At the high-skill end of the jobs that were opening up, primarily for machinists, one plant projected 250 new hires. Fifty of the slots had already been filled, but the rest of the openings were awaiting qualified applicants. Consequently, by the following spring, the director of the county employment training program and the county's economic development director were helping the firm make a pitch for skilled machinists from Buffalo to move down to the waiting jobs in Allegany County.

Most of the available jobs appropriate for people just entering employment were part time, paying $3.50 to $4 an hour, and without benefits, the kind of job, the director said, "suitable only as the second source of income in the home." The problem, however, is that for many of the people who take those jobs, this income has to stretch to serve as the household's primary income. Many may still need assistance in the form of food stamps, medicaid, or subsidized child care. Predictions of labor needs in rural New York indicate that the level of education and job skills required—even for entry-level positions—will continue to rise, further aggravating the mismatch problem.

The Young Adult Work Force: "What Happened to the Class of 1983?"

An interesting local perspective on the employment situation comes from a special study that was carried out in early 1989 by a four-county BOCES district in the central region of the state. Surveying the graduates of the class of 1983 from the eighteen component rural school districts, the study found several indicators that reflect the problematic regional job situation and the insecure fortunes of local young people entering the local and nearby job market in the mid-1980s. The survey probably underestimated young adult employment problems because it included almost no high school dropouts. Nonetheless, with 1,200 questionnaires mailed out, two-thirds of them to addresses within the four-county area, and a 30 percent response rate, three trends emerge strongly.

Many of these young adults are not yet stabilized in the labor force. Eleven percent of respondents were unemployed five years after graduation from high school, and 72 percent expected to change jobs in the next two years (42 percent of those answering the question expected to change jobs within a year). Earnings are relatively low. For men and women combined, five years after graduating high school, a quarter earned less than $10,000 per year, whereas 21 percent more earned between that and $15,000 (thus 46 percent earned under $15,000).

Earning levels for men and women differed sharply. For women, 53 percent were earning under $15,000, whereas only 28 percent of the men fell below this figure; a full 27 percent of female respondents were earning less than $10,000, but only 14 percent of the men were earning at this low level. The distribution of men and women graduates of the class of 1983 in the higher salary range shows the same relative advantage to men, with 23 percent of the men earning over $25,000, whereas only 10 percent of the women earned this much.

The lower earnings of young women in this area, compared to the earnings of men in the same age group, are a local-level reflection of the findings of quantitative studies of women in the labor force in rural America (McLaughlin and Sachs 1988, Slesinger and Cautley 1988). As the class of 1983 matures, three major trends will intersect: More rural women will be in the work force; rural adults with no post-secondary education will increasingly be limited to the lower wage levels and less than full-time work; and rural female workers will increasingly be single heads of households. Thus, the gender gap in salaries will become more critical in rural areas because of changes in family structure and household formation as well as changes in employment structure.

In this situation, as in others affecting rural communities, national and international economic forces have a significant impact because they combine with local social and demographic changes occurring at the same time.

PART THREE

Changing
Rural Populations

CHAPTER SIX

People and Places:
Demographic Change
and Local Response

Transformations in agriculture and the nonfarm rural economy, as well as new external forces, have caused some significant changes in the populations residing in small towns and the open countryside. Demographic changes are not just a matter of changes in numbers of people or characteristics of populations, however. They occur within and have consequences for places: They shape and are shaped by the economic, social, and cultural life of ·local communities.

This chapter will present an overview of major demographic changes but will focus on the changes occurring at the local level and their effects in bringing about a change in the mix of local interests and needs, in some places bringing about a noticeably changed community. Analysis of the local-level changes and responses is based primarily on materials from the four core research counties, Allegany, Chenango, Delaware, and Franklin. We begin with some local ethnographic observations.

SIGNS OF THE TIMES: OBSERVATIONS
AT A RURAL COUNTY FAIR

Summertime county fairs are useful observation points, being to some degree a stage on which the community not only entertains itself but also displays itself. Traditionally an agricultural exposition and an homage to farm living, most rural county fairs of the 1980s now include and represent a much broader cross-section of the community. Exhibits and exhibitors include the frankly commercial merchandise and entertainments and the full panoply of community services and agencies, as well as the agricultural organizations and cattle exhibitions. In several counties recently, fair organizers have attempted to reverse the slipping agricultural prominence at the fair, although among the throngs of fair-goers, out-of-town tourists and nonfarm residents probably outnumbered farm people by a wide margin. The 1986 Delaware County Fair, marking the hundredth anniversary of this venerable institution, presented a mixture of agricultural and nonagricultural displays that captured and projected the demographic and economic changes of the decade.

It was a beautiful August day, and the flat fields used for the fair, donated years ago by a local farm family, nestled against a backdrop of dark green hills. The first-day crowd was large, according to the car-parking attendants. Despite problems on many dairy farms that summer and the fact that forty county farms were just now in the process of going out on the government's whole-herd buyout, the long white dairy barns were filled with cows. Youngsters dressed in their 4-H whites were busily grooming and cleaning up after their prized animals. Each family was stationed near its row of about ten cows, with folding lawn chairs, a thermos of coffee for adults, cool-drink dispenser for kids, displays of ribbons won at past fairs, and the name of the farm and of each cow proudly displayed along the row. At their parents' feet little children played with miniature tractors and farm implements. Although there were fewer 4-H exhibitors than usual, the tension and excitement in the judging ring, the seriousness of the judging, and the handsome appearance of the calves and cows being shown gave no hint of troubles on farms. In other barns nearby, pens of sheep, swine, and beef cattle were waiting their turn in the show ring. An equestrian show at the edge of the fairgrounds was attracting many spectators.

Near the animal barns, exhibitors of large farm implements drew relatively few people and talked quite pessimistically about the slump in sales. There were at least as many garden tractors on display as field tractors. A pesticide applicator sat in his booth, arms folded across his chest, display literature on the tables in front of him, waiting for a serious farmer to come along. In the next booth, a table covered with a veritable flea market of pocket knives, tie clips, cloth wallets, teddy bears, and pins and bumper stickers with catchy sayings was doing a lot of business.

A few steps from the dairy barns was one of the major nonagricultural parts of the fair, the "commercial tent," which, despite its name, was mostly a display place for various community organizations and agencies to advertise their services. Each booth was staffed with a representative who could talk about the program. Cooperative Extension was there with photo displays and pamphlets, and so was the Public Health Nursing Service. The Community Action Agency was advertising Head Start and Weatherization for low-income households. The Task Force on Child and Family Development had an eye-catching display, as did the Red Cross, and there were demonstrations of the Heimlich maneuver for choking victims and dramatic posters warning of the dangers of drinking and driving. At a card table well stocked with pamphlets, volunteers for the Office for the Aging sat and chatted with each other and with passersby. The counselors of a special program that assists farmers in trouble to explore options and secure training or jobs were not at their booth because they found it better to talk to farm people in the dairy show barns, though in the booth they had left discreet papers with their phone numbers

Scattered in with these service agencies were booths or tables of several different real estate firms active in the county. Each had a poster-board display with photographs of properties for sale, with the usual real estate blurbs under them and in some cases the price. There were many sorts of cabins in the woods, a broad selection of 5-acre building lots in the hills and at the edges of farms, old farmhouses, and even whole farms. Fairgoers crowded around each of these display boards in little clusters, and it appeared that there were two distinct kinds of groups. One kind of grouping was local: They studied the photos and the descriptions and prices, and their comments were: "Oh, for goodness sake, that's Arthur's place. Will you look at what they're asking for it? $100,000 for that crate?!" "Why look! Denton's house is on the market. What do you suppose he's up to?" and "Would you look at that! Sam's asking $15,000 for a five-acre piece on the side of his woodlot! Can you believe these prices?!" An equally incredulous group of people would stop at the same display, study the pictures and the information, and exclaim excitedly, "Look at this one! Isn't that a beauty? Only $100,000. Not bad!" and "Now there's a cute house— and they're letting it go for a song! It's a steal!" and "What a view! Imagine having a cabin there! What a view from my rocker on the porch! Not a bad price, either, $3,000 an acre, compared to what Harry paid for his place." This scene of contrasts was repeated frequently throughout the day. It was not necessary to look at the clothes, to listen for the accent, or to ask where they lived. The divergent views expressed on local real estate were ample identification.

Here on exhibit in microcosm at this county fair, inadvertently or unconsciously, was the impact of population change, and of the agricultural, economic, and land-use changes that were all intertwined with it. Such a broad collection of activities, organizations, services, and interests arises out of a significant broadening in the make-up and interests of the county population.

OVERVIEW OF RECENT DEMOGRAPHIC TRENDS

The National and Regional Picture

Nationwide, the biggest rural demographic trend in recent decades was the one least predicted: "the nonmetropolitan turnaround" of the 1970s, in which for the first time in history rural America experienced widespread population gains and actually grew faster than metropolitan areas (Kenneth Johnson 1989, p. 301). The 1980 census showed that even rural areas not adjacent to metropolitan areas had experienced a turnaround of their historic trend of population loss, in that movement to rural areas in the 1970s exceeded movement away from rural areas. Taken by surprise and assuming that this trend would continue, some observers predicted a continued growth of rural areas, even a "rural renaissance."

However, while the numbers were still being analyzed in the early 1980s, the trend was already beginning to slacken. Since then, population movement reversed itself again in favor of growth in metropolitan areas and resumption of the dominance of rural-to-urban migration. Citing the net loss of over 600,000 people from nonmetropolitan to metropolitan areas in 1985–1986 alone, analysts now predict that "reduced nonmetro growth of the 1980s may signal a return to the generalized decline of previous decades" (Brown and Deavers 1988, p. 16). In the many rural areas where the 1980s has brought economic stagnation, moving from city to country has now been transformed into an economic sacrifice that fewer people are willing to make (Wardwell and Rowe 1988). Although there is still considerable urban-to-rural movement underneath a larger flow in the rural-to-urban direction, for the nation as a whole, rural areas are again suffering a net loss.

The loss of rural young people by out-migration, an age-old pattern in rural America, grows worse in periods of rural economic downturn, such as the 1980s, and remains a serious concern in rural communities. In 1988 the *Wall Street Journal* carried a story on the current rural exodus problem, covering rural America from Maine to Montana. In Eastport, Maine, it reported, "young people are leaving for the cities. Their parents watch them go with resignation. Why stay when there is so little opportunity?" In Dawson, Georgia, only two of twenty high school seniors want to stay in town. A senior explains the majority view: "You can't go very far here" (Charlier 1988).

Rural areas have "traditionally had a higher proportion of children, relatively fewer younger adults and middle aged persons, and a larger proportion of the elderly," reflecting "a higher level of fertility in rural areas, out-migration of young adults, and both in-migration of older persons and aging-in-place" (Brown and Deavers 1988, p. 18). These characteristics have not been significantly altered by the 1970s migration to rural areas or the net return flow to metropolitan areas in the 1980s.

The rural Northeast differs from some other areas of the nation. In the Northeast the rural population contains only small numbers of minority people, a fact that makes it more like Appalachia and distinguishes it from the rural South and Southwest. In the more densely populated Northeast, furthermore, the common size of rural communities is larger than in some other regions such as the Midwest, where, for example, in Kansas, 80 percent of the towns have fewer than 2,500 people. And many of the rural communities in the Northeast are situated quite near urban centers. This proximity factor, in a region with numerous metropolitan areas, means that rural demographic changes are tied closely to economic conditions in metropolitan areas and to residential preferences of metropolitan people. In the Northeast, the nonmetropolitan turnaround of the 1970s was not as great, nor was the reversal afterward.

Recent Population Trends in Rural New York

In New York the nonmetropolitan population turnaround had already begun around 1950. The rural migration gain during the 1970s was muted and was concentrated in places adjacent to the state's metropolitan areas. More remote counties grew only very slowly. During the period from 1980 to 1986, when the state as a whole experienced a slight population growth of 1.2 percent, rural counties close to metropolitan areas gained more people than they lost, but a number of the more remote counties lost population.

In the structure and characteristics of the population, recent decades have been marked by a convergence of demographic and socioeconomic trends in metropolitan and nonmetropolitan areas, and rural counties became "increasingly similar in a number of important ways" to metropolitan counties (Eberts 1984, p. 99). For example, in labor characteristics, the rise of service-sector employment and the increasing participation of women in the work force in rural counties have both closely paralleled metropolitan figures, with only a small and diminishing difference between metropolitan and rural areas (Eberts and Khawaja 1988).

However, not all characteristics have been converging. Population density, of course, is still a major factor differentiating rural New York from urban, a basic fact that is too often overlooked in government decisions, programs, and funding allocations. The small size and low density of rural populations have major consequences for all sorts of institutions, such as schools and hospitals, make delivery of community services costly, and dilute political strength in Washington and Albany. Rural areas also differ from the rest of the state in that they continue to have lower income levels and higher poverty rates. In rural New York, however, poverty and low income are not significantly associated with racial or ethnic minority populations, for minorities continue to make up only a very small proportion of the state's rural population, still around 1 or 2 percent in many counties in 1980, even though minority population growth in the state as a whole has been substantial.

LOCAL TRENDS: POPULATION LOSS, HOUSEHOLD CHANGE, AND AGING

For the local perspective, we turn to the four core research counties. (See demographic data in Appendix Two.) Continuing a decades-old pattern, these four counties, which are among those with the least urban influence (Eberts 1984), still disproportionately lose a significant fraction of their young people to out-migration. This loss has a major effect on both a county's growth and its age distribution. Because families in the childbearing years account for a relatively smaller segment of the local population, the birthrate is depressed, which means that natural increase of population is low and that there is a relative shortage of both children and young adults. The effect of this young-adult population drain is exacerbated in counties where in-migration has been minimal. The result is that the counties farther from metropolitan areas suffered a population decline in the period from 1980 to 1986 (Economic Development and Technical Assistance Center 1987).

Although Chenango County just managed to top the state's 1.2 percent growth rate for this period with a 1.3 percent increase, Allegany dropped by 2.4 percent, and Franklin by 2.5 percent, the state's largest loss. The only big exception to population stagnation in remote areas was the rapid growth in the area around Watertown, where Fort Drum military base was undergoing major expansion.

One important new trend in many rural areas of New York is that the number of households has been increasing faster than number of people. In some rural counties in the 1970s, population growth rate and household growth rate were approximately the same, whereas in others the number of households grew twice as fast as the population, which was the pattern nationwide (Fuguitt, Brown, and Beale 1989, p. 160). In the 1980s, faster growth of households has speeded up and become more widespread. For example, in Chenango County, where growth rate in population and households was about even in the 1970s, projections for 1980 to 1990 indicate that the number of households will have grown nearly four times as fast as the population (Hirschl 1987). This rapid growth of households reflects, among other things, the recent increase in rural areas, as in the state as a whole, of "female-headed households" or "single-parent families." Although unmeasured at this point, the increase in single-parent households was reported by schools, agencies, and planners in many rural communities. This trend gains even more significance because it intersects with another major recent trend, the rise in women with young children who are taking jobs outside the home. In terms of actual people, one and the same woman may be both a single-parent head of household and also a working mother with young children. At the aggregate level of the community, small towns may increasingly be made up of people who are part of several new trends at once. Rural social patterns and community institutions are sure to be affected by these demographic trends.

As a group, the more rural counties of New York have generally had a greater proportion of elderly people than the less rural counties, and in some counties this difference is now increasing, though aging trends differ widely among rural counties. Particularly in rural retirement areas, where in-migration of older people adds to the already high proportion of elderly people, aging of the population has significant impacts on local communities.

In Allegany County the over-sixty-five population was 11.6 percent of the total in 1980, but it has been growing steadily, mostly as a result of "aging in place," and was expected to reach 15.5 percent in 1990. Chenango's elderly population was 12.5 percent and Franklin's 12.8 percent in 1980, and neither is expected to increase at a rate faster than state averages. In Delaware County, however, an already large population of elderly is being swelled by in-migrating retirement people. Even by 1980, 14.7 percent of the county's population was over sixty-five. This high proportion of elderly is the figure projected for the United States as a whole in the year 2010, which means that in Delaware County the future was already here in 1980. (In rural Greene County, closer to metropolitan areas, the over-sixty-five population in 1980 had reached 17 percent.)

In a small place a population change that is only minor in absolute numbers can have major repercussions. Because rural communities are small not only in population size but also in formal and institutional structure and fiscal resources, even a small number of changes in household composition or a modest influx of older people may have a large impact on local institutions. For small counties and small communities, these recent and projected demographic changes are matters of considerable import, for they alter the makeup and interests of local residents and affect the mix of services that are needed and can be supported by the local population. Whether in providing day care for working single mothers or ensuing adequate public transportation and medical services for the elderly, the governments, agencies, and institutions of rural communities in the 1980s were all responding to, and trying to plan for, changing needs of their changing populations.

In Delaware County, where over a third of absentee landowners surveyed planned to retire to their vacation homes (Warren and Banks 1988, p. 7), service needs of the elderly are rising dramatically. "Our agency is each year more increasingly involved in meeting the needs of newcomers or people who have moved permanently into their secondary homes. The majority of these people, being from metropolitan areas, are totally naive about the unavailability of support services in the county. This friendly belief will continue as we can expect the current land boom to continue in all parts of our area. I personally feel that we are looking at a much larger entry than our demographics predict, and we are totally unprepared and ill-equipped for this influx and the consequent demand for services" (New York State Legislative Commission on Rural Resources 1985, p. 50).

RETURN MIGRATION TO RURAL COMMUNITIES

Underneath the new outflow from rural counties is a smaller in-migration, not all of which is for retirement. Along with young and middle-aged adults who move from urban areas to rural communities is a small population of return migrants, people coming back to their home communities after a period of residence "outside." Returning locals appear to fall into two distinct categories based on socioeconomic status, and the two are not equally welcomed by the receiving community.

The Desired Returnees: "Our Children" Returning Home

Each year a small but significant population of "returnees" comes back to their home county to take good positions in local schools, agencies, and businesses. Numerous local people have commented that there now seem to be more of these people coming back to their hometowns. Such returnees had earlier been part of the age-old pattern of rural exodus by which many rural communities lost their most ambitious and potentially productive young people; they were part of what is sometimes termed "rural America's most precious export crop." Although it is not known how many people are involved, this group of return migrants has a significance in local perception that is probably much greater than the numbers alone would warrant. These returnees are well educated, economically stable, and able to make a decent living in the rural environment. They have been successful "outside" but have chosen to return. Community perceptions of these in-migrants are highly favorable.

When these people had left the community, after high school or college, their parents had concurred in their plans to seek their fortunes in other places; but parents never stopped wishing that it might be otherwise. "We wish there could be more jobs here so that our children wouldn't have to leave" is a common refrain repeated in interviews and in citizens' remarks in public meetings. The phrase "our children" is not used as a specific reference to one's own progeny, though, but a classification of people, "the young people of the community," meaning *the community's* children. In small towns, many adults, not only the actual parents, had watched these youngsters grow up, attended their basketball games and their graduations, and then bid them farewell. And they always hoped that some of "our children," perhaps a neighbor's or a brother's child, if not one's own son or daughter, would come home.

> Stories of the returning daughter or son who gave up glamour and money to return home for a better quality of life were told in virtually every rural community as a kind of collective way of dealing with the sadness—a happy ending to console the older generation. Whenever people discussed the loss of young people, it was quite likely that the sadness of this would be countered by a favorite story about a young person, maybe even the speaker, who left town and got a good job elsewhere, perhaps as far away as Chicago, with good pay. But then the person became homesick and didn't like living there, so came back home.

In some localities, recent improvement in the employment situation has allowed some of those who departed earlier to return. Some of these returnees are middle-aged adults who have spent two decades or more in metropolitan suburbs, raising their children and working in their careers and have now come back home, where they take up a late-life career or perhaps start a small business. Other returnees in this category are younger adults who have gone out to college, worked for a few years in metropolitan areas of the state and then decided that the amenities and lower cost of living in the rural areas outweigh the high salaries of urban jobs. They may want to raise their children in a small town, perhaps with a backyard farm, and they are drawn by having parents and other relatives still in the home county. Some young, single adults are also moving back, finding that the career differential between metropolitan area and hometown has diminished somewhat in recent years. For those who grew up in the North Country mountains or the quiet wooded hills of Allegany County, the home area always seems to beckon.

These return migrants occupy important roles in the community. They work in planning offices, run employment training offices, and serve as school principals, probation directors, and so forth. In their off-the-job time they are serving as community leaders in various capacities, from scout leaders to coordinators of recycling campaigns. These adults were once the youngsters who couldn't wait to leave home to go to college and who vowed that after college they would never return, as there was neither career nor social life for them in their hometown.

A young woman in the Tug Hill area launching a career in environmental planning remembered, "When I got out of high school, I just knew I'd never come back. *Everyone* was leaving. None of my friends planned to come back here after college. There was *nothing* here to come back to. But now with the way things are booming around here, more of the people I went to school with *are* coming back. So when this job came up, I jumped for it."

A woman who runs employment training services recalled, "Most of the kids in my class left town. In the '50s and '60s, everyone wanted to get out. The feeling was 'You're a fool if you stay.' But after about fifteen or twenty years, most have come back. They like the life better here."

A leader in the local effort to create more jobs and get the county's people into more secure employment is a native of the county who has been here "all my life—so far—except when I was in the service." Now he hopes that his son, who wants to come back home, will find a suitable opening locally in the medical profession. He says, "Our kids will come back when there are jobs." When he writes grant proposals for economic developments, "bringing our kids back home" is an expressed objective.

Low-Income Returnees: "Locals" Perceived as "Outsiders"

In several rural counties there is also another pattern of returning: young adults of lower socioeconomic status who had left town but been unable to make their way in cities or other regions of the country, and so have returned home, jobless and broke. Although there are no systematic data on the size of this return population, its existence is documented in social service departments, community agencies, schools, employment training programs, and employment offices of several counties, and in the stories told by the returnees themselves. These return migrants, some of whom grew up in impoverished homes, generally had not completed high school. They left home seeking adventure, a job in Florida or Texas, or maybe a tour of duty in the military. But when jobs dried up in the Sunbelt, or the cost of living there outstripped their earning capacities, some of these young adults returned to their home counties, seeking a familiar life-style, a relatively low cost of living, and social connections to family and friends. Some of these returnees have been unable to find jobs when they first got home and have turned to welfare for support. But with the local employment situation now stronger, some are able to get a job, although they may need the services of job-readiness and job-training programs first.

For these return migrants, there is no welcome mat. Prevailing negative feelings about low-income people lead many local residents to distance themselves from these young returnees. This is accomplished in part through a collective misinterpretation of the facts: Residents claim that the new people in the village are out-of-staters, pointing as evidence to their Florida or Texas license plates. However, if pressed further about where these new people have come from, some residents pause a minute and then say, "Come to think of it, those people don't talk funny. They don't have a southern accent. So I guess maybe they're originally from around here. Maybe they've just been away a while." Nonetheless, a community belief persists that these low-income in-migrants have come from other states or counties and that the reason they came was to take advantage of the state's "generous" welfare payments and the county's various services, a belief that was common in several of the research counties and has been reported by other investigators in other states (Voss et al. 1986). By these beliefs, lower-income returnees are lumped together with any low-income in-migrants who might actually be from other places.

These returning low-income locals are not only categorized as nonlocals but are conceptualized, collectively, as temporary residents within the community and referred to as "transients," a term that further separates "them" from "us" and implies that "they" will soon be gone. In fact, some individual low-income returnees may move back out again, at least temporarily. But whereas the individual returns may be temporary, the phenomenon is not. Through using the word "transient," however, the community obviates the necessity of treating these residents socially as community members.

NEW YEAR-ROUND RESIDENTS

In some of the rural counties, people from "downstate" (the New York–New Jersey metropolitan area) and from other states have recently purchased or built houses and taken up year-round residence in the countryside or the villages. These residents join rural communities as individuals and couples, as parents of children in school, as local businesspeople, as taxpayers, as participants and officers in local clubs, as churchgoers and dog owners. Many are commuters who travel out to work each day. Some of these are hardly known by other residents, as they interact minimally in the community. But other commuters attend local meetings and coach Little League ball in the village at night: Even if they continue to be labeled "newcomers" for a decade or a generation, they are conceived and accepted as members of the community. In several rural communities, this new influx helps make a village come alive again, reversing a downward trend of decades.

One resident, who had earlier been part of this in-migration process, enthusiastically listed the improvements that have come as a result of the recent addition of new year-round residents. "New people in the village are attracting other new people, and the level of community activity and pride goes up. As some young families move in, also some young adults from the village are staying here to settle, instead of moving out to the county seat or a larger village. There is revitalization in village businesses, including a local newspaper, a revitalized spirit, more activities, more for local youngsters to do, and more community pride."

Some of these new residents make up a growing group of "backyard farmers," families with a 5-acre patch or a 40-acre spread, who raise a few chickens or sheep and keep horses, who contribute to the local feed dealer's business, and who participate in 4-H and the county fair. Their positive feeling about farming is appreciated in the community, although humorous comments may circulate about their near-complete lack of farming knowledge and their apparent assumption that money will make up for the farm experience they lack. Some of the backyard farmers have professional occupations that they conduct out of offices in their rural homes; some are making mid-life career changes; others are retiring early from urban professional occupations. As a group, they are choosing rural quality-of-life advantages rather than high urban incomes while their children are still young enough to enjoy the benefits of rural living and rural schooling. Many of these new residents have devoted considerable time and skill to local government and community organizations and are among the most active people leading efforts to preserve and protect the rural natural environment.

One group in particular, police officers from New York City, is represented in several of the rural counties. In some cases, these men spend a decade or so in a commuting arrangement, leaving wives and children in new houses in the country while they spend several days in a row in the city on an intense duty shift, then several days in the country with the family, and then back to the city again. Then, often before their early fifties, these men retire to their rural homes, perhaps taking up a new career there, taking a part-time job, or starting a business. These families are often cited by long-term locals as desirable new residents, active in schools and churches, contributing to the community in many ways, and especially appreciative of the quiet rural environment.

Despite the problems of farming in the 1980s, a few farm families have recently moved to upstate counties. The farm operators had been driven out of farming closer to metropolitan areas by rising real estate prices, taxes, and suburban development. "Real farmers" who come in to take over a farm that had gone out of business are welcomed and easily accepted into the formal and informal networks of farming people. In dozens of farm interviews, neither longtime farmers nor farmers who recently moved into the area made negative remarks about the other as a category, instead assessing each farmer or each farm operation on its own merits. In fact, although some of the farms in each of these counties are owned and operated by a third- or fourth-generation member of a family line, an uncounted but probably fairly high number of farms is operated by people not native to the county.

LAND DEVELOPMENT AND
THE NONRESIDENT POPULATION

As the areas nearer the New York–New Jersey metropolitan area have filled up with residential exurbia, development pressure moves to areas slightly more distant. Land development, sprinkling former farmlands with suburban houses, and spreading vacation cabins in the wooded hills, has come through the western Catskills region, moving through Delaware County from east to west. Second-home development, though slowed down in 1990, is currently making its way through Chenango, Otsego, and Schoharie counties, all bordering on Delaware. In similar fashion, the development boom of vacation or retirement homes is spreading through rural areas outside of other upstate metropolitan centers, in the Tug Hill area, and especially in the remaining available parts of the Adirondack region.

This land development boom is mostly in the hands of large interstate land development corporations, most notably Patten Real Estate, a Vermont-based corporation that operates in twenty-three states and bills itself as "the nation's leading retailer of rural land" (Kunstler 1989). The reach of this particular company is long, and it can transform local landscapes and local communities. In the North Country, the firm was referred to in an interview as "a wolf in sheep's clothing"; in the Tug Hill area, where citizens at a series of public forums on the future of the region expressed real concern about rapid land development, this firm was specifically implicated.

> One man introduced himself and said, "The reason I came over [to this meeting] is the Patten Corporation. . . . Every time I read an ad of something for sale, it's the Patten Corporation. I don't really know who they are. . . . But I'm getting tired of picking up the paper and finding somebody coming in and buying the little guy out and then turning it over into a big development for a huge profit." Another resident predicted that if restrictions on lumbering in the area were tightened, as proposed, the lumber and paper companies would not be able to continue to own the land and would sell out. "Who buys it? Patten . . . and the whole ball game is shot."

Recreational land development is not really a local demographic trend in the strict sense of the term, as it does not refer to people who reside in the area. And it is only happening in certain locations around the state. But where it is occurring, it is an important population trend, in the broader sense, in that it represents a change in the relationship of people and places. The land is being developed and resold by and to people who are not residents at all. Vacation- and retirement-home development brings only seasonal and temporary people. This development does not bring children for the community's schools, volunteers for its fire departments, or ministers for its rural churches. It is a "vacationland" phenomenon, long known in the Adirondack North Country but less familiar to people in other parts of upstate New York where the past has been agricultural and the land has been their own.

CHAPTER SEVEN

Perceptions and Frictions: Problems in Accepting and Absorbing Newcomers

In many rural communities there is an uneasiness about local population changes. One. theme picked up in many interviews is a communal perception that suddenly, quickly, and inexorably the community is undergoing major changes in its composition. Some of the colorful old-timers have died. The school has been losing children. New people are moving in, and they are bringing change to the community. This perception of population change is heightened by the contrast between present population realities and the image of the way the community has "always" been until now.

THE MYTHIC RURAL COMMUNITY: PERCEPTIONS OF STASIS AND STABILITY

The collective image of the recent past is of a community composed of people who had lived in it for generation after generation, a community where everyone knew everyone, where everyone was related to everyone, and where there were few newcomers. This perception of a stable population is part of the collective representation of many rural communities, not only in the United States but also in Europe (Thernstrom 1970; Wylie 1964, pp. 340–370). Still believing in this myth, rural Americans of the late twentieth century become anxious over what they perceive as a "new" mobility of the population and a "new invasion" of "outsiders" into a stable community.

In fact, the populations of most townships and villages of rural New York State show no such stability in the recent past. In Allegany County, for example, census figures from 1980 indicate more recent residency and higher turnover than locally recognized. In this county, after decades of a net population outflow, the standard perception is that the residents who still remain are all truly local people who have been here "forever." Census figures tell a different story.

In 1980, over 40 percent of the population had resided in the county for less than five years, a recency that can only partially be explained by the fact that the 1980 census, for the first time, counted the nearly 5,000 students on three college campuses as county residents. Leaving aside the townships where college students officially made up part of the 1980 population, we find that many other townships have approximately twice as many people who had come in during the five years prior to 1980 as people who had resided there since before 1960. In two of the most rural townships, around 60 percent of the population had arrived within the five years prior to the 1980 census, and only about one-quarter of the population had been there since before 1960. Nonetheless, the local perception is that these townships have had a stable population: "Yes, we've had new people moving in here recently, but mostly it's the same old families."

Perhaps the perception of a stable past continues because those people who do make up the long-term core of residents are more well known in the townships, have other relatives by the same family name who also reside in the area, operate the farms, occupy township offices, live along roads that bear the family name, and are generally more noticed. In contrast, some of the newer residents have been commuters who work elsewhere, may participate only minimally in community affairs, and have few kinship ties locally; so they have been less noticed. Rather than call into question the collective assumption that the past was stable, the response seems to be to exaggerate the suddenness and magnitude of the present "influx of new people."

Local attitudes about the speed and sweep of population changes can be picked up in many settings, and, again, the county fair served as a good barometer of local perceptions. In Delaware County the substantial influx of vacationers and retirees from the metropolitan area has been linked conceptually, even more than in fact, with the farm crisis. By the time of the 1988 fair, communal anxiety over these transformations was running high. One exhibit, put together by a township Grange, presented a strong statement of collective local feelings, cleverly executed in a large display booth. It portrayed starkly a dichotomous contrast between an idyllic image of the very recent past— just last spring—and an imagined scene of an unwanted future only a decade away; between a farming community and a resort-residential community; between "good" and "bad."

The main part of the exhibit, spread out in miniature over a large table, consisted of two displays: on the left, 1988, and on the right, 1998. The 1988 display showed a model farm, an idyllic "Crestwood Farm" with a big red barn, cows in the pasture, and the farmer on his tractor plowing his field. On the right was a model of what the same place was expected to look like in ten years. The idyllic farm had been replaced by a second-home development, with only a tiny farm beside it—and a sign in front advertising "Farm For Sale." The big entryway arch identifying the place proclaimed it as "Crestwood Estates" with "Lakefront and Prime Sites." Another sign warned, "Private Drive, Keep Out." Trucks loaded with building supplies were heading toward houses under construction. Many signs along driveways, on tree trunks, and fenceposts proclaimed "Posted," "No Hunting, Fishing, or Trespassing," and "Private." At the start of an especially long driveway to an especially elegant new house, the sign read "Dr. and Mrs. I. M. Rich." This exhibit was awarded a "best of show" ribbon in the Grange Hall and drew much comment and praise from local fairgoers.

THE CITY COMES TO THE COUNTRY

Another ethnographic vignette, from another setting, also depicts the rapid pace of change.

> In an annex of a township garage, the town clerk's office on an October day was frantically busy. Equipped with a portable manual typewriter as her most modern piece of office equipment, the clerk, a lifelong resident, tried to cope with the modern-day rush of business. A steady stream of cars, vans, and pickup trucks pulled into the driveway out front. People stood by the door or sat waiting on the folding metal chairs around the perimeter of the bare, cement-block room. As the clerk dealt with each individual or couple who came up to her desk, she was constantly interrupted by phone calls asking for some information or where to go and whom to talk with for some problem. One reason for the large number of people coming in that day was that deer season was approaching, and many local people wanted their permits for hunting. But the larger volume of business was in land and housing matters, people needing to get information or take care of matters pertaining to building permits, certificates of occupancy, title transfers, and taxes.

> As the clerk tried to keep up with the rush that afternoon, the changes that were transforming the township itself were being played out right in her office: Two distinct populations were juxtaposed in one place, people from two different backgrounds and with two different reasons for coming, people with two quite different relationships to the local space.

"City People" in Rural Areas

In those regions where new people are moving into rural areas, whether as permanent residents or pre-retirement vacationers, some of the anxiety about the speed of change may turn into negative feelings about the people who are the new residents—not as individuals but as a category. When local residents talk about "the city people coming in," what they mean is not the people in particular but the phenomenon. When questioned about their firsthand knowledge of "city people," some residents admit that they actually do not know any personally or that they have had only minimal interaction. Others say they really like their new neighbors, "even if they are city people." But the phrase "city people" stands for the whole process, so much speeded up in some places in recent years, that includes fragmentation of land, decline of farming, and loss of a community in which, it is believed, "everybody knew everybody." Even farm-owners who have bailed out their shaky farm operations by selling off parcels and who acknowledge that it has been helpful to have ready buyers nonetheless are uncomfortable with the influx of "city people" as a movement.

The changes are first noticed in connection with a weekend or summer population growth. Despite—or perhaps because—these recreation-home owners do not interact much with local people, their presence is noted, and "they" are perceived as "different." The changes are first noticed in the villages.

"When I walk along Main Street in town on weekends, I hardly recognize anybody."

"All summer long the sidewalks in town are filled with designer shorts and 'Banana Republic' clothes."

"The new people are so different from us—they even dress different—and they're really taking over now."

The summertime and weekend changes in traffic, store customers, and pedestrians are only the most obvious and first-noticed changes. Eventually, local people notice that the changes are more pervasive and not only seasonal. Lifelong residents realize that they don't even know the salespeople in the stores any more. Later, even more significant changes break through to consciousness.

"I don't know the president of the local bank anymore."

"In church I don't know too many of the people who are there."

The whole awareness of change has become crystallized around a clear dichotomy, "locals" and "city people." Other synonyms may be used for local people, such as old-timers or natives or farm people, but no matter which term is used for oneself or one's community of reference, the opposed term is invariably "city people." And around this term cluster a whole series of meanings that tell residents who have been here for a long time not only who those "other" people are but also who they themselves are and what their perception of community is. It is a handy dichotomy, used collectively as a way of explaining what is happening, as a way to sort people and to identify the self; it is the community's shorthand to describe the changes and the present situation.

In the absence of effective interaction between the two populations, negative perceptions form. Many of the "weekend people" come to their mountaintop hideaways purposely to escape and avoid interaction with people, so interaction with locals is both unlikely because of topographic isolation and limited because of preference for seclusion. A study of absentee landowners in Delaware County found that "it should not be expected that they are interested in the fate of communities in which their vacation homes are located. They will *not* join the volunteer fire departments, go to church dinners, nor contribute to local causes. In general, they will limit their role in the community to being consumers of community products and services. Yet even their product purchases may be limited, since they can likely get 'better deals' in the urban stores where they have permanent residence" (Warren and Banks 1988, p. 11). Even the early-retirement people who move permanently into their vacation homes tend not to become involved in local politics, churches, or organized social life. For some, this reflects their past: They may have had minimal community involvement in their urban environments and so may not be inclined toward civic participation, even in small communities to which they come.

Among the new permanent residents, on the other hand, whether they are commuters to urban jobs or retirees, many do become participants in local activities and events. As these people become more known in the community, they may lose the label "city people" and become reclassified as "newcomers." This represents a big promotion in the local scheme, for it signifies a transition from "outsider" to a membership status within the community, although further promotion to the status of being "a local" may not come for decades or a generation. These status changes also reveal that the term "city people" is not specifically a reference to an urban place of origin but to being an "outsider" in the community. And as such, "city people" contrasts most sharply with "farm people."

"Farm People" and "City People": Interactions and Perceptions

The contrast between "city people" and "farm people" is a leitmotif in local perception of population changes. These are categories, not descriptions of individual people, but as categories they serve to explain and order people's perceptions of other people. Even though the opinions and feelings of farm people vary as widely as do the individual people from any city, and even though individual farm people and city people may actually be good friends, the perceptual categories are a ready part of the collective belief system and the communal lexicon.

One farm family member scanned the valley and hillsides around her financially troubled farm as we talked. "My neighbors here, they're all city people now. There's a carpenter, a professional painter, and a New York City policeman who moved his family up here. He comes weekends and will move up here in a couple of years when he gets early retirement. They all like farmers. They are all sympathetic to our problems. I like them all."

A farm wife said, "Actually, it helps the farmers to be able to sell off little pieces of land, land that isn't good for farming. It provides the cash we need to manage our debts. And it's nice to see some of the old farmhouses that have been sold to outsiders are getting fixed up. But the city people don't become members of the community, and they don't farm. They fix up the farmhouses, but they don't farm. When you take away the farming, even though there are people living in the old farmhouses, it's just not the same."

The perceived contrast between farm people and city people shows up in ways of doing business and ways of relating to other people, not just in activities related to agriculture.

One farm woman said she tried to be open-minded about the new people coming up from the city—after all, neither her family nor her farming neighbors were true natives, having come in from other parts of the state or even out of state to farm here. But she expressed an awareness of personal contact lost as more city people come in. Her example: "We sold a 5-acre piece of land to a city person. He seemed nice to talk to—at first. But now every communication we have comes from his lawyer. And our lawyer says his lawyer is unpleasant to deal with. I wish the man would talk with us himself, personally, instead of doing everything through lawyers."

In one family, the farm had just been sold to a man from the city. "He seems like a nice person, and he says he wants to keep a few cows in the barn. But city people just have a different view of things. Like, one day he told us that my husband ought to charge our neighbors for all the little services we do for them, such as hauling someone's car out of a ditch with our tractor. But it's just not our way here to charge neighbors for services."

At a higher level of resentment are nuisance and complaint factors, in which each group has a perception that the other is causing a nuisance. Some farm people complain that vandalism to farm property and implements has risen sharply, so that "you can't leave your baler in the field overnight any more," although they recognize that the vandalism might be perpetrated by local youths, not just "city people." Damage to property, such as riding off-road and all-terrain vehicles on farmland and thereby harming crops and causing ruts and erosion, is also seen as caused by locals as well as city people. But several farmers connected the increase in vandalism and farm property damage with the increase in a population that knows nothing about farming. Operators of off-road vehicles, hunters, and even skiers have been known to knock down fences and travel through crops. But the purposeful removing of stones from stone walls, to be hauled away and built into the patio of some weekend home, is thought to be a new kind of transgression perpetrated by new kinds of people who do not understand or value rural life.

Tensions also arise over some of the unattractive aspects of farming. Both vacation-home people and those who have moved in as permanent residents profess to like the farming landscape: They like to see cows grazing in the fields, and they are favorable to farmers and farming—until the neighboring farmer spreads his stored-up manure in the spring or sprays pesticides on his cornfield. Then the complaints come. But, again, they come in ways that farm people think of as a breach of normal rural behavior. Farm people look to past norms, when an aggrieved neighbor would talk directly with a farmer whose cows had got out and trampled her garden. If the farmer delivered a truckload of well-rotted cow manure for the garden, this would settle the issue in a neighborly fashion. The pattern now is that instead of talking directly with the farmer, the new nonfarm neighbor gets on the telephone to someone in authority, even the police, registers a complaint against the farmer, and asks that it be investigated. An instance of this sort was all part of the workday of an agricultural agent at a county Extension office.

The agent returned a phone call to a new resident living in an expensive new house in the countryside. The problem turned out to be that the farmer adjacent to this man's property had just spread a winter's worth of stored manure on his cornfield. The odor was driving the newcomer family indoors, preventing them from enjoying their new patio, making them close all the windows on a lovely summer day, and attracting hordes of flies. The family wanted something done to stop this nuisance. The agent listened patiently to both the facts and the feelings. He then explained that the modern slurry system of manure handling, in which manure is stored in a short, wide silo and spread only a few times a year, preserves the nitrogen better—but it does smell worse when spread. The agent carefully explained that this system of manure handling is standard practice and entirely permissible in an agricultural district, right up to within a fraction of an inch of adjacent lands—no matter which way the wind is blowing. The agent also suggested to the new resident that the direct personal neighbor-to-neighbor approach might be worth trying: "Why not go talk to him. The least he'll do is give you a load of manure to help that new raspberry patch you set in."

These tensions are not new and not unique to this area, of course, as they are well known in any agricultural area where nonfarm people move in. As a recent article on "The Pastoral Paradox" claimed, "People like the idea of a farming landscape, but complain about the farm next door" (Dunphy 1988). The topic of farmers versus "flatlanders" is one of considerable humor in Vermont (see Bryan and Mares 1983), where the few remaining farmers have been inundated by people from Boston, New York City, and the whole megalopolis in between. Across the nation, "right-to-farm" laws have passed in virtually every state, attempting to minimize some of the nuisance conflicts that inevitably increase as nonfarm subdivisions penetrate farmland (Lisansky 1986) and urging dispute resolution rather than court action. However, such philosophically pro-farm legislation is only a small and relatively mild protection for a land-use activity, farming, that is becoming somewhat of an anachronism in some places—not only in the rural countryside but also in the public and political arenas.

Conflicting interests of farmers and their nonfarm neighbors came to a head in the late 1980s in acrimonious debate concerning pesticide spraying. In New York State, the Department of Environmental Conservation (DEC), backed by pro-environmentalist public opinion, required that farmers give prior notification to adjacent landowners before spraying pesticides. The regulations were bitterly fought by agricultural organizations, which claimed that pesticide use on farms was already sufficiently regulated through permits and other restrictions and that the new regulations were excessive and would force farmers out of business. As one farmer asked, "What if you can't get hold of the landowner who lives in New York on the day before you plan to spray? Or what if unpredictable weather conditions make it impossible for a farmer to say with certainty whether he will spray tomorrow or the next day—or whether he will take advantage of today's good weather and do it right now?" In spring 1989 the courts overturned this ruling by the DEC, less on its merits than on the principle that such regulations should originate not in an agency of the executive branch, but in the state legislature. The issue itself was not resolved, and it remained unresolved as the next planting season commenced.

In this issue as in others, the tension in New York's rural counties that contain considerable nonfarm population, whether as vacationers, retirees, or long-term year-round residents, is part of the more general national pattern throughout rural America. But it is particularly noticed in the more densely populated northeastern region because the scale of the population influx is so large, because of the rapid loss of farms in the 1980s, and because there are many more nonfarm people living among a dwindling number of farm people.

The Wealth Gap: Competition for Housing and Land

The perceived wealth of people who have recently come to the area is a major part of the social construction of "city people." Local people caught in tight economic times sometimes express resentment of the wealth of people who can afford fancier vacation homes than they themselves will ever own as their only home. The perception of affluence is often quite correct—at least by comparison to local economic standards.

A survey response from nearly 400 absentee landowners in Delaware County revealed that over 53 percent of nonresident owners had household incomes over $50,000, and 23 percent had incomes above $80,000, a level attained by only a few local people in a county where the median family income in 1980 was $16,072 (Warren and Banks 1988, p. 6).

Even more troubling to local people is that the wealth of "outsiders" and "newcomers" drives up the price of local land and housing to a point where their own grown children cannot afford to live in their hometown. Although the out-migration of local youth has long been a problem, it has generally been driven by the lack of local jobs, a problem that could not easily be blamed on anyone or anything in particular. But the out-migration now resulting from inability to compete in the spiraling housing market is new, and it has a more easily identified source: "wealthy city people." In the more scenic parts of New York State, the problem becomes acute, especially in the Adirondacks, where state regulations impose tight restrictions on land uses and homebuilding outside the hamlets. These restrictions limit the supply of housing lots and require large lots, thus forcing up the cost of housing above what locals can afford, given the low salaries paid in the region (Cohen 1990).

In rural places with rapidly rising land prices, an increasing proportion of low- and moderate-income families are finding mobile homes the only type of housing they can afford. However, in areas with major real estate activity and second-home development, where land prices range from $500 to $1,000 per acre (in Chenango County) on up to $3,000 or more an acre (for small parcels in Delaware), obtaining even enough land to set a trailer on is difficult for young families in a low-wage rural economy.

> "My oldest son, he's got a construction job, in excavation work. There's a lot of work available now in constructing new cabins and houses. He's very good at it. But he has to move from where he's living, and he can't find a place he can afford. The influx from the city has driven up the price of housing something awful. We're trying to help him buy land for a trailer, but even that has gone sky-high. Just recently you could get land for a trailer for only about $200 or $300. Now it's up to $1,000—just for a trailer space."

One result of the housing competition is that the dichotomy between "locals" and "city people" becomes visibly expressed in two diverging types of housing on the rural landscape, phrased by one interviewee as "architect houses and mobile homes." But the problem created by development has another facet besides land costs. With wealthier people owning more expensive homes in the countryside comes pressure to enact land-use regulations to protect the area from excessive development or from the "visual pollution" of mobile homes. These regulations may require a minimum lot size of 5 acres just for a trailer, thus considerably increasing the cost for young couples trying to establish themselves as homeowners in their own community. Another result of land-development pressures is that the stock of somewhat worn-out old housing that in the past was available to local people is no longer within their reach as these places, too, are desirable for outsiders with money to renovate. Rural gentrification thus puts local residents in a tight housing situation and often adds to resentment of outsiders who can pay high prices for land and houses.

The real and perceived wealth gap, and its effect on local costs of living, is one reason why local people are so aware of the consumption patterns of the weekenders and summer people, why expensive cars and fashion clothes become part of the collective image of "city people." The wealth gap also adds to a resentful tone of voice when locals say, "This county is just becoming a playground of the rich." In a number of localities, "the wealthy" are resented almost as much as residents at the opposite end of the economic spectrum, "the welfare."

> As one town supervisor predicted, "We will become the happy hunting ground for New Jersey. We will be bought up in 5- and 10-acre pieces by

people from the city. They will be happy to pay our taxes, but they will be noisy on weekends." Another town supervisor in another county commented, "We are afraid of people who come here with money. Will their affluence change our community?"

Pressures for Services and Amenities
Beyond Local Capacities or Wants

Most rural residents are quite accustomed to dirt roads and dark nights. But, they say, when people from the city move to the country, the first thing they want is to have the hill roads paved and the next thing is to have street lights. Wealth is an issue in this because local people fear that the newcomers, with their higher expectations for services and amenities, will push up local governmental expenses, which will push up property-tax rates. But also at issue here is a set of different perceptions and expectations about services and amenities appropriate for rural areas. If some of the tales of city people wanting upgraded services and expensive amenities are apocryphal or exaggerated, there is ample factual basis to support local people's perceptions.

In one county, some new year-round residents came as a group to a town board meeting and petitioned the town highway department to blacktop a hill road. The town complied. But the new surface caused such serious maintenance problems and costs that the town eventually returned the road to low-maintenance gravel.

In another locality, the pressure comes from weekenders. A town highway superintendent, who has worked on local highways for decades, claims that "city people" make demands on his department that strain his budget, his time, and his patience. On Fridays in the winter he sometimes gets phone calls from city residents telling him that they're coming up for the weekend and want the road plowed. Perhaps it is a back road with no year-round residents, no farms where milk must be picked up each day by the tank truck, and therefore it is low on the highway department's priority for plowing in a snowy winter. This rural highway superintendent, like others, may be caught in the middle of competing ways of using local land that create competing demands on limited service capacity. "To accommodate the demands of the new people I have to cut back on service to old-time residents, give them less than they used to get—and this leaves *them* unhappy. If I don't do what the weekend people want, they remind me how much they are paying in property taxes, and it is a lot, I know. But my highway budget can only stretch so far. And where farmers are concerned, we've got to keep their roads so's the milk trucks can come in."

One town clerk who claims to be "related to half the people in this town and friends with all the rest" captured a whole bundle of local perceptions and anxieties in her comments. "I don't mind sharing the beauty of my area with city people. But if they don't like it here the way it is, why did they come? They raise our taxes. And our young people can't afford a house here anymore."

BLACKS, SOUTHERNERS, AND
"OTHERS WHO ARE DIFFERENT"

The rural communities of upstate New York, by and large, have been racially and ethnically very homogeneous. Many rural residents claim that their community has no racism, although it would be more correct to say that they simply have not had the opportunities to interact with a diverse population and so have had no situations in which racial and ethnic stereotypes, ignorance, and prejudice would be acted out. Only in a few rural communities is there already a significant black population, as in cases where agricultural migrant laborers have settled out or where a specific local historical factor brought blacks into a community generations ago. Most of the American Indian population of the rural counties lives somewhat apart on reservations, as in the case of the Mohawk Nation (Akwasasne), of whom over 2,000 people live on the St. Regis Reservation in Franklin County.

Demographic projections for the first two decades of the twenty-first century show New York State's black and Hispanic population growing faster than the white population, so that by the year 2015, non-Hispanic whites are expected to make up less than 48 percent of the state's population (Bouvier and Briggs 1988). Although most of this growth will undoubtedly take place in the New York City region and the upstate metropolitan areas, it seems likely that the faces and voices of rural communities will also become more varied in coming decades. Economic factors alone, particularly high city rents and shortage of affordable housing in the suburbs will drive an exodus that will be racially and ethnically diverse. Some rural counties closer to the metropolitan areas have already picked up significant minority populations in the late 1980s. For example, Sullivan County (see Map 1.2), still officially listed as among the "most rural" but changing very rapidly, has recently gained a noticeable Hispanic and black population, mostly from the nearby New York City metropolitan area. A little farther from the city, a village in rural Greene County has also started receiving a new population that includes Hispanics and blacks.

The previous lack of significant racial or ethnic heterogeneity in rural populations, and the likelihood that the future will bring much more heterogeneity, is a matter of concern in several rural communities. At its best, the concern is with how to undo and change negative stereotypes and prejudices *before* the situations arise when they might be translated into action, how to prepare for diversity. Among more remote rural communities, the response to the first few people of different racial or ethnic backgrounds has been varied.

In one rural township the first black family to move in eventually left because of negative feelings expressed by some residents of the community. When a second black family purchased a house, a petition against them was circulated in the community. But they stayed and have won acceptance and respect as exemplary members of the community, the children participating actively and successfully in the local school, where, however, they are still the only blacks. The parents report that they now feel accepted in the formal community activities, and they are involved in informal neighboring patterns of visiting, borrowing, and helping.

In another county, a small group of blacks has lived in one community for generations, but the rest of the county has had very few black residents. As one young woman said, "With so few of us, you could never go to a prom at school because there was no one to go with who wasn't your brother or your cousin." In the late 1980s, some middle-class black families have moved to some of the smaller villages, one couple opening up a store in a refurbished building on a depressed Main Street.

In several communities of the rural counties, a black man or woman is among the vibrant, energetic, and forward-looking community participants, serving as an educator, minister, or human service worker, operating a government agency or working in a prominent position. Some community residents who have been concerned about the problem of local prejudices point with relief to these success stories and hope that they can serve as "stereotype-busters." Even the growing preponderance of medical doctors from Pakistan, India, and the Philippines has reportedly had an effect in "wearing down the stereotypes." For many rural residents, a visit to the clinic doctor is the first time they have ever heard a foreign accent. At first some were skeptical that these doctors would be accepted in the community; but the experience has generally been positive, in part because rural residents badly need the services of these physicians and also because the interaction is person to person.

In some places, however, the change in population make-up comes more quickly than the change in attitude, especially if significant numbers of people are moving in, or if those moving in are of a lower socioeconomic level. In some rural counties closer to the New York metropolitan area, the problem of accepting ethnically or racially different people may be exacerbated by the fact that the new population is largely composed of lower-income people squeezed out of the city by high costs and intolerable conditions. In these small towns, negative attitudes about poor people may compound ethnic or racial prejudices. In the distant North Country, a different situation may serve to increase racial and ethnic stereotypes. In the growing number of state prisons in the region, a large proportion of prison inmates are black and Hispanic. For some local residents, this inmate population has confirmed their stereotypes. A specific prison-related problem is that when the families of inmates travel to the far reaches of New York State to visit their incarcerated members, they may also spend time in the village, appearing to local people as a "crowd" on the sidewalk or in the fast-food restaurant, a crowd of people who are "different" and with whom there is no interaction. The subtle fears provoked and negative attitudes hardened in these situations may make it even more difficult for some local residents to interact easily when the community does gain a more racially and culturally diverse resident population. Some local leaders concerned about this issue have suggested that the negative attitudes could be reduced if more black and Hispanic employees of the state prison system moved to upstate communities as more prisons open up there. Such employees would, these leaders hope, hold well-paid jobs, buy average houses, and generally match the socioeconomic mainstream of the community, and would therefore be effective in helping the community overcome racial and ethnic prejudice. So far, however, upstate prisons have had difficulty attracting minority employees to these distant and perhaps unfriendly communities.

In some rural communities, decisions by federal government about federal facilities have brought major changes in the make-up of the population. For example, the U.S. Army's 1984 decision to expand significantly its Fort Drum military base near Watertown, at the western edge of the Tug Hill area, has meant a tremendous and rapid influx of population: 25,000 soldiers and their families, with housing built by the army and private developers not only on the base but in communities up to 30 miles distant (Smardon and Carter 1990). The expansion has had the economic impacts local leaders had sought for their regional economy, including a real estate and construction boom that created many jobs and a major surge in retail sales. The sizable influx of people has quickly created a much more heterogeneous population for many communities near the base, as black military personnel and their families move in. Because this sudden heterogeneity has come as part of a boom period when long-term residents feel more secure economically than they have for decades, the adjustment to population diversity has, on the whole, been reasonably smooth.

> Some small communities with federally supported housing for military personnel have doubled in population in just a few years, and the faces on the streets, in the new village park, and in the classrooms are more varied now. So are the voices. To at least some residents, the southern accents are harder to get used to than the racial diversity. Locals still notice that the salespeople in the malls, many of whom are army wives, have southern accents. Although there are some negative feelings toward "the army" and various complaints about traffic problems and the changed character of the area, both school and local government officials were cautiously optimistic in 1989 that the predicted racial tensions had not materialized. "Our people are learning quickly," they said.

Elsewhere in the state, scattered particularly along minor roads in some of the central part and especially in the western Southern Tier, is a smaller but growing in-migrant population of "people who are different." Amish people from Pennsylvania have been arriving through the last decade, settling along the back roads and taking over abandoned farmland. They remove electric wires and set to work repairing derelict old barns; they plow up overgrown pastures, thin out the forests and saw up lumber, and make quilts, cheese, and baked goods to sell by the roadside. In some of the rural areas where Amish families have settled, local people admit to being puzzled by the old-fashioned ways of the Amish, such as the absence of cars, trucks, and tractors; childhood immunizations; electricity; and house telephones (to say nothing of television). But the locals have high praise for the "hardworking," "thrifty" attributes of the Amish people and for their success in farming land that had been given up as "unfarmable" years before. Young Amish boys make steady workers on non-Amish farms, earning a reputation for working hard and not goofing off.

In Allegany County the Amish earned a new spot in the hearts of local people when a contingent of Amish men, in their distinctive hats and beards, attended the first public meeting concerning the possible siting of a radioactive waste facility in the county: The audience clapped as the Amish men filed in and sat down in the front row. They sat there silently as a group, then left as a group. As a county political leader said, "By their presence, they signified their membership in the county, and they were welcomed as such." For the county this was a demonstration that "they" were now part of "us."

STEREOTYPES, SCAPEGOATS, AND UNEASINESS WITH CHANGE

The terms "city people," "outsiders," "weekenders," and "people who are different" are group labels, ways of categorizing and referencing other people. The labels and the accompanying stereotypes are not an expression of feeling about the actual people one knows, however, but about the people one doesn't know or doesn't know well. Many local people explicitly state, in fact, that they like and get along with most of the city people they know. But like all group labels, these terms convey and perpetuate negative attitudes toward people as members of a group. Even the term "newcomer," used for people who may have moved in a decade ago, keeps these residents in a limbo category and reminds them of their somewhat separate status.

On a deeper level, these terms represent a collective expression of concern over the rapid pace of change in many rural communities and can be better understood in the context of this general anxiety. Some communities have experienced only minimal population and land-use change during the decade, but in others the pace of change has gathered sufficient momentum to make change, rather than stability, the most noticeable condition of the rural community. In the Tug Hill area, for example, caught in the pincers of the double impact of the Fort Drum expansion and land-development pressures for recreational use, concern over the rapid pace of change was evident in a series of public forums in winter and spring 1989. As the Tug Hill Commission surveyed and listened to public attitudes about "the present and future character of our town," the theme phrase of the meetings was, "There is nothing permanent except change."

Where an influx of new residents has occurred, it has generally coincided with other major changes happening at the same time. To some extent, negative feelings about the various other changes in their lives and their communities become translated by rural residents into negative feelings about the people who are now among them. In some places new people have arrived at the same time that there was a significant loss of dairy farms due to financial difficulties. The temporal association is often interpreted as a sign of causation: The population influx is seen as having brought about the farm loss.

A less-noticed reason why so much seems to be changing so fast is that long-term local residents themselves have been changing their own living styles. The traditional style of interpersonal interaction in rural communities has been gradually breaking down anyway, even without any influence from in-migrants. Longtime rural residents, like Americans everywhere, are doing their shopping at regional malls—so of course they interact less with local merchants, salespeople, and residents in the village. Rural residents, like Americans everywhere, are transacting their banking with plastic cards—so of course they don't interact with the local bank tellers. Thus, when they do walk along Main Street, not only do they not know the people they see in the village, but, even more unsettling, the people they see there don't know them. To some extent, this loss of knowing and being known by others results from local people's own actions as much as from the arrival of new people. But as these losses in social connectedness break through to consciousness, they are cross-referenced with observations made along Main Street on the weekend, and the whole uneasy perception of a changing local community is lumped together and blamed on a scapegoat: "city people" and other "outsiders."

Local people's diagnosis of the cause of their discomfort may be inaccurate and may overlook the role they themselves play in bringing about changes in the community; nonetheless, these perceptions and oversights generate strong feelings. When enough people have similar feelings, a collective explanation arises in a community, encoded in the frequently used phrases, "city people" or "outsiders" or "newcomers" or "different." These code words then become the basis for interpreting subsequent new information and experience. Inaccurate as the terms are, and unfair to people covered by them, a greater problem with such a collective representation may be that it prevents the community from dealing effectively with the situation of change, from valuing the incoming populations and benefiting from the vitalizing effects of diversity. The collective anxiety about "all these new people coming in" impedes sociocultural adjustment to a new demographic reality.

PART FOUR

Worsening Rural Poverty

CHAPTER EIGHT
Poverty in Rural Places: Patterns and Changes

The general public's image of rural America does not even include poverty; conversely, the public image of poverty does not include rural places. And so poverty, as real a feature of many rural landscapes as the hills, fields, and barns, goes quite unnoticed by the predominantly urban national population and inadequately addressed by federal and state governments. An endemic feature in many places, rural poverty now seems to be growing worse.

The complex causes of increased rural impoverization will be explored in the next chapter. The present chapter emphasizes local-level description. The purpose here is to present an overview of the changing patterns of rural poverty in this region. Before turning to local observations, however, an overview of the rural poverty situation on the national, regional, and state levels will help set the context.

RURAL POVERTY THROUGH THE 1980s: NATIONAL AND STATEWIDE TRENDS

Rural poverty has been increasing nationwide through the 1980s. At mid-decade, rural poverty was growing faster than urban poverty and was becoming more entrenched (O'Hare 1988, p. 6). By 1986, the nonmetropolitan poverty rate had reached 18 percent, virtually the same as the rate in the nation's inner cities, while the metropolitan poverty rate was only 12 percent and the national rate around 13.5 percent (O'Hare 1988, p. 6; Porter 1989, p. 26). Although at the end of the decade the inner city poverty rate again surpassed the nonmetropolitan poverty rate, the generally poor economic performance in rural America in the 1980s (Deavers 1988) is likely to lead to continuation of high poverty levels in many rural areas through the 1990s, particularly if the nation as a whole should experience recession.

The point, however, is not just that poverty exists in rural places, or that the percentage of the population below the poverty line in rural places is as high as it is in inner cities. Besides that, poverty in rural places is different from poverty in urban areas. It takes different forms and has different expressions from urban poverty because it is embedded within the context of rural places, rural economic systems, and rural sociocultural institutions. And the changes taking place in rural economic, demographic, and sociocultural patterns in the 1980s were causing qualitative as well as quantitative changes in rural poverty.

On the whole, the rural (or nonmetropolitan) Northeast has less poverty than other rural regions. Figures for 1987 show an 11.2 percent poverty rate in the nonmetropolitan Northeast, as compared to a rural poverty rate in the South of exactly twice that level, 22.4 percent, whereas in the West it was 18.3 percent and in the Midwest 14.4 percent (Porter 1989, p. 31).

In New York, as in most states, rural counties tend to fall below metropolitan counties in nearly all economic indicators. The counties classified as "most rural" together have had the highest unemployment, lowest median family income, lowest percentage of families in affluence, and lowest level of formal education attained; and their poverty rate was exactly tied with the New York City metropolitan area—both being far ahead of the state average (Eberts 1984). According to these indicators, the divergence in economic well-being between New York's rural and metropolitan areas has increased during the 1980s (Eberts and Khawaja 1988).

Unlike urban poverty, and unlike rural poverty in some other regions, a striking characteristic of poverty in rural New York is its racial and ethnic similarity to the majority, nonpoor population. The rural poor in New York State, as is generally true in the Northeast and Appalachia, are mostly white and non-Hispanic. Only in a few specific locations is there a racial or ethnic component, as in some places where blacks have settled out of the agricultural migrant stream and among some American Indian populations.

The increase in poverty in rural New York, as in most of rural America, is not primarily farm related. There is a scattered population of farm laborers, as well as some marginal farm operators, who have traditionally been poor. And farm labor jobs are part of the employment background of a number of rural poor people not now working in agriculture. By and large, though, the bulk of poverty in rural New York, and its recent growth, is related less to agriculture than to problems in the nonfarm economy.

Statistical Profile of Poverty in Rural New York: What the Figures Don't Show

The growing divergence in economic well-being between rural and metropolitan New York becomes more stark when we look at figures for specific rural areas of the state. The 1980 poverty figures for the most rural counties ran as high as 18.4 percent, compared to a national poverty rate in that year of 13.0 percent. Since 1980, poverty rates in these rural counties followed the national trend in rising steeply then falling—but only down again to somewhere slightly above the 1980 levels. In terms of per capita income, the most rural counties rank in the lowest third of the state's counties, usually at or near the bottom.

Aggregate profiles of rural counties, however, may fail to reveal just how serious poverty may be in some places within a rural county. Counties that in the aggregate are poor contain localities that are even poorer. For example, Allegany County, perennially among the poorest in the state, claimed the state's lowest income. Additionally, 20 percent of its population received some form of assistance from the Department of Social Services each month. In 1989 it had the highest rate of public assistance. But within this poor county several places were considerably poorer. In some of its more rural townships, more than 10 percent of the residents had incomes less than 75 percent of the poverty line. In 1985, one-third of the county's townships had a per capita income below 60 percent of the county's already low level, ranging down to two townships that stood at less than 50 percent of state's per capita income. (Excluded from these calculations are localities with significant institutionalized populations, in this case, colleges.) In other rural counties, too, intracounty variation in poverty rates is considerable: Some villages and townships have a poverty rate more than twice that of their county.

The extent of rural poverty is hidden by other aggregation effects too: In New York, as elsewhere in the nation, some counties that are not classified as either rural or poor contain within them some localities that are both very rural and very poor. (Nationally, there are an estimated 2.3 million people who are poor and reside in rural places that lie within metropolitan areas and who, therefore, are not officially counted among the nation's *rural* poor.) For example, Broome County, an upstate metropolitan county with a fairly large city, Binghamton, just made it into the top quarter of the state's counties in terms of per capita income in 1985. But Broome also contains some rural townships in which per capita income is only 67 percent of the county figure, and serious poverty exists. Adjacent Tioga County, slightly more rural, ranks fairly well in terms of per capita income and is not regarded as a poverty county. But in one if its very rural townships the adjusted per capita income actually decreased from 1979 to 1985, and official records show that more than 54 percent of households fell within Department of Housing and Urban Development (HUD) income guidelines for federal low-income home-improvement grants. In Essex County in the North Country, the fairly high per capita income level that results from a small number of quite wealthy people statistically hides one desperately poor township that was described by local human service workers as "tightly packed with need." In such places, where rural poverty is clustered within a few townships or villages, the healthy countywide income statistics make it difficult to obtain funds for special poverty-related programs.

On the local level in a number of places, various indicators suggest that poverty has been increasing significantly in the end of the decade. Certain county welfare departments, school districts, and other institutions report a new influx of low-income people arriving in their locality from elsewhere, some report an increase of local people falling into poverty now, and many report that few of the local people who were already poor have been able to escape from poverty. Unfortunately, statistics on poverty in the end of the 1980s are not readily available and are not fine-grained or recent enough to keep up with these changing situations on the local level. But when rural county departments of social services saw their AFDC (Aid to Families with Dependent Children) caseloads rise as much as 12 to 18 percent in 1989 alone, when a village food pantry finds itself running out of emergency supplies even more often, and when school teachers, social workers, and pediatricians all report more low-income families under more stress, then at these local levels the rise in rural poverty seems real enough, even though not precisely measured. In addition to the increase in numbers of poor people, some significant changes are making rural poverty more troublesome and harder to alleviate.

To provide local-level understanding of the worsening rural poverty situation, ethnographic research has been conducted within the four core counties (Allegany, Chenango, Delaware, and Franklin) and supplemented by additional observations, interviews and secondary data collected in the remainder of the counties in the three research regions, plus spot checks in other rural counties. Because rural poor people live in very different settings from urban poor people, this chapter's examination of poverty will concentrate on describing the kinds of rural places where poverty is located and the characteristics of that poverty.

PORTRAITS OF RURAL POVERTY:
THREE RESIDENTIAL PATTERNS

Three quite different kinds of situations are most likely to contain high concentrations of rural poverty: open-country residential clusters, small villages, and trailer parks. These three do not represent types of poverty or types of poor people, however, for each includes some people who are not poor and some who only occasionally fall below the poverty line. Additionally, people who are poor may move from one residential situation to another, and nonpoor people also live in these residential settings. These three are simply the kinds of places in rural areas where concentrations of poor people are likely to be found; differentiation among them is useful for analytical purposes and for policymaking and program design.

Pockets of Long-Term, Intergenerational Poverty
in the Open Countryside

Pockets of nonfarm poverty in the open countryside have been a persistent feature of the landscape in many areas of New York and throughout the northern Appalachian region. This is particularly the case where soils, topography, and market conditions made agriculture marginal and where poorer families who remained on the land did not

adapt well into the employment opportunities of the growing towns or cities of the region (Vaughan 1929, Brunner and Lorge 1937, Sanderson 1937). Many of the descendants of the difficult adaptation continued to live in the same open-country areas along back roads and remained economically poor and socially marginal. A few of the pockets of poverty of the central Southern Tier counties were the subject of long-term ethnographic research (Fitchen 1981). The situation, as it was in the 1970s, can be briefly summarized here.

Visually, such depressed rural neighborhoods are characterized by small clusters of dilapidated housing: run-down farmhouses, very old trailers encased in wooden additions, and shacks built of used lumber and tar paper. Space around the homes is strewn with old cars and car parts, building materials, appliances, snowmobiles, and other recreational equipment. There are no stores, schools, or public buildings. People must travel, often 20 miles or more, to towns and small cities where they work, go to school, shop, and tend to official business such as licensing cars, making court appearances, and applying for food stamps, or connecting with community agencies.

A greater problem than geographical isolation, however, is the social isolation of such rural pockets of poverty. Their social separation from the larger urban-based community is revealed verbally: They refer to it as "the outside world." Reciprocally, the people of the rural pockets of poverty are referred to by the larger community in such derogatory terms as "poor white trash," "the shack people," or "people who live like animals." Their social life is almost entirely confined to the immediate neighborhood or within a cluster of similar depressed neighborhoods that are linked by geographic proximity, kinship, marriage, car trading, and shared poverty and stigma.

Virtually all of the adults of these depressed neighborhoods had grown up in poverty, either in the same locale or in a similar pocket of poverty nearby, and they have remained chronically poor. Although most households generally have at least one person employed most of the time, they work in low-paying jobs on highway and public-works crews, on night-shift janitorial jobs, and on factory assembly lines. Most mothers of young children stay home with them, unless they can get a night-shift job or have a relative who will babysit. Most households hover just around the official poverty line and are easily kicked below it by an accident, illness, or loss of job. When the children of these pockets of poverty grow up, most settle close to home, often in a trailer placed in the side yard. Some return home after a brief residence elsewhere, seeking refuge from a larger world in which they are unable to participate effectively.

To survive in this poverty, people depend on a variety of strategies and coping mechanisms, with special emphasis on the informal economy, on minimizing cash outflow, and relying on a network of relatives and friends. People "make do" on their own to the extent they can, utilizing these social resources to substitute for inadequate financial resources. Though always short of money and never accumulating a cushion to boost them out of poverty, they tide themselves over from crisis to crisis, just getting by but never getting ahead.

Now, more than two decades after research in these pockets of poverty began, the same poverty is still there, not only in the few places where it was studied, but dispersed along back roads of many rural New York counties. This scattered poverty is widespread in rural New York, deeply entrenched, and now cycling into yet another generation. In several localities in the central region of the state, where I had earlier done windshield surveys and brief interviewing, the very same pockets of poverty are still there today—but the number of shacks, trailers, and people in them has grown.

In one neighborhood where I had done intensive research, recent inquiries indicate that although a few of the children I tracked through the 1970s have broken out of poverty, most of them now exhibit the same problems of inadequate education, unsatisfactory employment, tenuous marriages, poverty, and low self-esteem that enveloped their parents. As adults, they now commute daily in beat-up cars to low-paid jobs in the nearest urban center. Most have spent the last decade in place or simply moving around from one such pocket of poverty to another, never generating enough momentum to spin out of their poverty and social marginality. Another generation of children, larger than the last one, is now growing up in the same poverty that enveloped their parents and grandparents. Some of these children have already been identified by schools, public health officials, and family courts as children at risk.

In other parts of the state, where such isolated pockets of poverty also dot the countryside, these, too, are long-standing, intergenerational situations. In almost every county where research was conducted, a variety of local people, including schoolteachers, Head Start staff, public health nurses, and welfare caseworkers, were unanimous in pointing out on a county map the location of such pockets of poverty. And these local workers have all indicated that the residents of these depressed neighborhoods have not become less poor in the last decade, nor have their numbers decreased.

Poverty in Villages and Small Towns

The second residential expression that poverty takes in rural New York consists of clusters of low-income people living in rental apartments in small towns and villages. In virtually every one of the research counties, at least one or two villages fit this pattern. Many such villages are located on the extreme periphery of a county, in several cases straddling the border between two counties, rather remote from the jobs of any urban center and the services of a county seat and from the high housing costs of its more built-up areas.

One such village, located under 15 miles from a county seat, sits at an intersection of a through-traffic state highway and a minor state road. In the 1970s the village was the home of about 400 families, shopkeepers, retired farmers, and blue-collar workers commuting to factory jobs in the county seat. The population of the village became more economically depressed as employment in the county seat dropped. Some residents moved out of the village and the area, leaving behind an even more economically marginal population, including families just barely getting by, elderly people, a number of widows, and some housebound and disabled people. School enrollments that had been shrinking for years sank precipitously. In the early 1980s, several businesses folded, real estate prices were "down in the bottom," and the surplus of houses, deteriorating but available, grew.

A few young families with small children moved in, attracted by the low-cost housing that would enable them to stretch out their meager income from a low-paying job, unemployment benefits, or welfare. This trickle of new young families became an influx as some of the old houses and vacated store buildings were purchased by outside investor-landlords who converted them into multiple-family residences and rented out apartments. Several old homes were divided into three or four units; one of the larger old houses was "chopped up" into a dozen apartments holding upwards of twenty-five residents. Each household was paying $300 to $350 a month in 1988 for apartments that were generally known to be substandard but had not been inspected. The tenants were young adults, single individuals and couples, and women alone or with young children, most of whom had previously been living elsewhere in the county.

One house that formerly held a single family now contains four rental units, each of its side entrances now leading to a separate apartment, and four electricity meters lined up on the front porch. Extra cars, some no longer operable, fill its driveway and one side yard. Bicycles, scooters, strollers, and used tires are scattered on the front lawn. Two rental trailers sit beside the house on what once was a side yard.

Many of the tenants of these apartments are on public assistance, some entirely dependent on welfare, others combining employment and partial assistance, including food stamps and medicaid. Many are unable to find

work or lack reliable transportation to get to a job if they had one. Both men and women tend to work part time and odd hours. Some women work nights in the larger town, in the shopping mall or fast-food restaurants, leaving a husband or boyfriend looking after the children.

On a typical weekday, young men are working on cars, watching over small children at play on the front step. Very young mothers push their babies in strollers along the sidewalks to the laundromat or to the pay phone by the drug store. The one remaining grocery store has a constant stream of customers using food stamps and of small children buying soda pop and keeping the teenage cashier busy. The corner gas station also has a convenience mart, which does a brisk business in videotape rentals and beer. The post office is particularly crowded at the start of each month, when welfare checks arrive. Two churches struggle to keep going, and their small congregations alternate the task of operating the emergency food pantry. The number of people coming for government-donated food or emergency food has steadily increased from about fifteen families coming sporadically in the early 1980s to sixty households being served at most distributions, about half of them coming quite regularly.

This small-town or village poverty, like the open-country pockets of poverty, has precursors in the past. Back in the Depression era, after decades of population decline, some small towns and villages experienced growth in population, but mostly in poorer people, because of "movement from the open country to villages and small towns" (Sanderson 1937, p. 22) and "migration from cities to cheaper homes and low taxes of villages" (Brunner and Lorge 1937, p. 68). More than half a century later, a similar phenomenon is again apparent in many rural counties: Some small towns and villages are gaining an increasing number of low-income people. And the factors underlying the present situation are quite similar. Today, as a result of recent decades of rural population loss, houses and store buildings in some rural villages have become vacant. Absentee landlords (either family heirs or outside investors), unable to sell or rent these buildings for their original purposes, have cut them up into apartments, which they now rent at rates that are considerably lower than rents in the larger towns or nearby cities, though not usually quite low enough to fit within the shelter allowance of welfare or the budget of low-wage earners. Thus, some small villages have become de facto low-income housing sites.

Although the phenomenon of impoverishment of small villages is not new, it seems to be increasing at the present time. More villages are affected, and more poor people are living in more cheap apartments in these villages. In some of the research counties, some of the low-income people settling in these villages are part of a return migration of young adults coming back home. Many are young adults who have grown up locally or nearby and have only recently fallen into poverty as a result of low earnings, single parenthood, or both. In counties closer to metropolitan regions, more of the low-income in-migrants appear to be from the urban area and its adjacent counties. Although this latter group is not at all well counted or documented, records from some county agencies and interviews in several counties indicate that it is composed largely of people unable to keep up with rapidly escalating urban housing costs, people moving to rural areas to find cheaper housing, to follow their friends, and to seek a better life in a small community. Being potentially mobile because the service-sector jobs they have may also be available in rural areas or the welfare that supports them is transferable, some low-income people are resolving the shortfall between income and housing costs by moving from urban areas and from the county's more dynamic or larger villages to small villages and hamlets.

At the same time that some lower-income people are moving from more built-up areas to small villages, there is also a centripetal movement inward to some villages. Some of the poorer residents of open-country pockets of poverty, especially young adults who grew up in kin-based housing clusters, are moving inward to nearby villages and towns, creating a small but growing pattern of in-migration. This centripetal movement results in a concentration of young adults who grew up nearby—and poor—settling into the old buildings of the hamlets.

According to such diverse sources as a director of a local office of the state Employment Service and a probation director, both of whom had grown up in the area, as well as a county social services commissioner, there is an increasing number of young adults, still in their teens, perhaps still in school, who leave the parental home in a rural pocket of poverty to move to a larger village. These young people may combine school, part-time jobs, and welfare support in varying proportions, seeking "independence" from parents, "excitement" to replace the "boredom" they experience at home, and companionship and social interaction among peers. To stretch their financial resources in the village apartments, these young adults settle in what one school superintendent described as "nests of individuals living together." These arrangements are fragile and frequently disrupted by shifting personal attachments, disputes over household finances and rent, problems with the landlord over late rent payment and damage to the property, and unanticipated changes in status such as becoming a parent or landing in jail.

In most cases there is no public transportation serving these villages, and many of the residents are unable to provide their own reliable transportation to the larger towns where the jobs are. People arrive assuming that they can rely on a friend or relative or their own old car to get to work in town or at the regional mall, but many find themselves stranded by the difficulty of providing their own transportation, yet unable to afford to move closer to where the jobs are. Absence from work may be a common result, or simply not getting a job at all or having a series of short-term jobs alternating with periods of being unemployed.

Employment counselors find that many of the long-term unemployed men and women who live in these villages simply have no adequate means of transportation. Riding with friends, patching up cars that barely pass inspection, driving after insurance has expired, and hitchhiking are common—but unreliable. "Transportation" is frequently listed, and usually accepted, as a "barrier to employment" that releases a food stamp recipient, for example, from the work requirement.

Some critics, such as one local political leader, claim that such people are not really stuck and argue that "if those people had any motivation, they would move out of that antisocial, degenerated place where there are no jobs, move into town [the county seat] where there are all kinds of stores advertising for cashiers, baggers, clerks, and stockboys." But as a county planner said, with considerable feeling, "The idea that the rural poor can move into town and take jobs is a *sick myth*. There are no jobs accessible to them that pay enough and no housing that they could afford on the jobs they could get." And so some hamlets and small villages continue to attract more low-income residents.

Rapidly Growing Trailer Parks and Informal Trailer Clusters

Just at the edge of one of the villages described above, nestled against farm fields, a trailer park that was started a decade ago with only a few trailers now holds a few dozen, and preparations are under way to add fifteen more. Like several other new and growing trailer parks in this township, and like many throughout rural New York, this one

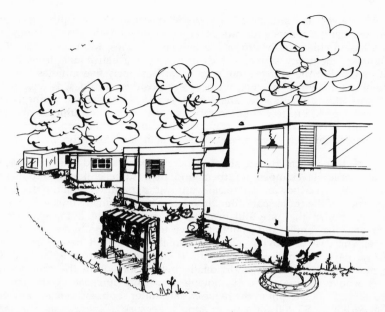

holds a concentration of lower-income residents. Some are owners and some renters of their trailers; a few have been here several years, some arrived only recently, and some expect or hope to move soon.

This is one of the cheaper trailer parks in the area, charging $120 a month in 1989, discounted to $105 if paid by the first of the month. Water and septic system are provided, though inadequate, and tenants pay their own utilities; additionally, a $300 security deposit has been instituted, even for current residents. Many of the thirty-five households in this park are living at or below the poverty line, though as two residents explained, there are people who are long-term poor and others, such as themselves, who are currently poor because of limited earning power and a growing family but who had not been raised in poverty and did not expect to remain poor. "These more stable families have mostly been in the park for several years, they keep their lawns mowed, don't allow junk to accumulate around their yards, and they watch their children both indoors and out." But one section of the park has a higher turnover of residents, fewer people employed, more noise at night, and more children unsupervised. Residents of the former type resent the bad reputation some tenants have given the park.

The park contains close to 100 children, the majority preschool and elementary school age. Most of the men work in the city, as do many of the women. Men who work night-shift jobs and unemployed men hang around the park in the daytime, working on cars and running in and out of the village. Mothers who are employed commute to work, with their husbands if they are married to an employed man, but find that $100 a week goes to child care in the village or within the trailer park, for the long commute means long babysitting hours. Mothers staying at home with young children refer to themselves as "stranded housewives" because few families have more than one car. Residents with cars usually take riders to the city for shopping—for a fee. In children's health or accident emergencies, women call the village volunteer emergency squad. The closest clinic is a half hour's drive; to walk with a child to the village store requires at least forty-five minutes. The local school, about which parents express very positive attitudes, is now packed full and adding new space. The school provides bus service to the edge of the trailer park, but few children can stay after school for athletics and other programs because of limited transportation home afterward. Many of the trailer-park children have no supervision at home after school.

One resident indicated that she and her husband would like to move out, as the trailer is cramped for them and their three children and they are troubled by what they feel are socially unhealthy conditions and the stigmatized reputation of the trailer park. But although they have finally finished payments on their trailer, they are still just able to meet current living expenses for their growing family and unable to save up toward the move they hope to make. The cost of moving a trailer, "unless you buy it new from a dealer and he pays to move it to your site, is outrageous," from $500 to $1,000. To move the trailer to an individually owned lot within the county's rural areas would involve not only moving costs and purchase of the land but also about $5,000 to put in the required sand-filter septic system and anywhere from $1,000 to $5,000 for a water supply. Because of these costs, this family has felt confined to stay within trailer parks. But other trailer parks, nicer or closer to towns, are too expensive—"you can't afford a place there. Besides, those parks are already full and have waiting lists." As this woman said, "You can *get* on a waiting list, but you can't *live* on a list."

Not all of the mobile homes in the parks and in the open countryside are owned and occupied by people who are poor, for many lower-middle-income families find a mobile home the only affordable form of home ownership. For a number of families, a trailer represents a step up, a more spacious, more private place to live, a home of their own rather than living with parents or in-laws. For some, the "mobile home" they presently rent or own is part of a dream of becoming "upwardly mobile," and in some cases a family has made the transition, living in their trailer on their property in the country while building the house, and eventually moving into the house and selling the trailer. However, the older mobile homes, generally referred to less pretentiously as trailers, are a hallmark of rural poverty, spatially and temporally associated with an increase of poverty. Often the trailer becomes permanent housing rather than an interim step. For the most part, trailers do not usually turn out to be as good an investment as their buyers had hoped: Resale value after several years of family wear and tear is usually considerably depreciated.

For people of insecure and inadequate income, perhaps hovering just around the poverty line, trailers are "the housing of choice"—a choice severely constrained by low income and low earning potential and by the high cost of other forms of housing. The older trailers that many lower-income people own or rent are inadequate in terms of space and quality. Many are expensive to heat, burning up a lot of kerosene and leaking a lot of heat to the outdoors, and in midsummer they can be unbearably hot. Furthermore, they are not necessarily cheap in proportion to the income their occupants earn, or to the housing allowance from public assistance.

The purchase of a reasonably good used trailer anything less than a decade old (and thus built after some minimal construction and safety standards were instituted in 1975) may involve as much as $10,000, even up to $20,000. One family that purchased a new trailer figured they would be making payments on it until 1999. Trailer-park rents, too, are a burden for lower-income residents. Even the cheaper parks charge a trailer owner over $100 a month just for the lot with its sewer and water service and electrical hook-up, and they charge from $250 to $350 a month to those who rent a trailer. In one community, trailer rent in a tightly packed park was $200 to $250 a month, plus electricity and kerosene for heat. At the time, the housing allowance for a family of three on welfare was about $150.

Particularly in rural townships with high poverty rates, low per capita income levels, or both, mobile homes are becoming ever more prevalent, including individual trailers on privately owned lots that most occupants would prefer but many cannot afford, and also in parks and informal groupings.

In Chenango County, for example, where 13.6 percent of the population was in mobile homes in 1980, in ten of the twenty-one towns, more than 20 percent of the housing was mobile homes. In one township, the figure was over 29 percent and in two others over 25 percent. In the late 1980s, permits for all types of new housing were increasing, but mobile homes were claiming an increasing share of the permits issued. In 1987 and 1988, just over a quarter of the new-housing-unit permits were for mobile homes, whereas in the first half of 1989, 45 percent of permits were for mobile homes (though there is some problem in comparability of figures because the "doublewides," counted as houses rather than mobile homes in the earlier years, are now counted as mobile homes). Some townships, however, issue very few mobile-home permits, because of minimum 5-acre lot restrictions or outright limitations on mobile homes. But in the most rural and poorer townships, the ratio of mobile-home permits to house permits ranges from two to one, through four to one, on up to seven to one.

In many rural areas, nearly all trailer parks are full. There is increasing crowding of trailers within each trailer park and increased crowding of people within each trailer, as tenants double up, trying to keep housing costs down or fulfilling obligations to relatives and friends by providing them temporary shelter. Many trailer parks show signs of recent, current, or planned growth: new driveways prepared, new pads and hookups developed, more trailers in the park, and more mailboxes hanging off the edge of the structure at the entrance to the park. Some of the trailer parks are growing rapidly enough to have a noticeable effect on elementary school enrollments. In one school district that had been experiencing declining enrollment for years, two trailer parks have recently been established and expanded. Each morning a school bus nearly fills up at each trailer park.

As a result of continued demand for inexpensive rural housing, informal roadside trailer clusters are sprouting up on the rural landscape in many locations, typically two to four old trailers sitting in the yard next to an older farmhouse. (With fewer than three trailers, these groupings do not come under much regulation or licensing as a trailer park, and three can share a single septic system.) Although the physical condition of the trailers, their water and sewer systems, the driveways, and other amenities may be barely adequate, these trailers fill a market niche: helping to satisfy a desperate demand for inexpensive and readily available rural housing—in essence, emergency housing. In one new trailer cluster, all four trailers were rented to young, single women heads of households on welfare. For none of these women was this considered a desired form of housing: It was a stopgap, the only housing available within the welfare allowance, the only way they could maintain independence from parents, previous husbands, or boyfriends. There is no other slack in the low-income rural housing supply.

Other factors are now affecting the balance of supply and demand for rural mobile homes. In some localities, better health code enforcement has resulted in the disappearance of some trailer parks. When one large trailer park on the edge of a city was finally closed down by the county health department for violations, however, the ousted residents had difficulty finding substitute low-cost housing in an already tight market. Those who owned their trailers were suddenly thrust into a unique form of homelessness: owning a trailer but having no place to put it.

Elsewhere, new land-use regulations prevent the addition of any more mobile homes, either individually placed or in parks. In some rural areas adjacent to economically expanding urban centers, mobile-home park tenants are subject to displacement to make room for more profitable uses of the land. Park owners are tempted to convert to newer, fancier mobile homes for higher rentals or may decide to build apartment houses, condominiums, or commercial buildings instead. Responding to this situation, New York State has recently instituted a "Bill of Rights for Mobile Home Tenants" intended to protect tenants' rights to a year's lease and provide legal protection in eviction proceedings. In 1988 the state set aside a $9 million fund to provide low-cost loans to help trailer-park tenants purchase their parks if they are put up for sale, and then to run them as housing cooperatives.

Somewhat akin to mobile homes on individually owned parcels of land are the winterized cottages and cabins that have become low-cost homes for purchase or rental. In many scenic areas of the state, along river edges, lakeshores, and in the remote hills and mountains, some modest vacation cabins built a generation or two ago for seasonal use are now being lived in year-round by people with small incomes. Having been neglected by owners or heirs, or located in areas no longer desirable as vacation places, these dwellings have become unrentable as ordinary vacation lodgings and so may be sold or rented to local people. Such a cabin, perhaps with a trailer grafted on, provides inexpensive housing, but the quality may be substandard. For example, winter heating may be inadequate and costly, and septic and water systems built for occasional seasonal use are likely to be inadequate to the demands of year-round family living. Furthermore, the remote locations may not be conducive to connecting to the jobs and services of the community. In some localities, such remote cabins are occupied seasonally in warmer months by low-income families who move back into towns for the winter months, doubling up with friends or relatives there

IMPLICATIONS FOR COMMUNITIES

The worsening rural poverty affects not only individuals and families but also communities. "Impoverization in place," by which local people who were not previously poor are being knocked into poverty as a result of changes in employment and family circumstances, creates problems for communities and their institutions, especially if the community as a whole is in economic decline. If, moreover, a community becomes a catchment for a larger surrounding area of poor people needing low-cost housing, the problems are compounded. Some villages, by the very fact that they do have low-cost rental housing available, serve to alleviate pressure elsewhere in an area, relieving larger and more prosperous parts of a county, or surrounding counties, of a sense of responsibility for addressing their own poverty problems. The slide downward of some small communities, such as the villages described here, though not entirely recent or sudden, appears to have picked up speed and angle of descent in recent years.

Though some local individuals and organizations are working to hold and improve quality of life for their community and whoever lives in it, the problem is beyond their efforts, its causes beyond their control. As families and households that social workers term "dysfunctional" move to, within, out of, and back into such a rural community, so too the community may become dysfunctional.

One concerned local resident, who deals professionally with law enforcement problems of discouraged people in deteriorating communities, phrased it clearly: "What has broken down is *community*. The problem is not just the poverty, the lack of money, but the fact that there is no sense of belonging or oneness. In these communities, there is no longer community, no longer a community to give the support—and the criticism—that young people need."

The community's reputation may also deteriorate. As an increasing proportion of its residents are stigmatized individuals, the community itself becomes a stigmatized community. It becomes labeled as a "slum," a "dump," or a "welfare town." Like the deteriorating conditions of its housing, the community's reputation declines, and the whole process spirals downward. Then in a self-fulfilling prophesy, more low-income and struggling families move in. Communities skidding downward are not apt to be effective as social settings and institutional matrices for their low-income residents. And as earlier research indicated (Fitchen 1981), when communities and their social institutions are weakened by worsening poverty, they become less able to meet the needs of their impoverished residents.

CHAPTER NINE

The Dynamics of
Rural Impoverization:
Causes and Processes

The phenomenon of rural impoverization in New York, the creation of more and worse rural poverty on top of that which already existed, is the result of a complex interweaving of several different forces and changes that are part of nationwide trends. Except for rural counties within the sphere of strong urban economies, the decade of the 1980s has brought either impoverization in place, outward dispersion of poverty from metropolitan areas, or some combination of the two, keeping some rural counties poor. Similar patterns appear to be operating in other rural areas of the United States as well. In the Appalachian region, rural counties that were desperately poor in the 1960s have diverged markedly: Some of those located close to a metropolitan area have been transformed out of poverty, whereas more remote counties have been unable to make any sustained improvement (Applebome 1990). Several specific causes of worsening rural poverty have been identified through local-level research in rural counties of New York State.

The key factors underlying rural impoverization are found in three intersecting segments of contemporary rural society: employment problems, housing shortages, and changing family relationships. These three together produce a fourth factor, high frequency of residential mobility, which exacerbates poverty and its consequences for people and for communities. These four factors are all part of the changing rural scene discussed throughout this book; worsening poverty is inextricably tied to the other major changes presently occurring.

INADEQUACIES IN RURAL EMPLOYMENT

The relationship between poverty and work in rural America is not as simple as might be supposed. Nationwide, the rural poor show a strong commitment to work, as evidenced in the consistent statistics showing that a greater percentage of rural poor people than urban poor people are employed quite steadily (Shapiro 1989). But in many rural areas, for reasons discussed in earlier chapters, available employment simply does not yield adequate income. Furthermore, even in a time of unusually low official unemployment rates, there are many among the rural poor who are not working. Case materials, selected from interviews and observations and from reports of public agencies in the three research regions, illustrate the broader problems.

Working Rural People: Increasingly at Risk of Being Poor

Sandy is twenty years old. She lives in a trailer park in a small village and is sole provider for herself and her one child. The welfare department wanted her to get a job, and she herself desperately wanted to get off welfare. The only work she could get was a thirty-hour a week job, at $4.05 an hour, in a supermarket in town. This leaves her below the poverty level; even with continued food-stamp and medicaid benefits, she has insufficient income. Sandy interviewed at a fast-food restaurant for a second part-time job but found it impossible to combine the shifts of two jobs, as the restaurant would not inform her until each Friday what her next week's schedule would be. Besides, she still would not have had health benefits. She decided not to pursue the job. Eventually, when she got too far behind in the rent, Sandy moved in with a friend.

In the later 1980s, as rural unemployment dropped so dramatically in most rural counties, it was initially accompanied by a noticeable though less dramatic drop in AFDC cases. But, significantly, many of those now holding jobs are falling below the poverty line or just barely keeping above it, and by 1990 welfare caseloads were climbing quite rapidly. The reason behind this descent or return to poverty lies in the nature of the jobs people hold: Earnings in new kinds of employment are simply inadequate to support more than the worker alone; they fall far short of supporting a dependent as well. Many of the available jobs are only suitable as a second income in a family and may even be advertised as such. But many of the people seeking jobs may need to provide the primary family income.

The recent welfare reform (Family Support Act), designed to help move people from welfare to work, will not help this woman or thousands of others like her escape poverty if the only jobs they can get pay subpoverty wages (see Bloomquist et al. 1988). Increase in the federal minimum wage, to $4.25 in 1991, should benefit some rural workers, but those just at the new level will still fall short of the poverty line. In 1989, at the common entry-level service wage of $4 to $4.15 an hour, a woman with two children would be in poverty even if she worked full time (see Ellwood 1987, pp. 13, 25). Because many service-sector jobs are only part time, such a woman with one child would fall below the poverty line unless she made substantially more than minimum wage. Even the new manufacturing jobs, which currently start at around $4.50 an hour, leave many families, including two-worker families, very near the poverty line.

Difficulty Getting and Keeping Jobs

Joseph had grown up in the county, mostly in its outlying areas. Family problems following the death of a parent and inability to get along with a stepparent, combined with a perception that "school had nothing for me," led him to quit school and leave home at age fourteen. For a few years, Joseph slept in cars and in basements of abandoned rural houses. Alcoholism, a perennial problem in his family, affected him early, and he admits to heavy drinking for a number of years, and also to doing drugs. Much of his life has been spent, he said, "wasting myself." He flitted from job to job, place to place, and in and out of personal attachments and family arrangements. The work history Joseph recounted indicated a pattern of quitting jobs abruptly, either discouraged over the low pay, impatient about not getting results (money) quickly enough, or unable to get along with a boss or other workers. Recently, Joseph entered an alcoholism rehabilitation program. Then as a condition for continuing to receive welfare support (Home Relief), he entered a job-readiness program, in which he gained not only job-seeking skills but some close interaction that helped him realize that he does actually possess marketable skills and that he could learn to control some of his problem behavior and thereby enhance his ability to stay employed. Soon, however, the lure of a temporary construction job in another area interrupted his training. A year later, Joseph was still employed as a laborer in construction, earning $7 an hour, although his employment situation was still not entirely satisfactory.

One particular aspect of the problem of entrenched intergenerational poverty is that some young adult men with no physical disability have difficulty obtaining adequate jobs because they have a poor work history. The high rural unemployment of the past decade took its toll on a whole cohort of young people who grew up into joblessness in the late 1970s and early 1980s. In a tight job market, marginally educated young men from the rural pockets of poverty had been unwanted, and they became even less wanted as their years out of the labor force increased. Some became chronic Home Relief cases, picking up only minor informal employment with relatives and friends. Even now, in the current period of low unemployment, many of these young men are considered "unemployable."

The long history of poverty in some areas has also created employment casualties among women, especially women who are now in the middle-age range and no longer have small children at home to care for. They may need a job to augment a husband's meager or precarious income or to move off welfare, but many of them have never been employed, or perhaps not since their high school years; and many have weak formal education and job skills. A surprising number do not drive, have no license and no car, although some single women can drive and may even own a vehicle but cannot afford to pay for a needed repair or for insurance. The problems these women must surmount, in terms of barriers to employment, include the same problems of age and lack of job history and job skills that make it difficult for middle-class displaced homemakers to get their first jobs. But the problems are compounded by the erosive effects of a lifetime in poverty: physical disabilities or poor health, including alcoholism, malnutrition, extensive dental problems, obesity, diabetes, and unresolved gynecological problems (Roe and Eickwort 1973). Many of these women exhibit high levels of stress and low self-esteem, and they are constantly worn out by the demands that other family members, including children and grandchildren, make on their time and energy (Fitchen 1981, pp. 68–71). A summary of the eight women who participated together, along with two men, in an intensive job-preparation program indicates these barriers to employment. All eight women had been long-term social services clients.

One woman in her late forties had been out of the labor force over ten years. She had clerical skills but little confidence in herself and had no transportation available. A second woman was unable to read or write—despite having a high school diploma. She had worked during high school through school placement jobs but had few job skills. At twenty-one, she was also bogged down in family troubles involving an abusive husband with alcohol problems. A woman in her fifties was bothered by numerous health problems, had minimal employment experience, no driver's license, no high school diploma, and no confidence that she could earn an equivalency diploma. The fourth woman, a mother of three teen and preteen children had never worked outside the home and had no transportation or driver's license. She had made several attempts to improve her situation, including earning her GED, but lacked confidence in her abilities. A mother of four teen and preteen children presented positive characteristics: some work experience, a GED, and transportation. But health problems, personal appearance, and limited self-esteem kept her from seeking any more satisfying and remunerative work than cleaning and occasional home health care. Another woman, in her thirties, with six children, had neither a high school diploma nor a driver's license. Her work experience was limited and her hygiene poor, and she and her husband were somewhat overwhelmed by behavioral and health problems of their children. One woman not only had a GED but also had completed a nurse's aide course and had worked briefly in that field. But her personal life—a bad marriage and eventual divorce, temporary loss of her children to foster care, and dependence on a boyfriend for transportation—had been too much for her. The eighth woman in the group had no work experience, no training, and no high school diploma. She did not drive, and her family life had overwhelmed her: Her two teenagers had just returned to live with her.

Some excellent comprehensive employment training programs have now been put together in several rural counties to help long-term unemployed people overcome such barriers to employment. Some pre-employment programs are long-term and work intensively on life skills as well as job-seeking preparation and job skills. One transitional training program emphasizes "job survival skills" for people who have just been hired by a local manufacturing plant and are receiving job training there but whose minimal previous employment and lifetime of poverty might diminish their likelihood of being able to keep their new jobs. These training sessions are intense, intensive, time-consuming, and expensive;

and for all that is put into them, there is no guarantee that trainees will get jobs or that the jobs they get will be able to support them.

> The training session I observed was the fourth afternoon of a five-day voluntary program. There were five men in the group, plus a woman who was absent that day. Four of the men had been born and raised in the county. Participants had been given many exercises all week, with written and oral material to help them learn how to talk about the skills they had, to think about the kinds of jobs they wanted, and to sell themselves to a job interviewer or personnel officer. They had spent the morning practicing application interviews, and in the afternoon they were doing simulated interviews that were videotaped to be studied and critiqued on the final day. Despite the supportiveness of the trainers, it was an incredibly nervous bunch of men, their anxiety expressed through joking about needing to leave or needing a drink. There was nervous laughter, reticence, and much cigarette smoking as they tried to explain to the role-playing "employment officer" that they had years of experience in construction or janitorial work, that they could operate a backhoe and were reliable family men. Strain was in the air, and, in fact, one trainee could not go through with the exercise; relief at the session's end was palpable. There was also great camaraderie and supportiveness among this group, none of whom had known each other before the week began.

> Unfortunately, however, this was not one of the more successful job-searching training groups. Even during the classes, the staff felt that this particular group offered an unusually large number of employment barriers. After one year, only one class member was employed: He was earning a locally good wage of $6 an hour. One had enrolled in a two-year college program in the county but had since dropped out. Five of the original seven were unemployed one year later.

As in so many programs for undoing the legacy of poverty, the mixed success rate only points up the tremendous deficits with which some people are starting. Without such programs, the long-term unemployed people, the chronic public assistance cases, would have only the slightest chance of ever becoming economically independent and rising above poverty. With such intensive, concentrated programs, people with the most difficult problems can at least make several steps forward, and some will surmount their barriers and move along toward economic independence and some security. Job-preparation and job-seeking programs can provide a major boost for people otherwise deemed "unemployable" and may help local employers fill their expanding labor needs. But no matter how good these programs are, they cannot lift people out of poverty if the jobs to which they graduate pay them no more than poverty wages.

A TIGHTER RURAL HOUSING SITUATION

Housing quality in rural America is actually worse than in urban America, according to statistics on rates of housing inadequacy, and is worst of all among rental rural housing. In 1983, 25.5 percent of renters in nonmetropolitan areas around the nation lived in inadequate dwellings (Apgar and Brown 1988, p. 16). Comparison of poor households in metropolitan and nonmetropolitan areas shows that "the nonmetro poor occupy a disproportionate share of physically deficient housing units" (Lazere, Leonard, and Kravitz 1989, p. 25). In rural areas of New York, low-income people have always made trade-offs in their housing, accepting substandard or inadequate housing in order to cut cash expenses and, if possible, remain independent of welfare (Fitchen 1981, pp. 96–98). Now, however, costs are rising, but the housing quality is getting no better and in some cases deteriorating. In some areas, even paying increased rents and accepting inadequate housing does not ensure being able to find and keep a place to live.

> Caseworkers in one rural county's department of social services report that the most frustrating aspect of their job now is trying to find housing—let alone adequate housing—for their clients. "The department makes up lists from advertisements in the free press to give to clients, and the clients go looking—and looking and looking and looking. Even in this rural county, we are putting more and more people in motels for a night or two while they hunt for a place. Eventually, a client comes across someone who knows someone who knows of a place. But then there's someone else who desperately needs a place."

Substandard Housing:
An Ongoing Problem in Rural Areas

In the open-country pockets of poverty in New York, much of the owner-occupied housing—worn-down farmhouses, tar-paper shacks, old trailers, and converted school buses—is still as substandard, structurally unsound, or lacking in adequate wiring and plumbing as it was in the 1970s. In some of the burgeoning trailer parks and the new trailer clusters along back roads, water and sewer systems are unable to meet increased loads or state codes. Many of the trailers still occupied by low-income people predate the imposition of even minimal safety standards in construction and materials. In the villages and hamlets, rented housing may be of no better quality. In several instances where vacant houses and store buildings have been converted into low-rent apartments, local caseworkers have stated that these apartments probably would not meet code if there were inspections. Substandard village housing units are rarely condemned by local authorities, however, in part because of the lack of alternative low-cost housing. In one village, over one-third of the 100 housing units along a few streets targeted for a special housing improvement project were deemed substandard. In twelve of the houses, twenty-three substandard rental apartments were identified, nearly every one of them owned by an absentee landlord.

Rising Rural Housing Costs

However inadequate, housing in rural areas is now becoming more expensive, largely as a result of greater competition among an increasing number of poor people for a limited number of low-cost homes, but specifically because ownership is less flexible now and renting is becoming both more common and more costly. In the open country, stricter land-use regulations, building ordinances, and state housing codes now prevent low-income families who own their own modest homes from using their traditional strategies to provide cheap makeshift housing for themselves and their extended families. At the state level, for example, the uniform fire and building code officially prohibits people from moving into a partially completed home and then building, modifying, completing, and extending the house gradually over many years as family needs change and money and used building materials become available. (Several attempts to modify this restriction have failed to pass the state legislature.) In some open-country areas, rural gentrification has reduced the number of inexpensive old farmhouses available for local people. It has also further curtailed the strategies open-country people use to provide housing at minimal cash cost. For example, a couple may now be prohibited from using a converted school bus parked in the back as a temporary home for a grown daughter just separated from her husband. Local prohibitions on trailers on individual lots in open countryside further restrict poor people's housing options and increase their costs.

The rising cost of rural housing is particularly acute in rental housing. Already during the 1970s, the "rent burden" (percentage of income that must be devoted to rent) had been increasing in rural areas faster than the state's average increase, coming to equal the rent burden of central cities (New York State Division of Housing and Community Renewal 1984, pp. 2–31). Although in some villages and hamlets surplus homes resulting from population losses have provided a stock of low-cost housing, increasing demand for small-town apartments has pushed rents up much faster than incomes, which have actually dropped for many workers. Rents vary considerably throughout rural New York, but a typical range recently paid by low-income families for substandard or inadequate apartments in small upstate villages has generally been between $250 and $350 for a two-bedroom apartment, depending on remoteness and condition. By 1989 these apartments were renting in the $350 to $400 range. For families headed by women on public assistance, the shortfall between welfare shelter allowance and increasing rental rates for barely adequate or substandard apartments has grown considerably in the last few years. For example, it was reported by welfare caseworkers in one county that two-thirds of the rents paid by their clients exceeded the shelter allowance by more than $100.

Competition for space in mobile-home parks appears to be increasing too, and rents are rising: For example, a "low-cost" park in 1988 was charging under $100 a month for pad and hookup but in 1989 raised the rent to $120, which was still about the lowest trailer-park rent anywhere. As the supply of trailer-park space falls behind demand, rents rise further. Only for the comparatively small number of rural poor people accommodated in public housing or with federal subsidies is rent kept at 30 percent of income.

Low-Income Renters and the Insecurity of Tenancy

In the past, many rural poor people had the security and limited cash expense of owning a place to live or having parents who owned a place, even if it was just a crumbling farmhouse or an old trailer with a plywood addition. But this security is increasingly being replaced by the precariousness of tenancy, as more of the poor people in rural areas today have neither land nor relatives with land. Even if property is available within the family, people are no longer so free to put their own trailer or shack on it because of tightened land-use and building restrictions.

The problem with renting is not only that rent payments take up so much income but that they require a cash outlay on a regular basis. Many of the tenants in trailer parks and in the small-town apartments are women with children trying to get by on welfare payments or on their minimum-wage service-sector jobs or young couples trying to make a go of it on a patchwork of jobs. Some have repeatedly been forced to move out of an apartment because they get behind in their rent as housing costs outdistance their earning power. If they can find another place, they face a large up-front cash cost in deposits before they can move in: The total of the first month's rent and a security deposit can easily top $700, and there are other charges to pay, such as electricity or phone installation fees. Housing and employment problems are thus intertwined. It is in the light of the tenuous employment situation of so many young households in rural communities that the increasing proportion of those who rent rather than own their homes causes such a problem. For single mothers, the rent burden is often the reason they are unable to make it on their own, the expense that sends them to welfare, keeps them on welfare, or makes them return to it, or that causes them to move into the apartment of a boyfriend.

Low-income renters have little legal protection, minimal financial savings, few housing options, and little social or community commitment to ensure their access to housing. The chief resource they have at their command is a network of friends and relatives who can sometimes provide emergency housing. But these friends and relatives, too, are increasingly apt to be low-income renters, people similarly at risk of losing their housing.

One specific case that arose in spring 1989 and affected over 100 low-income families in rented apartments in one community indicates the precariousness of tenancy for rural people with marginal incomes. This case, a threatened conversion of a tract of low-cost rental housing in a central New York village into condominiums, illustrates the vulnerability of low-income people to market-driven forces in housing.

> Located at the edge of this village of approximately 4,500 people, this multifamily rental housing is home to nearly 700 people. About sixty-five buildings, most containing four or more two-story units, line the roadways circling up the hill. Many buildings are in disrepair, the exterior siding, windows, doorways, and roofs only suggesting the delapidation and shabbiness found inside. Children play along the streets; young mothers walk the mile to town with little ones in tow; men work on cars in the parking areas in front of the buildings. The buildings look like old-style military barracks, and look like they should no longer be in existence, let alone inhabited. Appearances are not deceiving in this case. The buildings were constructed in 1940 by the federal government as temporary housing for workers at a local defense-related plant, as the nation was gearing up for war. After the war the government sold the buildings, and the first few owners resold them to others. The buildings are now owned by several different landlords, some of them absentee. The main reason people live here is that rents are low, ranging from $155 to $250, with an average of $210 in 1989, which keeps tenants in "the projects" despite the deteriorating physical conditions, some unhealthy social conditions described by a county official as "a melting pot of social problems" (Cunningham and Grace 1986), and the stigma attached to the place. Rents elsewhere in the region are beyond reach for most families, as about 80 percent are below the poverty line and 40 percent are on welfare. And so "the projects" became and remained for forty years a de facto low-income housing project for three contiguous counties.
>
> Suddenly, in January 1989, a downstate real estate developer announced that it had made an offer to two of the larger landlords to purchase some two dozen of the buildings, 112 units in all. These buildings would be stripped down to their still-sound structural elements, rehabilitated, and turned into townhouses to be sold at $50,000 each. Conversion work would be done unit-by-unit, with tenants displaced gradually over several months beginning April first, when the down payment from the developer was due. Disbelief and shock followed the announcement and then turned to anger and panic, as over 100 families worried about when they would have to move out, where they would go, and how they could afford any other place to live. All tenants were keenly aware of the scarcity of other cheap rental housing, not only in this county but in the two contiguous counties as well. At the time, only six apartments were advertised for rent in the entire village; their rents were well above what most "projects" tenants could pay and had just increased in anticipation of the surge in demand. What little public housing exists in the three counties had years of waiting lists.
>
> Although many residents said they had always hoped eventually to move to a "better place," a bigger apartment with privacy, or a trailer in the country, virtually all were devastated by the sudden, unexpected specter of being thrown out when they had no place else to go and no money to get a place even if they could find one. For children and parents alike, the greatest concern besides mere physical shelter was that kids should remain in their school through the end of the school year and hopefully for good.

Some tenants frantically began packing all their belongings and went on living in a swarm of cardboard boxes and piles of possessions, waiting to find out what would happen. Residents quickly turned to the full network of their relatives and friends within 50 miles: Parents, parents-in-law, former boyfriends, parents of former boyfriends, sisters and girlfriends, acquaintances on the job—anybody would be asked and asked again if they knew of any places available near them. Some tenants scanned regional newspapers provided by the newly formed Housing Assistance Office and telephoned about the few places listed, usually to find them already rented. Driving around the village and the countryside to follow up leads became a major activity after work and on weekends for entire families.

April 1 came, and the developer did not come across with the cash, so the deadline was postponed a week, then another and another. More anxiety and insecurity. Then a May 1 deadline passed, and with no cash in hand, the major landlord announced that the deal was off. Thus in the end there were no actual evictions. However, this landlord immediately gave notice to tenants that all rents would go up by $50 the following month. A high level of anxiety remained, and residents still felt very insecure. "There are probably other buyers out there who will come through with the money. It'll happen sooner or later and probably just when we're least expecting it." Over the summer, a number of families did move out—but their apartments were quickly filled with replacement tenants, also poor.

Rural Homelessness: A Hidden but Growing Problem

Poorer rural residents are extremely vulnerable to sudden changes in the local housing market, particularly to upscaling of housing. Rural gentrification has the same disastrous effect on poor people in the country that it does in the city—displacement. As more people with meager incomes get displaced, even if no more poor people arrive, there are more and more people playing a game of musical chairs for fewer and fewer inexpensive houses and apartments, most of them substandard or inadequate. For most, the moves they make bring little improvement, usually worsening their housing situation—and often at a greater cost.

Rural displaced people do not end up like the urban homeless, however, for there are no heating grates for them to sleep on and few community shelters for them to go to. For those fortunate enough to have access to relatives, one solution is to buy an old cheap trailer and set it in the relative's yard. For many rural people who find themselves without a home, the first recourse is to move in "temporarily" with parents or other relatives. As was found in earlier research, poor rural parents routinely offer their grown children a home to which they can return: "You can always come home if you need to." They double up, squeeze in, and stay until the situation grows unbearable or the welfare department threatens to close their case. Then they move on to someone else's place. If the host relative or friend cannot take the whole family, a child or two may be sent to live with another relative for a while, or a teenager may sleep in a car in the yard. But doubling up with relatives and friends becomes more difficult as the housing situation tightens for everyone. If the host is only a tenant rather than an owner of the residence, there is the possibility that the landlord will increase the rent on a per-person basis or require that the "guests" leave. Doubling two families in a trailer or apartment that is already too small for one often leads to intense friction, and so the extra family moves on yet again, becoming part of a growing rural population living at the edge of homelessness. But this is a hidden population and a hidden problem, and so it remains uncounted.

In April 1990, as the Census Bureau was taking extra care to count the urban homeless, Terry and her four children were still inadequately housed and on the edge of homelessness after two years of "bouncing around" among several locations in her county. When her marriage suddenly broke up, she and her four children stayed with her sister in town, then moved to a temporary residence in a small trailer cluster. But this location proved difficult, for at the time she had no car, so she moved into a village apartment. When this apartment proved unsatisfactory, they moved again. At present, she and her four children are crowded into a two-bedroom trailer in the country. Although she is "sick of moving," Terry is again searching for a place. She asks, "Why can't I find something worth what I'm paying? If I could just find a place to call home, to last a couple of years. . . ."

Some federal funding for homelessness assistance can be used to help some of the potentially homeless and "sometimes-homeless" population, if local agencies are creative in adapting the somewhat restrictive urban-based definitions of what constitutes homelessness. Some public agencies use earmarked homeless funds, and some private organizations devote their scarce resources to help these unhoused people to pay the security deposit to enable a person to rent an apartment that they otherwise could not get for lack of cash to cover this up-front cost. Some agencies have persuaded landlords to spread out the security deposit over several monthly payments, although many landlords are unwilling to do this because some tenants may move out with only a small payment into the deposit but a large amount of damage.

The condemnation of a trailer park for health reasons or the planned upgrading of a single privately owned low-income housing development can quickly overload the capabilities of any local agency and its available "homelessness funds." There is no slack in the system to absorb such losses in the stock of inexpensive housing. Only by innovative planning and creative funding schemes have some communities been able to tackle the rural homelessness problem.

In Clinton County, where an already serious low-income housing shortage existed around the Plattsburgh area, the homelessness problem was exacerbated by Southeast Asian refugees awaiting permission to enter Canada and by the closure of a trailer park where the trailers were literally falling into the crumbling sewer lines. Available motel space was diminishing, as the older motels were now being upgraded again for tourist business, and the cost of sheltering homeless people in motels was draining the local budget. Through an exemplary cooperative effort by local and state agencies, politicians and social service workers, housing was constructed outside the city limits but accessible to shopping and public transportation. The project, opened in early 1990, includes a mini-motel for emergencies and apartments of one, two, and three bedrooms. It is run by a not-for-profit agency, together with the county legislature and the Department of Social Services. Rents follow a sliding scale, so that tenants on welfare are charged exactly the amount their grant allows for housing, no more. The project has a built-in source of extra revenue in that it can lease or sell road-frontage property for commercial or residential use.

INSTABILITY AND INSECURITY OF FAMILY RELATIONSHIPS

Although the decrease in two-parent families, as a statistical norm, is a nationwide trend and not limited to lower income people, it has recently been growing significantly among the rural poor (Duncan and Tickamyer 1988, Gwynn et al. 1989). Ethnographic study of rural pockets of poverty in the early 1970s showed families in which there was considerable marital strife, often involving violence and temporary separation, but couples basically stayed together: Their marriages were enduring, if not peaceful (Fitchen 1981, pp. 105–123). There were indeed single mothers with babies, young women who had not yet married and were, in many cases, still living at home with their parents or perhaps living with the father of the baby. But the expectation, and the eventual reality in most cases, was marriage, though not necessarily to the father of the baby. In the late 1980s the picture had substantially changed, even in the open-country pockets of poverty, but more in the small-town and trailer-park areas. The growing incidence of single mothers and one-parent families in rural communities is attested to by a wide variety of local institutions. In almost any Head Start classroom, in elementary classrooms in poorer districts, among the women enrolled in WIC or in EFNEP, at least half of the population reflects single-parent households. In one school district with a 1980 poverty rate of 20 percent, school records at the end of the decade indicated no more than 45 percent of children living in two-parent households.

Better statistics on the percentage of rural families, even if available, would be only partially helpful, though, for the common rubrics "single mothers" and "female-headed households" lump together a considerable variety of causes and configurations. One component of this population is the very young women who have not been married but have become mothers. (A sixteen-year-old can leave home and receive public assistance to set up a separate household.) They may be living alone or living with, but not married to, the father of their child or children, or living with a different boyfriend. In many cases, their male partners are also young and may have a poor employment status. A quite different configuration of "single mothers" or "female-headed households" includes women who have been previously married and then separated or divorced. Such women may have two or more children and might be at least in their mid-twenties. The static and misleading terms also underestimate the temporariness and instability of family arrangements and the decoupling of marriage and parenting. Even the term "two-parent family" may be misleading in that it conveys a sense of stability that is simply not there in some cases.

These fluid and fragile family situations, though common and no longer much noticed in urban contexts, strike rural community agency workers as quite new and as rapidly becoming more prevalent. Rural educators and caseworkers express concern over the effects on children and the ability of community institutions to provide what the family does not.

> Elementary school teachers have attached a name to a phenomenon they see every week: "weekend anxiety syndrome." They say it begins on Friday and continues on Monday. It involves a noticeably higher level of anxiety and agitation in young children just before and after the weekend, and it is caused by the fact that many kids go to the other parent for the weekend or spend the weekend in a different home situation. Preparing emotionally for the change, or calming down after it, comes out in brooding, withdrawal, regressive behavior, misbehavior, or aggression at school.

> A probation officer reviewing records of presentencing investigations (PSIs) was emphatic and concerned about the deteriorating and fragile family situations he finds. "The overwhelming majority of the PSI cases have a family that is divorced, remarried, not married, or living with the nth spouse. Often when we do the family history, we find as many as four, even six kids in a family with that many different last names. A PSI family is apt to contain half brothers, stepsisters, and a series of stepparents. Often the kids don't get along with each other or there are stepparent-stepchild problems. These kids grow up feeling that relationships are impermanent, and in this setting they don't learn right and wrong. The kids lack discipline and affection. The mother or father may be so intent on getting through life and on the momentary courtship that the kids really lack any parent at all. They become peer focused. And they end up in the courts."

> A mental health counselor working in a rural county cited the case of a seventeen-year-old boy with divorced parents. He had been staying with his mother and siblings, but there was serious friction between him and one of his siblings. He moved away to a city to live with his father and the father's new wife, but they eventually threw him out because he got into minor troubles and drugs at school. His mother had him brought back home, but new difficulties arose between him and his mother's boyfriend, which deepened the rift between him and his sibling. The boyfriend threatened the mother that either the kid leave or else he, the boyfriend, would leave. This mental health professional went on to generalize: "Kids in these situations are confused, unsure of being loved. They go live with one parent, testing for love, testing that parent. Then they go to live with the other, again testing.

They harbor fantasies of their parents reuniting—but the fantasies don't come true. These are kids seeking love, kids insecure, feeling unsettled, even guilty. This may really be a case of a lengthy depression. But it is acted out in school in such a way that the child is labeled disruptive and/or learning disabled."

RESIDENTIAL MOBILITY WITHIN
AND BETWEEN RURAL COMMUNITIES

Community research has revealed a great deal of movement from one small-town apartment to another, from one village to another, from trailer park to trailer park, from trailer park to village, to open-country, to village again, and so on. It is usually the lower-income people in these settings who are doing the most moving. Their moves tend to be circumscribed within a fairly localized region, usually within a county or perhaps two adjacent counties.

In general, young adults appear to be the most mobile, for they are the ones dealing with the most difficult situations of poverty and stress, trying to support themselves and their children on inadequate employment or meager welfare, dealing with numerous agencies and programs, and seeking to finish growing up and putting their lives together. Though their family configurations and specific needs differ, their stories, told in interviews in their present homes, reveal certain common themes.

One young single mother had moved seven times in one year since she and her baby had fled from a violent boyfriend, staying temporarily with different relatives in already overcrowded housing, moving into a condemned building, then into an apartment she could not afford, and then living with her girlfriend until the welfare department ruled that out, and eventually ending up in a roadside cluster of trailers.

One woman, aged twenty-four, grew up in a small town in the county. Soon after graduating from high school, she and her boyfriend moved to an apartment in a larger town in the county, where their first child was born. Evicted from that apartment just before their second child was born, they found a house in a nearby town. Later they moved again, ending up in a large cluster of low-quality apartments. She and her boyfriend then split. Two years later, she and her new boyfriend and their child are living in an apartment near the first boyfriend. The oldest child is with his father down the street; the second child is with her. Now, because of impending sale of the apartment, she is frantically looking for another place to live.

One couple with two preschool children has moved eleven times in the six years of their marriage. Tomorrow, they would be moving again, but this would be "a good move" and an easy one, to an adjacent apartment that would have the two bedrooms the Department of Social Services requires the family to have if it is to continue receiving support for a child with special needs. Their present location, where they have been only two months, is spotlessly clean, their possessions stacked and packed. The couple has cycled through nine communities, all within the county in which they were both born. Substandard apartments, trailers with leaking roofs and fire hazards, places where inadequate air circulation exacerbated a medical problem, the marginal income, and the special needs of one child—all these and more had kept this family on the move.

A young couple and their toddler had just recently moved into the largest apartment they had ever had. They had obtained it with the help of the county's community action program, which also obtained federal rental assistance for them. The couple had moved back and forth in the county and nearby, quite often living with his or her parents, grandparents, or siblings, and had briefly stayed with another sister out of state. When I asked this young woman, "Where did you live before you got this place?" she thought but a split second and replied, "In limbo."

This residential mobility, mostly too fine-scale and too recent to be documented in any census or other statistical material, seems to be increasing noticeably. For those who move, it can become disruptive and exhausting. Moves across county lines require a great deal of paperwork, trips to the county seat, delays, and confusions in transferring or starting up assistance such as AFDC, food stamps, or medicaid. Some forms of housing rental assistance are not transferable across county lines. For children, frequent moves across school-district lines create stress, difficult adjustments, and serious loss of continuity in learning. When possible, families will accept sacrifices in housing quality in order to avoid crossing county and school-district lines, unless there is a compelling reason to leave a particular county or school system. The mobility is not only a problem for the people themselves, however, but also for community institutions and agencies, whose records and observations provide at least a window onto the scope of the problem.

A Head Start director familiar with the local school districts says Head Start children, who by program guidelines are almost all children from low-income families, "are the *movingest* children of all." The high mobility of these three- and four-year-olds stresses not only the children but the program. After denying admission to waiting-list children because the program is full, the staff then has to bring in these children in midyear. If there is no waiting list, then recruiting for new children must be undertaken. And what if the child that left this month comes back two months later? Another Head Start reports that it enrolls youngsters in the spring and works out bus routes, only to find that when the bus goes to the trailer parks in the fall, it's a different set of kids.

Many schoolteachers commented on the high mobility. Most indicated that mobility within their rural districts or between districts is not new, especially for children from low-income families, but they were all emphatic that the problem has become much worse in the last few years. "The constant *movement* of kids," one teacher said, "is *much* worse now than it used to be. Families

move all the time, especially at the end of the month, often in the middle
of the night, with no warning."

In one district the year began with eighty-five children in kindergarten, lost
some children, but gained more, so that the total went up to ninety-five
during the year. Then came a net loss again, and a return to eighty-five by
year's end. The difficulties in having appropriate levels of staff and space,
to say nothing of the extra care needed to fit these young children into
classroom activities and networks, posed an added strain on the school that
year. In a fourth-grade classroom of twenty-two children, eight children came
in and eight left in one year, including three new children in the classroom
in one month. In this same classroom, half of the children had recently
experienced multiple changes in family living, including more than one change
in a stepparent or mother's boyfriend, or moving from the home of one
parent to the other.

The high residential mobility is most noted in schools that have a
growing population of children from low-income families, and within
these schools teachers and principals alike note that it is the children
from lower economic levels who are the most mobile. If there were good
data and projections on this mobility, perhaps the schools could document
the need for a program similar to the state's special migrant-education
programs that work with children of agricultural migrants. But absent
the kind of hard information they'd like to have, schoolteachers and
administrators simply "know" from their own observations and experiences what is happening, and some schools are working hard to respond
effectively. Some small schools have been extremely creative in dealing
with the problem, adapting school practices to the inescapable fact of
high levels of mobility of lower-income families. In one school, the
principal emphasized that with a certain amount of upheaval in the
lives of some children, particularly those from lower-income families
who move frequently, it is important that the entire school make kids
feel welcome and wanted, whether they've just arrived, been here all
along, or come back again after a recent departure.

This principal stated, "When one family of kids has moved in and out a
few times, we never really say good-bye to them. We expect them back. We
plug them into classes for September so that we will be ready for them when
they show up in October. When the kid comes back, he is expected—and
he feels like he's come home again."

IN-MIGRATION OF POVERTY
TO RURAL COMMUNITIES:
A NATIONAL TREND?

In some rural communities, particularly those closer to metropolitan
areas, local agencies report a very recent and significant increase in low-
income people moving in from elsewhere, particularly from an urban

area or the towns close to it. In the absence of adequate quantitative data on this perceived trend, the best available source is the records of welfare departments, employment offices and employment training programs, schools, and other programs where new residents would furnish their last address before coming to a locality. In some counties this perceived movement is too new even for these agencies to have compiled accurate documentation. Two agencies reported that they were so swamped with applicants that they had simply not had the time to look at the records to see where all the people were coming from. But directors and administrators expressed with some certainty that what was happening was part of a movement of low-income people from urban or urban-fringe areas to rural communities. This movement, a social services commissioner reports, is the explanation for a sudden 15 percent increase in welfare caseload in one year, at a time when longer-term local residents have been moving from welfare to jobs. An employment training office reports a "big out-of-state influx" appearing in case records. And one county agency reports an increasing number of its clients have recently moved in from the neighboring county. As 1990 began, a number of agency administrators, trying to get a handle on what was happening, were deciding that indeed it would be necessary to tally up the intake records, so as to document their impressions and indicate to the agency and its funders why budgets are being overspent and services stretched.

When poor people who had been living in urbanized areas move to rural areas seeking cheaper housing and a better quality of life, or move from one rural county to another in search of a better job or affordable housing or better social relationships, the outlay for service and welfare costs rises in the receiving county. (The "sender" county pays the first month's welfare costs only.) In New York State, as in California and only a few other states, the funding arrangement for public assistance (welfare) requires a local input. Although the formula for local matching funds varies with the type of case, on average a county may pay one-fourth or more of the cost of every case on the social services rolls. Thus, rural counties that are receiving an influx of poor people are finding themselves charged with paying not only for their own low-income residents but also for people who have moved in from elsewhere. Meanwhile, the cities or counties that "export" poor people have relieved themselves of the responsibility of assuring affordable housing, and by doing so they have effectively reduced their service needs and their local welfare costs. Some counties perceive themselves as being on the receiving end of other counties' conscious efforts to reduce their poverty problems and poverty-related spending. The added cost to the receiving locality, as well as the stress on service and educational programs, is locally seen as a burden that has been unfairly shifted from urban to rural areas, from some counties to others, or across state lines.

Redistribution of poverty within New York State from urban to rural areas is as yet unmeasured and appears to be occurring only in certain localities. It may occur where there are bus or rail lines from a metropolitan center, where there is not only a supply of low-cost housing but also a grocery store, a post office, perhaps a pharmacy and clinic, and a school as minimal public services needed by incoming families. Undocumented as this trend is at present, it bears watching and needs measuring. And New York is not alone: The same trend has been cited informally and in print by community program personnel, rural mental health workers, and rural social scientists from around the country as existing in their areas also. In the northwestern states, for example, urban-to-rural movement of poor people, coupled with rural-to-urban migration by people with better incomes, may account for "pronounced growth in the number of welfare recipients in the region's less populated areas," where AFDC caseloads "have as much as doubled in the past decade while populations . . . have remained stable or even declined" (Harrison and Seib n.d., p. 85).

This trend is nowhere sufficiently documented or studied. One comprehensive policy-oriented study of recent demographic and economic trends in the nation's rural villages does, however, point to a broader occurrence of the pattern described here for rural New York. "The process of centralization of population and business activities over several decades has resulted in residential and commercial property vacancies and consequent low property values in many villages when compared to areas in or near larger cities that have experienced growth. Village housing and other real property may therefore appear attractive to prospective residents or entrepreneurs. A related factor is the demographic structure of villages with their high proportion of elderly residents and single-person households. The potential for turnover in housing may therefore be relatively high in villages as mortality and moves to other residential settings create vacancies in existing houses. This condition, along with the addition of specific housing for elderly residents common in many villages, should continue to depress village housing values" (Johansen and Fuguitt 1984, p. 207). One study, conducted in California, specifically cites the urban-to-rural migration of the poor: "Another factor in the high rates of poverty in California rural areas is due to the in-migration of persons already poor. The comparative advantage of living in areas with a lower cost of living may attract some poor to rural counties. . . . The poor simply cannot afford the cost of living in some urban areas and so have been moving out" (Gwynn et al. 1989, pp. 55–56).

Newspaper reports from other states, including Michigan, Washington, and California, add another kind of evidence for the pattern. From California, for example, a series of articles under the heading "Urban poor seek second chance in rural America" discussed what the reporter termed "an emerging and troubling trend that . . . the low-income and the destitute are abandoning the cities for greener pastures in rural America" (Cervantes 1988, p. 8). Welfare directors and county officials in several regions of California were quoted as saying that welfare caseloads in rural counties were being driven up by migration from the cities, while at the same time urban welfare rolls were diminishing. The articles cite broad-scale Census Bureau statistics that show that whereas 14.7 percent of the people who moved from metropolitan to nonmetropolitan areas in 1976 were below the poverty line, in 1986 a smaller number made the move but 22 percent of them were poor.

There may be different situations propelling urban poor people to move to the countryside in different regions of the nation, but the pattern has a basic sameness around the country: On the one hand, there are the escalating housing costs in urbanized areas, some of them spawned by metropolitan resurgence. On the other hand, there is a surplus small-town rural housing stock, with vacant and often deteriorated buildings. Into the gap come investor-landlords, who rent out small-town housing to low-income people, both locals and in-migrants fleeing escalating housing costs in more high-priced housing markets elsewhere. As more people of limited means compete for inexpensive housing in small towns, even substandard rural housing will become increasingly costly. Vulnerable people will be made more mobile, and disconnected from sustaining institutions and informal social ties, they will fall deeper and deeper into a hole. Some rural communities, too, will spiral downward as they become de facto low-income zones.

A COMPLEX, TROUBLED SITUATION
IN SOME COMMUNITIES

In retrospect, the situation in the open-country pockets of poverty in the 1970s seems less depressing than some of the present rural poverty situations. Where there were stable jobs, family-based support networks, enduring marriages, and home ownership then, now in many rural places there appear to be inadequate jobs, fragile man-woman relationships, smaller and weaker social networks, and a mobility and insecurity of housing tenure that keep many people on the edge of poverty—and some of them on the edge of homelessness.

The increasing numbers of poor people in some communities, the fact that some of the low-income in-migrants may be racially or ethnically different from the majority of the local population, and the increasing residential mobility of some of the low-income families may all intensify problems of stigmatization. New residents who are poor may be negatively conspicuous in the community: They may be using food stamps in the local grocery store; they may keep the church people busy with emergency food services; their children may hang around the main-street stores and sidewalks because their upstairs apartments lack space indoors or yards outdoors; the adults may hang around on the sidewalks or in a local cafe or tavern during the day because they have no jobs, or only part-time jobs or night jobs. The stigmas are strong, and the epithets stinging. Poor residents are often referred to, individually and collectively as "low-life," "the welfare," or even "wellies," which is not only a derogatory term but often an inaccurate supposition. The feeling of not being wanted exacerbates the problems low-income people have in settling into a community and thereby may contribute to their further mobility.

The continued and worsening rural poverty described in the previous chapter is a result of a complex interaction of causes discussed in this one. Employment inadequacies, housing shortages, and family instability all interact with each other and all share in causing a worsening of poverty in a number of rural communities. Each of the three is a problem in itself, but each contributes to or exacerbates the others. And together they contribute to the phenomenon of increased geographic mobility, which in turn exacerbates the other problems. Where in-migration of low-income people is occurring in addition, this can be one more factor in a deteriorating community situation. Together, these trends explain why, despite falling unemployment, there is more poverty in rural America now, not less. And they explain why rural poverty is becoming qualitatively worse. These trends are not unique to rural poverty, of course, and in many respects they closely resemble patterns in urban poverty. But they are quite new to many rural areas, and in the rural and small-town context, these trends may destabilize both people and communities.

PART FIVE

Providing Community Services in Changing Circumstances

CHAPTER TEN

Problems in Meeting
Rural Service Needs

In many rural communities, the entire spectrum of community or human services appears to be operating under growing stress. A pervasive perception, voiced by people who administer mental health agencies, operate programs for the elderly, run youth programs, coordinate services to the handicapped, or provide emergency food, and by many others as well, is that there are more people with needs and more needs than there are services to meet them. Unmet problems seem to grow faster, and also become worse faster, than the combined local service-providing capacity can handle. Administrators, "frontline workers," and counselors all seem to agree. Their institutions or agencies and their people are working harder and serving more people, but the problems they deal with are getting both more frequent and more intractable. In large part, this increase in workload is a result of broad societal problems of the decade taking their toll even in small or remote rural communities. Only to a slight extent is it attributable to more sophisticated or systematic detection and diagnosis of people in need.

The other part of the reported stress on rural community services is that the resources of money, staff, and institutional capacity have not grown as rapidly as the needs. Even where services are growing, need constantly outpaces capacity. Starting with the federal Budget Reconciliation Act of 1981, major cutbacks in federal funding diminished the ability of some local programs to serve all who required assistance. From housing subsidies to food stamps and medicaid, tightened federal guidelines for eligibility, combined with reduced federal funding, meant that many federally assisted programs were being spread increasingly thin. Some could serve only a portion of potentially eligible people: For example, in most counties only about half of the children who qualify for Head Start can be accommodated, despite the public and political popularity of this program. Budgetary tightness rippled through local community services, straining even programs that were not federally funded, as local monies from private sources, such as United Way contributions, had to stretch farther to cover local needs. There was tremendous pressure on local government budgets from programs and agencies that all needed extra local help to make up for the federal shortfall. Then, too, village, city, township, and county governments as well as school districts were all competing, each to meet its needs from the pockets of local taxpayers—just to continue services at levels the community had provided in the past. For a time, the federal revenue-sharing program helped relieve some of the sting of decreased direct federal funding for local programs, giving local governments the responsibility to allocate federally collected tax money among local operations. The subsequent demise of federal revenue-sharing resulted in significant reduction of the total money available locally and ushered in an era of even tighter budgetary constraints for local community services, with worthy causes competing even harder for shrinking local dollars.

Rising need and inadequately rising resources affect urban as well as rural services, of course, and receive considerable attention. But some other recent trends that are less commonly noted have been particularly detrimental to services in rural communities. Three trends especially affecting rural community services will be discussed in this chapter: the drawbacks of a cost-effectiveness model for human services in rural areas, the inappropriateness of certain urban-based trends in service delivery, and the persistence of some outdated rural attitudes toward human services in general.

CONSEQUENCES OF A COST-EFFECTIVENESS MODEL FOR RURAL SERVICES

Perhaps the most significant trend in human services in recent years, an insidious and far-reaching trend that has especially major impact on rural areas, is the application of economic rationality and a balance-sheet mentality to the provision of services. The gradual insertion of economic language and metaphor into planning and policy, and into funding and conducting community services, has been pervasive, percolating down from federal through state and local governments. The primacy of the bottom line and the doctrine of cost-effectiveness have become so generally accepted as to permeate virtually all community services, and they do so not as a theory or a debated approach, but as a policy orientation that shapes program design and funding, as a set of underlying assumptions about community services.

The vocabulary of this economic model, uttered at local government meetings, written into grant proposals and annual reports of agencies, and institutionalized in service delivery and program strategies, stresses "cost-effectiveness," "efficiency," "cost-benefit analysis," and "the bottom line." In a time of "scarce financial resources," the "allocation of funds" becomes not only a matter of distribution but a policy function: Determination of which programs will survive and how they shall operate is made not by local citizens or by service deliverers and others close to the situation, but by state and federal authorities with control over funding. The economic vocabulary subtly shapes the way governments and administrators think about and evaluate community services, from education to welfare, from care of the elderly to community development.

Marketplace measurement of programs is particularly unfavorable to rural community services simply because it costs more to serve a dispersed population than a concentrated one. Because the cost-effectiveness model judges a program's worth not in terms of *what* it does for people or communities but *how much it costs* per person served, it aggravates the effect of the higher cost of rural services. It contributes to the increasing centralization of services, and leaves some rural populations underserved, as can be illustrated with a few of the many concrete examples encountered in research. The examples presented below all come from rural New York, but there is ample evidence that the situation is much the same, if not worse, in states that are more rural than New York, where the cost-effectiveness model may be even more detrimental to the provision of community services.

Rural Hospitals and Rural Health Care

From the rural areas of Texas, Illinois, Colorado, and Washington, as well as New York, recent press coverage and Senate hearings have documented what locals knew all along: Small rural hospitals, long the backbone of health care in large, sparsely populated areas, are under increasing marketplace stresses that are being exacerbated by government cost-containment efforts and policy decisions of hospital consolidation. From 1980 to 1988, 161 of the nation's 2,700 rural hospitals had been forced to close, mostly since 1985, and 600 more were deemed "on the brink of closure" (Senator John Melcher, D-Montana, chairman of the Senate Aging Committee, in *New York Times*, June 14, 1988).

In rural areas of New York, as elsewhere, it has been increasingly difficult for small hospitals to keep up with state-of-the-art medical technology, and this has compounded the problem rural areas have long had in attracting and holding good doctors. In a viscious circle, the doctor shortage then weakens the hospital, and this, in turn, makes it even harder to attract doctors. However, the "inevitable" trend toward centralization of hospital facilities and reduction of medical services in remote areas has been hastened by both state and federal policies. As one local health care planner said, "What the market fails to do in terms of destroying rural hospitals, the state will do. And what the state doesn't accomplish in closing rural hospitals, the feds will."

In New York State, some rural counties have recently been fighting off attempts by the state Department of Health (DOH) to close one or more of their small local hospitals. Some hospitals were closed, others have won a temporary reprieve, and many more are still very nervous. In some instances the state DOH has been helpful in loosening some rather restrictive regulations pertaining to both acute and long-term care facilities, and rural hospitals now have a lower minimum "bed utilization rate" of 65 percent as opposed to 80 percent in urban hospitals. But, still, many rural practitioners feel that it's an uphill battle, a battle in which the outcome has already been decided against rural hospitals.

Some federal health care policies create a penalty for rural hospitals that is significant and increasing. In particular, medicare and medicaid reimbursement rates average 37 percent lower for rural hospitals than for urban hospitals. Medicare reimbursements have increased slower than operating costs at rural hospitals, and the shortfall is growing. The federal government's recent cost-containment effort called "DRGs," or diagnostic related groups, established diagnostic classifications, and for each one set a maximum length of hospital stay that will receive full medicaid and medicare reimbursement. In rural areas where adequate out-patient services are not available, patients may have to remain hospitalized longer, but the reimbursement rate will be reduced.

Another key element in the health care system in rural America is the local ambulance squad or volunteer emergency medical team, and this, too, is a medical care institution under stress. Local ambulance squads, most commonly volunteer crews connected to local volunteer fire companies, provide emergency medical care as well as transportation to hospitals. But federal support that had enabled small communities to purchase ambulances, obtain medical and communications equipment, and train personnel ran out after 1981, and most state governments, particularly those hard hit by the farm crisis or oil crisis, were unable to take over this funding. Nor have local governments been able to increase their funding to help with spiraling costs for insurance and medical supplies. Resident donations and user assessments hardly cover the operating costs. Despite tenacious efforts by the members of such emergency squads, the system is at risk: Equipment purchased earlier is now wearing out, and local fund-raisers, such as chicken barbecues, are hardly up to purchasing $40,000 ambulances.

Rural Mental Health Services

The impact of applying an economic worldview to rural human services is also well illustrated in the mental health field. Nationally, the community mental health centers that flourished in the 1960s and 1970s were seriously underfunded in the 1980s (Wagenfeld 1988, p. 7). Obtaining funds or medicaid reimbursement for the preventive mental health work that many practitioners see as especially needed and appropriate in rural areas has become increasingly difficult. One of the reasons for this difficulty is that it is hard to justify prevention programs in the language of cost efficiency. State mental health funding does not make it easy for localities to document need for or effectiveness of prevention programs; and local agencies find that it is easier to document a cure than a prevention. In particular, state funding creates a disincentive for working with children who are at risk of mental health trouble but who are not yet diagnosable as mentally ill. As one clinic director said, "We don't have many real psychotic kids. What we have is kids at risk for trouble, kids who have been sexually abused, neglected, who have alcoholic families, or who live in poverty."

Another impact of the cost-effectiveness model is sometimes referred to by local human service planners as "the tyranny of numbers," and this operates with a particularly strong bias against rural areas with small populations. Rural areas do not have "the economies of scale," and in the economic model, economies of scale become directives for funding, a situation that was illustrated by the head of a rural mental health clinic.

"Out here, we lack the economy of scale. For example, we need an alcohol crisis center, but the regulations for such a center require eighteen staff people for a twenty-five-bed unit, which is the minimum allowable for anywhere but New York City, where the minimum is thirty beds. Here in this county we only have about twelve cases a year that would need such a center— but they really do need it. Without more help from state funding we cannot have such a program here; our tax base simply would not support it.

"We have too small a program and staff in some of our activities to qualify for full state funding. For example, we cannot have an alternative-residence program for teens, a day treatment center, or a 'psycho-social' club for young people because the state makes regulatory demands that we can't meet. You have to have a certain amount of time devoted from a variety of professional staff. In this county we would need about thirty-five people in a day treatment center to make the break-even point to pay for all the services the state requires that such a program must have. But here in this county we might have only ten people, not thirty-five, who need a day treatment program." As this director concluded, "To get mental health assistance here, you almost have to be crazy!"

Services to the Poor

The "cost-effectiveness" model and "efficiency" emphasis in human service delivery has had an increasingly negative impact on distribution of services for low-income residents in rural areas. It is simply more costly to serve small, dispersed populations of poor people than large, concentrated ones, not only in terms of the obvious higher cost of transportation but also in that when the service is actually taken out to the more remote areas of the county, there are fewer people there to be served. Because of the higher per-person cost and the smaller number of persons to be served, decisions are made at federal, state, and local levels that "we simply cannot afford to serve those rural areas."

Within any rural area, poor people residing in the most remote areas are likely to be the least-served population, a situation that results from the interaction of two trends: the peripheralization of poverty, in which people forced out of the county's larger population centers by higher housing costs move to the further reaches of the county, and the centralization of services, in which most services are available only in the county seat or some other central place. The effect of these interacting trends is recognized by many local human service practitioners: Case-workers, schoolteachers, visiting public health workers, and probation workers express real concern about the underserved peripheries, but they work for agencies and programs that are so strapped for operating funds and so dominated by the cost-effectiveness model that they have withdrawn funding and programming from these rural areas. Following the federal and state model, service to remote sections is withdrawn or reduced or never extended in the first place and is concentrated in regions where the greatest number of people can benefit from the least amount of expenditure.

One casualty of this trend is the Head Start program. In most rural counties, Head Start centers exist in the larger, central villages, but there may be absolutely no program available to the children out in "the boondocks." In a remote section of one county, for example, two villages located only three miles apart and totaling nearly 4,000 people have no Head Start programs, not even the scaled-down "home-based" version. More than three-quarters of the downtown section in one community was considered low-income in a housing survey conducted for a grant application. Of the children in one of the elementary schools, 87 percent were labeled disadvantaged or disabled in terms of poverty, broken homes, and domestic violence. A local survey showed a sufficient number of eligible children. Yet there is no Head Start program because of the shortage of funding from the federal government, coupled with the prevailing economic model, in which allocating scarce dollars to centers already in existence is more efficient then starting up a new program. Localities that did not have a need or desire for a Head Start program in the beginning have not had an opportunity to add one because the federal funds did not substantially increase during the 1980s. Increased budget allocations for 1990 are still insufficient to fill these gaps.

Ironically, another victim of the domination of cost-efficiency mentality in providing services to the rural poor is the antipoverty agencies themselves. Even in rural counties, many of these agencies have gradually focused on larger population centers, dropping the services of an outreach worker assigned to each rural township in favor of assigning outreach workers only in the more concentrated areas of population. At the same time, some of these agencies have gradually pulled inward from the field to the office, reducing their outreach staff and requiring clients to come to the central office.

EFFECTS OF URBAN SERVICE DELIVERY
TRENDS ON RURAL SERVICES

Services in rural areas are increasingly shaped by urban-based models. Although professionals and rural professional organizations do exist in various human service fields, including a national rural mental health association, a community mental health association, a subfield of social work called community-oriented social work, and such practitioner and scholarly journals as *Human Services in the Rural Environment* and the *Journal of Rural Community Psychology*, these institutions swim against a current of urban-based programs, urban training institutions, and urban-trained practitioners. New patterns and trends in service delivery that work well in urban and suburban areas often become the standards and patterns throughout the nation, emulated widely because they work in areas of large populations. But when they are extended to rural areas, they may be less appropriate and less effective (Martinez-Brawley 1990).

Proliferation of Specialized Programs

Despite a decade of limited growth and even reduction in the level of funding available from federal, state, or local services, the number of agencies and programs involved in delivery of human services in rural areas has grown dramatically in recent years. The proliferation is evidenced, for example, in a rural county's directory listing available services, or "where to turn for help." In counties that recently had few services and no central listing, current lists include many programs, groups, agencies, and separate programs within agencies. For some counties, the recent proliferation and specialization also brings a new need: coordination of services within the community to avoid overlap and to minimize friction among agencies and programs competing for the same funding. In some cases programs developed by different groups or agencies may become more concerned with guarding their own turf than with overarching community goals. These problems resulting from specialization can be minimized or overcome, as has been the case in some counties, although doing so takes an extra commitment.

Specialization is also evident within programs, as in the growth of single-purpose programs as a mechanism enabling the agency to apply for special grants that occasionally become available outside of regular operating monies. However, the resulting fragmentation within an agency may weaken overall unity. For example, as the "antipoverty" agencies or "community action programs" set up originally by the Economic Opportunity Program of the War on Poverty lost public and government support, they not only lost considerable overall funding but had their funding broken up into a series of sources. Simply channeling and combining all the separate funding streams coming into the local agency requires considerably more fiscal and administrative time and attention. (Parenthetically, the common phrase "funding streams" is surely a misnomer or perhaps an oxymoron, as funding hardly flows but comes in intermittent trickles.) Regulations, accounting procedures, calendar years, reporting forms, and so forth may be different for different funding sources. Applying for grants and requesting grant renewals for many separate programs becomes a major activity. Only an exceptional agency with an exceptional administration and board can keep its eye on so many operations and also keep uppermost in mind the central purpose that is supposed to tie them all together. Some agencies fall short, not because they lack dedication but because fragmentation makes it harder to keep a sense of focus and purpose.

Standardization and Professionalization

As with specialization, the trend toward professionalization of community services is primarily an urban trend that may be less appropriate in rural areas. In some cases the professionalization results from rising standards within the service-providing field itself (as in upgrading, licensing, and credentialing), but it is also driven by requirements embodied in new governmental regulations attached to funding sources. Although in most cases professional requirements have been established or upgraded in the interests of providing better services, not all of these requirements are appropriate for rural low-density areas, where populations are sparse and concepts and realities of service delivery may be quite different. In some communities, very capable local people who have been doing a job well for many years may be "credentialed" out of a job, having to turn it over to a more "qualified" candidate. In other cases higher credentials may deter some capable local applicants who probably could perform adequately even without meeting new standards of formal education and certification.

One example of possibly inappropriate and certainly problematic profession-alization is a series of requirements to upgrade the capabilities of local ambulance crews. Higher levels of training now required of emergency medical technicians (EMTs) take so many hours that fewer rural people have taken the training recently. Farm people and others say they simply cannot take the time from their work to get the required training for joining or continuing in local ambulance squads. Consequently, many emergency squads are so understaffed that they now operate only on a part-time basis.

Another example was a recent proposal of the state Board of Regents that all local libraries be required to have directors with master's degrees in library science, at a minimum salary of $20,000. The regents intended that incentives and opportunities would be provided to make it feasible for any small-town librarian to get this training, but local people who can barely afford to keep their high school or college graduate librarian working three afternoons a week balked at this proposal.

The effect of increased professionalization in rural communities is connected to the problems rural communities already have in offering salaries sufficient to attract and keep good professionals. One of the perennial problems of many rural communities is that the generally low incomes and wage scales in private-sector employment, whether in farming, manufacturing, or services, tend to become the local standard for professional salaries as well.

Outreach workers in some antipoverty programs are notoriously underpaid. In one county outreach workers, all women between the ages of thirty and sixty-six, receive salaries for a thirty- to thirty-five-hour-a-week job ranging from $7,500 to about $12,500. Head Start salaries in several counties start at $8,600—for classroom teachers for a ten-month job of thirty hours a week. Proposed federal mandates for upgrading the professional training required of Head Start staff may exacerbate Head Start's financial tightness, despite increased federal funding budgeted in 1990.

If rural counties are to attract and keep able planners, administrators, social workers, and teachers, they clearly need to raise salaries enough to make the jobs attractive. Mandatory state or federal requirements for higher credentials might only aggravate the problem, however, particularly if no extra funding is forthcoming to offset the increased expense. If the credentials are boosted but the locality doesn't augment the salary commensurately, then it is assured of not getting any good outside candidates at all, which, in turn, confirms a local perception that "we simply can't get qualified people to fill that position." And so vacancies are perpetuated and agencies go understaffed or continue to operate under "acting" administrators. Increased professionalization of services and service providers may thus sometimes be counterproductive for delivering services in rural communities.

Both higher professional credentials and increased specialization of services, as urban-based trends in service delivery, may be particularly disadvantageous in rural areas because of the added factor of the cost-efficiency ideology. If services become even more costly in rural areas as a result of further specialization and professionalization, then the cost differential of serving dispersed rural people as compared to concentrated urban people will only increase. In the end rural areas will continue to lose services.

THE LEGACY OF OUTDATED RURAL ATTITUDES ABOUT HUMAN SERVICES

Human service needs have reached a level of citizen awareness, public discourse, and public agenda more slowly in rural areas than in urban and suburban areas. Several central differences between the urban and rural sociocultural environment underlie this slower development in rural areas: (1) the presumed (and sometimes actual) adequacy of rural social systems to take care of their own people through informal means rather than through formal institutions and programs; (2) an almost legendary rural commitment to "independence" rather than "dependence" on government programs; (3) the small and dispersed number of people with similar service needs; and (4) the belief that most of the problems that human services address hardly exist in rural areas because they are "urban problems." Acting on this traditional rural ethos, local political leaders often oppose public expenditure for "social work" and other "soft items" such as community mental health programs, voting instead for other needs they see as more pressing, such as roads and bridges, highway equipment, and landfills.

Contrary to the mythic-romantic notion, however, many of the standard societal problems have long been present in rural New York as in much of rural America. Mental illness and suicide rates have been fairly high in rural areas of the state, accidental death rates are significantly higher, and births to mothers aged fifteen to nineteen have generally been higher in the rural areas (New York State Legislative Commission on Rural Resources 1987, pp. 17–26). Alcoholism has long been recognized as a serious rural problem, not only by courts and rehabilitation programs but by local residents in general. Vandalism and petty crimes have long been accepted as part of community life. But if these behaviors were consciously noticed at all, they were also taken care of by the community on an informal, ad hoc basis.

The realities can no longer be dismissed. Public anxiety is mounting over rapidly rising crime rates, public perception now admits that drugs have become a serious problem locally, and concern has risen over the apparently rising number of young single parents in the community. Indicating the new level of awareness of such issues, some rural schools now use breathalyzer tests in school to detect and deter student drinking, which an administrator for the ninth and tenth grades called "a huge problem." Many schools now admit publicly that teen pregnancy is a problem locally, and of course all schools now have drug-education programs.

Even though there is a new awareness of social problems, however, there is still a lag in many rural places in perceiving and understanding them, a misdiagnosis, and an undercommitment to addressing them. The perceptual lag consists primarily of dividing social problems into "old, familiar problems that we've had with us all along" and "new problems that have come in recently from the cities." On the "old" side of the dichotomy, local people often list alcoholism, illiteracy, low labor skills, poverty, and teen pregnancy. On the opposite side, "new" problems include drugs, crime, single parenthood, and family breakdown. Not even listed by most informants are the growing but underperceived problems of mental illness and suicide among young people and children, and homelessness. Dichotomizing social problems as old or new, local or city-generated, even though providing rural people with a framework to organize their perceptions of recent change, may actually impede public willingness to support programs to address the problems. The old ones are simply "just there," "always with us," "part of the rural landscape," not something requiring attention or money. The new ones are seen as unwanted and unwelcome intrusions from the city, which, it is hoped, might just go away if ignored. As it is often expressed, "They're not problems *we* created, so I don't see how we can be expected to solve them." Based on this pattern of thought, local politicians and much of the citizenry have resisted increasing local taxes to support or expand community services.

Even the old problems that still hang on have changed and are not "just as they always were." For example, illiteracy and low job skills, both long-standing problems indeed, now carry a much higher cost to the individual and the community than they did in the past, when anyone willing to work could get a job in the local plant or on a nearby farm, making up in muscle and time whatever was lacking in literacy and technical skills. Similarly, teen pregnancy, which has long existed in rural communities, now occurs in a changed social context. No longer are young mothers so likely to marry the father of the child or remain in the home of their parents, who provide food, shelter, and child care in an extended-family atmosphere. As family support systems have become less able to care for teenage mothers, and farms and factories have become less able to use unskilled or semiliterate labor, communities have found themselves with more individuals who are unable to cope with the modern world. Some rural people are ahead of their fellow residents in "owning up to" the social problems that exist in the rural countryside.

> One country probation officer, "a local from way back," takes an analytical perspective on the increasing caseload of problems that comes his way. "Without community and extended family, people don't look out for other people. The extended family, in the sense of others in the community who feel they should look out for you and to whom you feel a sense of obligation, is necessary. The community is necessary. Traditionally, the community reinforces the family, but now there *is* no community to do that; people don't know each other now. In the old days people were really rural, really scattered, but individuals were not isolated. Now, there may be ten people in a trailer and each one of them feeling isolated. But people can't live isolated lives without psychological disturbance. This is why we're so busy in the courts and the probation system."

> In this long and thoughtful interview, I asked, "Where do these problems come from?" and his answer was as follows. "These are society's problems, and they are *our* problems. The problems we have here are not 'city problems'; they're our own problems. And despite what many people think, it's not true that most of the troublemakers here come from outside: Most of the probation cases I handle were born here or spent most of their lives here. Crime isn't moving in from the city; it's almost exclusively domestic. The intruder is us."

As the cumulative community-level impact of these changes surfaces to conscious level, realization gradually comes—though resisted by much traditional rural ideology—that society's problems do not fall into a neat urban-rural dichotomy. They are society's problems, and the rural community is inextricably part of that society. Gradually, with a heightened awareness that the full range of individual and societal problems exists even in their small town, more residents are now turning for help to local government, to schools, to Albany and Washington, and to the whole human service field. More rural people appear ready to press for—and to pay their share for—adequate human and community services.

CHAPTER ELEVEN
Local Innovation and Cooperation

Although growing community needs have frustrated the efforts of professionals and volunteers alike, of residents, taxpayers, and parents, as well as those who require services, innovative and spirited attempts to meet the needs have sprung up in many small communities. Effective local initiatives, in addition to meeting specific local needs, offer some general lessons about providing community services in rural places. They also demonstrate the enduring strengths of rural people, institutions, and communities.

NEW LOCAL INSTITUTIONAL EFFORTS

Innovative and cooperative efforts come from three different directions. Institutions long established for other purposes, such as rural churches and schools, have been active and creative in trying to fill in service gaps while carrying on their more traditional roles. New, informal groups have been assembled by ordinary citizens who feel some common need or interest, and new, formal organizations have been incorporated specifically to fill gaps in the local services. Additionally, some existing service agencies have altered their services or mode of operation, or even defied prevailing trends, to ensure that community service needs are met.

Activities of Local Churches
in Meeting Community Needs

Rural and small-town churches play an important, though insufficiently recognized, role in community services. To survive problems of dwindling membership and growing operating costs, some rural churches have merged, streamlined their operation by sharing clergy, and encouraged lay people to take on more responsibility for church activities. But the small size of a congregation often belies the strong commitment of these women, men, and teenagers to improving the well-being of their community. As individuals, and often as designated representatives of their church, they sit on the boards of community agencies, initiate and run community celebrations, organize community efforts to address unmet needs, sponsor a child or a family in difficulty, network with the formal agency structure, help in local fund-raising activities, and keep their congregations apprised of the service needs of the community. Small and financially weak as some rural and small-town churches may be, many of them continue not only to operate their own religious and social programs but also to play an increasingly important role in local community services, from operating emergency food pantries and used clothing exchanges to donating their basement for use as a Head Start center.

Ministerial groups and social ministries supported by their churches have been active in rural issues, such as the plight of migrant farmworkers. In the southwestern counties of the state, several churches took the lead in working with various community agencies and groups, particularly Cooperative Extension, to develop community consciousness about the farm crisis situation and to coordinate efforts to reach out to troubled farmers.

In Allegany County local churches play a varied role in filling service gaps. Several village churches are now involved in the operation of self-help groups recently formed under the aegis of the local antipoverty agency. A social outreach committee of one church hosts and operates a latchkey program at the church to provide after-school care five days a week. Another small-town church provides a foster grandparents volunteer program in a small school to increase the attention and time available for children with developmental disabilities.

Initiatives of Rural Schools in Response to Changing Needs

Some rural schools have also become more involved in community issues and needs. In the late 1980s many rural school enrollments bottomed out and began to grow again. Many are still small, and sentiment is still strongly against merging into larger districts, as has been demonstrated by resounding defeats of merger proposals in several recent votes. Realizing that the school is the community's central institution, and often its only public building, some rural schools are now taking a more active and more diverse role in the community. Some schools have become catalysts in raising public awareness of community service needs and have been actively engaged in working with community agencies concerning the needs of local children and their families.

Responding to expressed community need for after-school child care, one school has instituted a special after-school program with a late bus home. But this is not just recreation time. Taking advantage of the availability of space after the school day and of the captive audience of children in it, several of the community's service agencies have been encouraged to schedule regular "outreach" activities into the program, including mental health counseling, dispute resolution, Scouts and 4-H, nutrition education, and health clinics.

Closer interaction between schools and community services may become a more standard format for service delivery in rural communities in the future. Using school facilities and transportation as well as utilizing the input of school staff familiar with children and their needs can help overcome some of the fragmentation of services that otherwise reduces service effectiveness. Use of school facilities in out-of-school hours means that services can be delivered to rural children efficiently, because of minimized transportation costs, in a regular and organized fashion and in a place where children and their families can feel comfortable. In some communities, creative arrangements are being developed for sharing social work and counseling staff between school districts and community agencies, and in several districts the local county department of social services works closely with schools concerning at-risk children.

One intriguing example of innovative ways that rural institutions have coped with changes in populations and needs comes from a small school in central New York with a high poverty rate. This school's Morning Program has earned high marks from the state education department and has now been adopted by several other schools. The program arose out of concern about a growing incidence of poverty and a high rate of turnover of children. The program's specific goals, which are reinforced in a variety of other approaches and activities throughout the school, are to make children feel good about themselves, each other, teachers, administrators, and the school; to involve them in group activities; and to convey "certain positive values." In the driest terms, the morning program is a daily twenty-minute assembly for the entire elementary school of about 600 children. But an on-site visitor can easily feel the liveliness and warmth it generates.

The younger classes of children file into the gym of the South New Berlin School, and sit down in vague rows on the floor, accompanied by the teachers at the front of the gym who are singing and clapping, with arm and body motions. Five teachers are up at the front of the room, others gather in back then circulate among the kids. More active songs are played on the tape player as older elementary children come in, and the entire group claps and stomps to the music. Five children in the front join the teachers as leaders. Officially designated members of the welcoming committee, some from each grade, circulate to give an individual welcome to the few visitors (one parent, a family group, and myself). Nearly everyone joins in a spirited rendition of "You Are My Sunshine." The assistant superintendent, using the microphone, calls out, "Good morning, students!" and gets a cheery, roaring response. All children rise for the pledge of allegiance and then sing "This Land Is Your Land." The assistant superintendent introduces some young visitors, younger siblings, or relatives visiting school for the day; a child introduces her mother, grandmother, and baby sister. It is Misty's birthday, and she is called to the front and given a card while the crowd sings "Happy Birthday." Misty is not pressed to respond. Next comes "the word of the week" game and other word games, with enthusiastic clapping for all participants. Riddles about baseball are followed by an award of merit to each classroom from a nursing home to which the children had sent cards.

Throughout this part of the program, the assistant superintendent and all teachers use first names of children. The students are attentive and well behaved, raising their hands and participating. Teachers are energetic and supportive, leading in songs and games, but also encouraging individual children. The special feature of the day is a visit from the high school boys' baseball team, in uniform. The coach runs volunteer children through a humorous drill, and there is much excitement when a teacher has her turn to be up. After this, the assistant superintendent compliments the children on their performance in a recent fire drill, saying, "You ought to clap for yourself." They do, enthusiastically. He calls out, "Have a good day, everyone." Kids line up by classes and go out to more music. Teachers and children wish each other a nice day. Older children put away the dozen chairs. The spirit and enthusiasm of the children as they leave the gym is a complete contrast to what I had seen as sleepy children stumbling off the school bus into their classrooms just a half hour earlier.

In another small-town school, the principal emphasized the advantage of a school in which people all know each other and there is a feeling of "family," which she regards as especially important for the many children with unstable home situations. As if to prove her point, the following interaction interrupted our interview.

A second-grader stands at the open door to the principal's office and catches her attention. "What is it Peter?" Without preamble or explanation, he answers, "I forgot my note." "What note?" the principal asks. "My walk note." "Oh. Where are you going to walk to? Is Marie [the day-care giver for this child] still in Florida?" "Yes." "Where are you going today?" "To Cindy's—but I don't have a note." "Well, I'll call your Mom. Is she at work today?" "Yes." The child turns away and then skips past the secretary's desk. The principal writes a note on her pad with the mother's name and asks the secretary to phone her at work.

After this interlude, the principal explained that many children go to babysitters after school, but that most of the child care comes from high school students. Therefore the elementary school ties its day to the high school schedule, to avoid having elementary school ending before high school does. As yet, there is no after-school program, and the space, money, and personnel to make it happen seem beyond reach.

Formation of Informal Self-help Groups to Meet Local Needs

Following the pattern familiar in urban and suburban areas, but with some time delay, rural communities are now adding a whole spectrum of support groups and self-help groups that provide support to people who are going through particular problems or have been caught in certain difficulties. Whether the circumstance is marital violence, cancer surgery, being the parent of a teenager, or being the adult child of alcoholic parents, support groups have sprung up that bring together people in similar situations.

The support group phenomenon was slow to come to rural communities because, in large part, they already had informal neighborhood support systems that were easily activated, particularly in times of pain, grief, and misfortune. Furthermore, traditional rural code followed by many individuals and institutionalized in the operation and mores of the community, held that personal troubles should not become public affairs. Particularly where local governmental sponsorship or funding is involved, this traditional ideology has made rural communities hesitate to support the self-help movement for addressing the problems of changing family and social patterns. For example, rural ideology and official opinion have only slowly come to acknowledge that marital violence exists within the community, that it is a serious problem, that it is sufficiently common to form the basis of a group, or that going public and forming a support group is "the right thing to do."

Gradually, however, changes in the social life of rural communities, combined with weakening in family structure, have left people more vulnerable, but at the same time less likely to find assistance and support through informal networks in the community. The self-help group phenomenon, so accepted in larger communities, seems to have overcome traditional resistance as more groups are formed for more problems.

At the height of the farm crisis, farm wives in Delaware County formed a support group to enable them to talk through some of the emotional and social problems that came along with financial crisis on the farm.

In several rural counties a battered wives or domestic violence support group has recently been formed. Almost as soon as such groups are formed, they reach optimal size, and so additional groups are established. The scope also grows, and the emphasis shifts toward self-help as well as emotional support.

In 1987 Allegany set up a local "crisis support team," the first such support group in New York. The problem identified is "critical incident stress," or CIS, and it afflicts the volunteers in the ambulance squads, emergency medical teams, and fire departments of small communities. These volunteers have a lot of serious and grisly cases to deal with, a high rate of auto and farm machinery accidents, long distances to travel to hospitals that may mean less chance of the patient surviving, and less adequate facilities. Above all, in a small community the victims of accidents, fires, and serious illnesses are likely to be people that these volunteers know, even their own relatives. The crisis support team, made up of specially trained members of a volunteer group, helps people who have participated in critical incidents deal with both the acute and delayed stress reactions.

Elsewhere, a new women's group, called "Take a Break," includes young mothers, most of quite low income. These women meet twice a month at the Rural Services Center that was recently established by three very active and dedicated Catholic sisters in a small and poor hamlet on the distant edge of a county far from the county seat, where most agencies and programs are located. For the preschool children who are brought along, the mornings provide socialization experiences they will otherwise not receive until they are in kindergarten, as there is no Head Start in this rural part of the county. For the women it is both a needed social group and an opportunity to learn new skills and ideas. "At first they mostly talked about their problems," reported one of the organizing nuns. "But now they've gotten tired of hearing each other's problems. Now they want real programs, so we've turned to county agencies for expertise." The group has recently had a nutrition class from the county Extension Service and a Red Cross program on emergency care at home. For one session they requested a videotape dealing with problems in "broken families." Another meeting was devoted to women's health. The mothers also discuss the future for their children, and because of their expressed concerns about the lack of regular preschool programs, the sisters have been working with the county to get a commitment to setting up a Head Start center in the area. The Rural Services Center sees its role as facilitator, encouraging these women to encourage and support each other, and the sisters report that indeed the women have taken on an attitude of caring and concern for one another: "If one of them hasn't seen one of the others for several days, she may get worried and call us up at the center to see if that other woman is all right." Some of the women who live outside the hamlet now arrange their own carpooling to get to the center. Some of them also come in to help sort and stack for "clothing days," when about 125 local families come in to select from piles and piles of clothes, good used clothing and also new items, including jeans, socks, and underwear donated by stores and churches in the city.

Whatever their purpose or interest, these varied support groups are similar in that each has a parent organization within the formal structure of the community, an official sponsoring agency, church, or voluntary organization that helps it get started, provides some space or services, and may provide funding or be a conduit for funds. The groups are informal, loosely structured, quite narrow in stated purpose; they are run mostly by the participants themselves and are thoroughly unbureaucratic. They can even dissolve themselves, as a farm wives support group did. They tap into the formal human service network as necessary. Above all, these groups satisfy real and perceived needs for which there is no other adequate and available response, either because of changes in formal and informal social organization of the community or because the needs are too new and undefined to receive full institutional recognition yet. Their flexibility, low cost, and informality make organized support groups an adaptable tool in the provision of community services in rural areas. Their emphasis on informal social contacts is appropriate to traditional rural social preferences and effective in contemporary rural settings.

A Larger Role for Nongovernmental
Organizations in Community Services

One significant development in meeting rural needs has been the increased role of single-purpose, nonprofit or not-for-profit corporations in providing community services. For specialized groups of the local population, such as the elderly or low-income families or handicapped children, services are increasingly being provided by private organizations that are funded either through outside grants, by contracts with local governments, or some combination thereof. Local governments are stepping back from producing services themselves to providing them through contracts that are paid for with money that the state channels to localities for various social purposes. Some of these nonprofits have been able to put together some very effective patchwork quilts of grants and loans from a variety of federal, state, and private sources to accomplish goals that local people consider important. Housing rehabilitation is just one example.

A private not-for-profit corporation founded in 1981 in Allegany County receives its administrative funding from the New York State Division of Housing and Community Renewal, through its Rural Preservation Program. The funding for most of its projects comes from the federal Department of Housing and Urban Development (HUD). With her careful attention to details and her strong personal involvement, the executive director of this three-and-a-half-person outfit modestly admits that she has established a good track record in getting grants—without ever hiring a consultant. The majority of the corporation's effort is targeted in one small hamlet where housing is particularly run-down, with a high rate of rental occupancy by low-income people as well as substandard owner-occupied homes. It is a community where the county's welfare clients and working poor come to find cheap rental apartments, and where many who own their homes cannot afford to fix them.

Since its founding in 1982, the corporation has made seventy-eight low-interest home-improvement loans to homeowners who, according to the director, "otherwise would have been unable to make needed repairs or improvements due to their limited incomes." Then, with a $.5 million HUD grant, the corporation purchased and restored a historic but entirely crumbling home on Main Street, turning it into nine quality rental apartments that will be rented to low-income tenants at rates not to exceed 30 percent of their income. Next, this active corporation compiled a high-powered application and was waiting hopefully—"prayerfully," said the director—for HUD approval of a $400,000 Community Development Block Grant to fund rehabilitation of houses and apartments in a particularly deteriorated section of the village. On July 1, 1989, amid the publicity of investigation of alleged scandals at HUD, the grant came through. Other proposals are in the works and other projects already under way. Together, these efforts will go a long way not only to providing better-quality housing at affordable rents, but to turning the whole community around, helping it recover from what the director calls "an insidious disease" of physical decay that has taken its toll on the community's functioning and on its reputation.

An advantage in this privatization of community services is that the service-providing agencies have more autonomy from local politics and official community ideology. Whether using the services-by-contract model in which state funds are channeled through county governments to service agencies, or relying mostly on outside federal grants to support community programs, the new modes may allow programs and services to move out ahead of somewhat outdated traditional thinking that sometimes permeates the official stance of local governments. The variety of patterns of operation is itself one of the major benefits, allowing programs to be closely tailored to local situations and needs.

Attempts to Continue to Serve the Periphery

Underserving of rural people living on the periphery of the county does not have to be the case. Although some counties maintain very few services near their borders, preferring to require residents to travel inward to offices in the county seat, a variety of modes for reaching and serving the more remote areas have evolved in counties and agencies where commitment to serving the periphery remains strong. In some places a department of social services, a community action agency, and other services and agencies maintain either satellite offices or outreach programs as well as a central office. In some cases the cost of operating a satellite office is minimized by a coalition of agencies and services sharing the facility and by cooperation among workers from different programs who serve the same remote areas. Examples from field observations indicate that whereas many programs and agencies have centralized their services, a few programs have made a commitment to continuing to serve rural people despite the prevailing doctrine of cost efficiency in service delivery.

In St. Lawrence County, the state's largest and one of its poorest, twelve neighborhood centers or outreach bases are operated by the community action agency. Each center is a fairly autonomous satellite, sponsored in part by the local community and responsive to the particular needs of the area. In one village center, located 20 miles from the county seat, a local church covers the cost of rent, utilities, and salaries of workers other than the director. Located in a storefront on Main Street, this neighborhood center, like others, is a busy place. People drop in to look through its thrift shop for good used clothes. While there, they may check with the outreach worker to see if the expected phone call on a medicaid problem has come in and might look over the list of apartments for rent. They can find out about various programs available at or through the center, such as well-child clinics, WIC clinics, Head Start, parents' anonymous, and the expanded emergency food program. They may also talk informally and confidentially with the director about personal or family problems, perhaps picking up some suggestions about options to consider. They leave with a few clothes, a phone message, information, and a boost that enables them to face a problem at home. The director, who seems to know everyone in town, plays an advocate role for people with the department of social services and other community institutions, helps people sign up for various kinds of programs and assistance, and facilitates their networking with each other. This center has its hands full already, but it is making some changes to keep up with the changing needs of the area's low-income population, especially their outward displacement caused by the impact of Fort Drum expansion not far away.

LOCALIZED SOLUTIONS TO LOCAL PROBLEMS

To give an indication of local efforts, either alone or in cooperative combination with outside sources, four innovative efforts from different rural communities around the state will be briefly described. Many more examples could be cited, and some have already been described in earlier chapters. The selection of material presented here illustrates some lessons that can be learned and some common approaches that make such programs the successes they are in meeting rural community needs.

Building a Town Hall to Meet State Regulations: Volunteer Labor and Local Pride

One rural township with just over 2,000 people had a town hall building that had always been adequate to its needs. When new state regulations required certain features in all town halls, including handicap accessibility, the Davenport Township government in Delaware County was in a quandary. Failure to meet new requirements would leave the town vulnerable to a lawsuit for failure to comply, and the town's insurance would not cover such a suit or fines if the town was knowingly in violation.

> "We couldn't stay there and risk a lawsuit," said the town supervisor. "So we bought the old Grange building that was in disrepair and moved it down the road onto some land we purchased. We've built a new foundation that is an entire ground floor, and then placed the old Grange building on top." Feeling that there was no sense in applying for federal or state grants to cover this project, town officers decided to fund part of the project out of taxes, but to do most of the work themselves. And work they did! Even in the midst of haying season, farmers and other local people donated many hours of volunteer labor. The evening I stopped by for a guided tour, in June of 1987, there were four men and two wives working on plasterboarding and trim-finishing in the new ground floor. Some of the workers were professionals, donating their services at night, and the quality of work in the building reflected their expertise and dedication. A ramp entrance had been constructed, and a new handicap-accessible bathroom had been installed, complete with special fixtures. There are three small offices and a vault for town records, as well as a meeting room. When I returned two months later for a monthly meeting of a farm-crisis counseling program, the ground floor was essentially completed: Walls had been smoothly finished and painted, doors fitted and hung, construction debris was mostly cleared away, and the coffeepot was on. Next summer, renovations would start in the upstairs, the old Grange hall. "By doing most of the work ourselves, with volunteers and using our own town labor and equipment, it's cost the taxpayers very little— and still we were able to decreases taxes this year. Besides, now we'll really have a good town hall!"

By two years later, in summer 1989, the exterior of the building still showed its dual origins, though the old shingled Grange hall sits quite comfortably on the wood-sided, poured-concrete ground floor. Near the front entrance is mounted an official blue and white sign indicating the handicap entrance. The front part of the ground floor has become the new post office for the hamlet, with a steady stream of cars and trucks pulling into the parking lot through the day. The ground floor meeting room, completely finished and furnished, is too small for the courtroom needs, because, as the secretary reported, the number of court cases, mostly highway cases, has been increasing steadily. Thus the postponed work on the upstairs, to create an adequate courtroom, becomes more urgent.

A Literacy Volunteer Program in the North Country: Satisfactions of Teaching and Learning to Read

Literacy Volunteers of America, a well-known nationwide program, was started in Syracuse, New York, by a woman who saw the great need in her own city back in 1962. In an old county office building on Main Street in Malone, Franklin County, the coordinator of the local Literacy Volunteers program enthusiastically talks of his program's progress in its two years of existence. "I knew when I started this program that there was an illiteracy problem out there, but I had no idea how great it was. There are whole families of people in this area where no one in the family reads or writes. It's a *huge* problem."

The director's enthusiasm and dedication leave him oblivious to the constant buzzing and lighting of houseflies as we talk. He and his family have been in the North Country a long time. He's been involved in volunteer work most of his life, "because there's such a need, but also because you get such good results." He had retired a few years ago from a sales job, and then as a VISTA (Volunteers in Service to America) volunteer became coordinator of the fledgling local Literacy Volunteers program. In just two years, the local program has greatly exceeded its initial goals: teaching eighty students with over 100 trained and carefully matched tutors. The director worries especially about young adults who are unable to read, but elderly people, too, are important in his efforts. Currently, the star pupil, who has been featured in newspapers and in a recent video presentation, is eighty-one years old.

The director, using ingenious methods, has been quite successful in getting funds and attracting volunteers and has tinkered with the tutor training to adapt it to the schedules of volunteers, who come from all walks of life. What stands out most, however, is his dedication and sensitivity to the people who need the literacy tutoring, to the problems of low self-esteem and embarrassment that make it difficult for them even to admit to their problem, and to the need to tailor the tutoring program to their living situations. His program is infused with a can-do attitude. "In rural areas, we have to do things a little differently. We have to be flexible to make programs meet people's needs." The director himself comes into the office early to tutor two students before they go to work in the morning. He advertises the literacy program on early-morning radio, telling people over the air, "I'm always in my office by six o'clock in the morning, there's no one else around, the back door's open and the coffeepot's on. Why not drop in and find out about some of the programs we have going?"

A Nurse Practitioner in a Small Rural School:
Foundation Funding and a Dedicated Practitioner

In most schools the nurse's office is one of the busiest locations in the building; research interviews conducted with nurses in schools were interrupted many times for priority matters of children needing attention. In between the usual tummyaches, skinned knees, administering of fluoride tablets, and telephone calls to mothers at work, the staff of the nurse's office, no matter what their official titles, are a key element in warm interaction with children. In a few schools around the state, some new functions have been added to the usual soothe-and-wait approach: a carefully restricted program of primary medical care that is a tremendous asset in a rural place where other frontline medical care may be scarce.

Originally funded by a private foundation with a long record in encouraging innovative health care programs, and bolstered by special enabling legislation in Albany, the Robert Wood Johnson School Health Programs have been underwriting the training of school nurse practitioners and the purchase of medical equipment for a school nursing facility. These were pilot programs, and, unfortunately, only a few school districts have picked up the costs of operation and salary. But in one rural case the school board is convinced of the value of the program to all the children, to parents, and ultimately to the entire, spread-out community.

The Harpursville School District lies within an upstate metropolitan county but is quite a poor area, far from hospitals, and very rural. Most parents sign up for the program's highest option, that of primary care, which includes periodic physical examinations, vision and hearing tests, updating of immunizations, urine testing for diabetes, a blood test for anemia, a health history, and treating children for certain minor illnesses when school is in session, including prescribing medications if indicated. There is no charge for any service, whereas a strep throat culture would normally cost about $20 and a doctor visit at least $25 and would involve considerable travel problems, especially for families where the husband has the only car at his job, a half-hour's drive away and there is no public transportation. With about 500 prescriptions written during the 1987–1988 school year (for a school enrollment of slightly over 1,000), it is estimated that about $10,000 was saved for local parents. But beyond that, the benefits are in improved health care, including more attention to preventive and follow-up care. By 1989 children were graduating from sixth grade who had been in the program since kindergarten.

A child who has stayed home sick may be brought to the school to be examined without charge, and in the majority of cases, which so frequently involve ear or throat infections, a prescription can be written. If a child starts to feel bad while in school and comes to the office, the nurse practitioner will examine the child on the spot. If the ears or throat hurt but do not yet evidence a fully developed infection, she will instruct the child to come back in again the next day, at which time she can prescribe if appropriate. Even the prescriptions for the fall outbreaks of head lice can be written from the school, saving a trip to a doctor and making it much more likely that all infected children will get the effective treatment. The nurse practitioner also takes an active role in educating children about their own health. She places on the child the responsibility for taking the medication and coming back to her office for a final checkup (usually in ten days, when the course of medication is completed) and, in cases of ear infections, for a hearing test.

This school nurse practitioner sums up her philosophy and that of the Robert Wood Johnson program as follows: "Why not provide almost full health care to kids while they are here in school? Why *not*?" She closes the interview with another emphatic mission statement: "We give these kids the very best—not the minimal, but the ultimate."

Working to Solve the Rural Transportation Problem: The Town and Country Transit

Transportation has been cited as a major rural problem by all sorts of human service agencies and by the general public throughout rural New York. Nationally, with deregulation of transportation, rural bus routes that are less profitable get dropped, aggravating a transportation problem that was already serious in the more rural states. But connection of rural people with services has been made even more difficult because of centralization of services.

Putting together the funding and the institutional framework for rural public transportation is itself a major task, on top of the more pragmatic concerns of vehicles, maintenance, routes, schedules, and public acceptance. The Town and Country Transit in Chenango County was the first of its kind in the state, an attempt to replace overlapping but underused routes of several different service agencies with a unified countywide bus system coordinated by the community action agency. The agency has thirty-four vehicles and a wide variety of routes and schedules designed to connect outlying villages and countryside with the small county seat, where most of the county's specialized services are located. For the most part, the transit system serves clients of the seven county agencies, including the Office for the Aging and Association for Retarded Citizens, that grouped together to form the system, and it carries all of the children for Head Start. But the transportation is available to the general public, and people of lower income can obtain a pass to ride free. The transit system was set up as a demonstration project and received funding through a state rural transportation bill. Subsequent state funding has allowed some other counties to design and implement their own coordinated public transportation systems. In Chenango there were start-up glitches to overcome, and improvements are still needed to increase "ridership," but the transit system works.

The blue van-bus starts its run on a May afternoon from behind the headquarters of the community action agency, Opportunities for Chenango. With two women riders already aboard, Kris turns into the parking lot in the center of downtown to pick up two passengers from the county's mental health and development training center. Next, she picks up a man on his way home from medical appointments, and then swings over to the BOCES center to pick up two sisters, one aged four, the other just turned five, who had been at speech therapy for the day. Having buckled the girls in their seatbelts, Kris negotiates smoothly through the traffic of the small downtown, and drives carefully along two-lane roads past valley farms and through wooded hills, skillfully dodging potholes, stopping at railroad tracks, and waving to residents outdoors on a bright spring day.

In this unique rural transportation service, Kris is not only a driver but also conversationalist, informal therapist, and a caring, friendly person. As she drives along country roads, she keeps up a constant patter with the passengers. She consciously encourages the two little girls from speech therapy to talk: She resumes the song she started to teach them on last week's ride, plays word games and rhyming with them, and then sends them into giggles by singing a song with the words all mixed up for them to correct. Finally she drops them off at their home in a hamlet at the far edge of the county; Kris carries on a brief conversation with the mother as she turns the van around in the driveway and then turns her conversation to the other riders, chatting lightly about the day and the scenery, getting riders to check for the family of Canada geese on a pond. She coaxes a withdrawn mental health patient to interact with her and with others on the bus. As Kris lets each passenger off, giving assistance if needed, there is a pleasant good-bye and often a bit of humor: "Watch out as you step down, now; there may be snakes in the grass there." Coming back toward town over an hour later, she picks up two regular paying customers who use the bus as part of their strategy for getting home after work. Today she did not have the frequent round-trip passenger, an elderly lady who sometimes rides the entire route just to get out of her house and have some people to talk with.

For effective delivery of the whole gamut of human services in rural areas, from health care for the elderly to education of the very young, or conversely, from health care of the very young to education for the elderly, better public transportation is clearly a high priority. However, provision of rural transportation is not a substitute for decentralization of services through satellite centers and outreach workers.

LESSONS LEARNED FROM LOCAL EFFORTS

As these examples—and many others not presented here—demonstrate, *it can be done*. Specific community needs *can* be met, even in rural areas, even as needs are growing and changing. The rural can-do philosophy is a major asset that goes a long way to devising and implementing innovative solutions to community service needs. One motto often cited by individuals with exciting and effective programs is "Damn the torpedoes; full speed ahead." Others cite the adage "If

I have a good idea for my program, I'd rather ask for forgiveness afterwards than beg for permission first." Effective rural programs utilize a lot of local talent and a commonsense approach supplemented by judicious use of outside or professional help when needed and appropriate. Creative individuals at the head of agencies, some of them long-term residents, others recent arrivals, can accomplish a great deal in rural communities to move human services out of service delivery ruts and into a proactive mode.

Local efforts to meet particular needs can also be very effective in building community problem-solving capacity if the *process* of resolving a problem is given at least as much attention as the product. In a process-oriented approach, there is more opportunity to build up and build on local strengths. It can also be used to broaden community participation, loosening decisionmaking and planning from the grip of professionals who provide the services.

Rural service needs are not effectively addressed by urban-derived programs, and simply aiming urban solutions at rural problems may miss the mark completely. Even worse results accrue when urban solutions are applied but with only a fraction of the urban funding levels, based on per capita formulas. An inappropriate program that is underfunded to the point where it couldn't even begin to work is doubly wasteful. Meeting rural needs requires much more than simply delivering prorated urban services. Even where impetus or funding for a program does come from outside, whether state or federal government, exciting results are most likely to happen when plenty of allowance is made for rural initiative and innovativeness rather than handing down a preformulated program.

Some of the most exciting programs operating in rural communities are aimed not only at the service needs of individuals but at supporting the community and institutional structure to enable it to do a better job, both informally and formally, in meeting the needs of members. Greatest lasting effectiveness comes from enabling existing community networks and institutions to improve the total social environment of the community rather than simply increasing local people's dependence on services being provided from the outside. Emphasizing the problem-solving capacity in existing institutions and the community-building aspects of meeting local needs can also help to avoid the fragmentation of services among agencies and institutions. In areas with small populations, changing local needs, and decreasing outside funding, fragmentation and turf battles among service-providing groups are unaffordable. Additionally, these divisions are anticommunity in that they prevent community publics from effectively getting involved in designing, funding, and overseeing their own services.

The lessons drawn from these community examples point to some key benefits of the capacity-building, problem-solving kind of community development in which local talents and local ideas are given free rein to design and implement community-appropriate solutions to the community's own problems. This is a broader and more lasting concept of rural community development than the sometimes narrow focus that concentrates only on physical infrastructure and on economic development, such as building roads and attracting factories. It is a concept of rural community development that emphasizes *institutional* infrastructure and *social* development, and that enables a community to become more effective in attacking such specific problems as physical infrastructure and economic development. It enhances the community's ability to meet its own needs.

PART SIX

Changes and Challenges in Local Government

CHAPTER TWELVE

Leadership and Local Government in Flux: Changes in Who, What, and How

We always used to think that local government was the stable bedrock of our community, that it would just go on and on, always doing what it has always done. But it's not that way at all. Local government is in flux now.
—A rural township supervisor

Significant changes are occurring in the composition of political leadership, in issues facing local governments, and in modes of conducting and financing government services. And the governmental changes are gaining momentum and force because they are connected to the many other changes occurring at the same time in rural communities, the agricultural, economic, demographic, and social changes. It is a time of political flux, but the direction of change is not fully established and the speed and direction of change varies in different communities. In responding to new challenges, some local governments appear to be moving into new modes with new ideas and new people, some are reverting to tried-and-true formulas for getting by in hard times, and some appear to vacillate between one direction and the other.

In New York State, the layers of local government, each with jurisdiction and responsibilities that are somewhat distinct but also overlapping, include the county, the component townships, the incorporated villages within them and, where they exist, cities. Although on each level the responses are diverse and still evolving, observations in several rural counties reveal some patterns—and some problems.

SHIFTS IN POLITICAL ALIGNMENT AND INFLUENCE: CHANGES IN THE WHO

In past decades, rural governments were characterized by stability and by longevity of people holding offices. Farm people and an agricultural orientation prevailed, and older men carried on much of the business of local government. An unwritten political code made it unlikely that an incumbent who sought reelection to town or county office would ever face a primary.

As one county legislator said, "The rural areas have never had competition to get on the county board." He cited the example of a once-respected but now very sleepy old man who consistently won reelection to the county legislature, even though he had become an embarrassment to members of his own party. "People in his township will not run against him despite how ineffective he is." There were no primaries within his party to consider another candidate. The opposite political party, greatly outnumbered in the district's registered voters, did not even put up a candidate to oppose him.

New Faces in Public Places

Kinship and length of residence in the community remain important in local politics. Some township boards are still family affairs, with several members related to each other and many of them long-term residents in the area.

> Three people with the same last name hold positions on one board of a dozen people; a man serves as town justice in the same township where his mother is supervisor; a husband and wife serve together on one board, a father and son on another, two brothers on another; and in one town a father and daughter hold office. In several cases, township offices have traditionally been held for generations in certain respected families, often farm families, with sons taking over an office relinquished by retiring fathers.

The late 1980s, however, included more challenges to long-term officeholders than had generally occurred in the past and a loosening up of the solid "ownership" of certain offices and committee assignments. Some of the old family "dynasties" are dissolving, and some of the traditional assumptions and agreements about leadership are now subject to questioning. In local elections in 1988 and 1989, the trends were mixed: In some townships and villages nearly all incumbents were running unopposed in quiet elections; in other places there were "unheard-of" Republican primaries, both parties ran candidates for most offices, campaigning was unusually active and voter turnout unusually large, though still much less than 50 percent in most places. There were some major upsets, but even in upsets the trend was bimodal in that some localities ousted long-term officeholders in favor of "new faces," whereas elsewhere more recently elected incumbents were ousted in favor of more traditional candidates who were said by their backers "to have a country sense of values and maybe know how to pinch a dollar better."

One of the most noticeable characteristics in local governments now is turnover of officeholders, with a statewide rate figured at about 36 percent (according to the New York Department of State). The turnover is due not only to contested elections but also to the nature of the job: More officeholders are now stepping down after a single term. Some new and capable township supervisors report that the heavy time commitment for minimal salary, the complexity of recent state and federal regulations, the threat of lawsuits, the blizzard of paperwork, and the realization that there is really very little decisionmaking latitude available to local governments all made township government less a rewarding civic activity and much more a headache.

The age profile of elected officials appears to be declining, although this trend is slow and spotty. In one county in 1988, of the fifteen legislators, only two were under fifty, one was in his fifties, and the rest were over sixty; but the 1990 board had a considerably lower age range, as some of the older board members had either decided not to seek reelection, or had been beaten in primaries or district elections. The decline in age is likely to continue where new resident populations have arrived from nearby cities or where a younger generation of local people becomes involved in politics as new issues, such as environmental quality, arise.

Although women have long served on township and village boards, their positions have generally been limited to very clear gender-specific roles of lesser prominence. In the majority of cases, township supervisors are male and clerks are female; village and city mayors are male.

A review of the members of local governments during 1987 and 1988 in five counties (Allegany, Chenango, Delaware, Franklin, and Clinton) revealed that in 102 townships, there were only seven women supervisors, but there were eighty-nine women clerks. Of the two cities in these five counties, both had male mayors, whereas of the thirty-seven villages, thirty-one had male mayors.

Now, one or two women sit on most county legislative boards and in some cases occupy crucial leadership and committee roles. As 1990 began, history was made in one rural county when the legislature inaugurated a woman, who had served on the board for eight years, for its top leadership position. She was proclaimed in the local newspaper as the first "female chairman" of the county board.

Declining Political Role of Farming

Farm people, both lifelong residents and recently arrived farmers, have traditionally been active in local politics and government. Many farm people continued to hold local office even as their farms were going through tough times recently; other farmers who sold their herds and no longer have the incessant demands of milking cows have just joined local governments and community boards. Nonetheless, farming interests appear to have gradually lost some influence in local politics, a slippage that is reflected in the make-up of locally elected governing bodies.

The chairman of a county board of legislators, a former farmer and long-time legislator, sat in his office in the courthouse and talked of the changes in county politics and government over the years. He pulled from his shelf the county directories from previous decades and perused the lists of county board members. "Twenty years ago in this county, this board was all farmers," he said. But as he glanced down the list, he modified his statement: "Well, mostly farmers." Besides farmers, there was a logger, an undertaker, two merchants, an insurance man and someone from industry, a schoolteacher and "a retired lady teacher," a school accountant, and a lawyer. Then he went down a current list for the end of the 1980s and found only one retired farmer and no one still in farming.

The decreasing role of farming in local politics is mostly attributable to ascendance of other interests and is related to changes in the make-up of local population and the local economy. But it has also come about because the local farm population has become a very diverse group. "The farm population" is no longer, if it ever was, a unified constituency or influence. The range of political inclinations, educational and experience backgrounds, and personal stakes in the local community is now as broad as the range of farms.

In some counties the decline of farm influence in local politics and decisionmaking is also due to changes in structure of county government that took place in the late 1960s. At that time, twenty-six of the forty-four rural counties underwent a change from a governing board composed of township supervisors to a body of separately elected county legislators who have no responsibility for township government. This latter form tends to disconnect county government somewhat from township so-ciopolitical traditions and thereby weakens the farm influence. In the eighteen rural counties where this change did not occur, township supervisors still serve as county legislators, so more farmers may sit on the county board; but their voice in government decisions has generally been diminished by a system of weighted voting, in which each su-pervisor-legislator has a vote proportional to the population of her or his township.

Shifting Interests and Alignments

Along with a more fluid roster of elected officials, there are new alignments and new dynamic tensions, based mostly on economic in-terests. These shifts show up at the ballot box and in the organization of local legislative bodies, through election of officers and assignments to powerful committees. Although the alignments and competing interests are complex and in flux, they are often interpreted as farm-nonfarm schisms, as "farm interests" competing against "the business and industry interests."

For example, in two counties farm people complained that county tax money was being spent to expand and improve a small local airport that, they said, would be used only by executives of manufacturing firms. Meanwhile, nonfarmers complained that the special agricultural districts give farmers a tax advantage while throwing the tax burden disproportionately on business and nonfarm residents.

In some localities, recent in-migrants to the community may cause further shifting of political alignments. A few local politicians expressed concern that new residents might vote as a bloc in opposition to the more traditional coalition of interests bound together by long-term local residence: "After all, the weight of a vote is the same for people who have been here two days as for people who have been here two hundred years." However, there is as yet little evidence of such bloc voting.

The shifts and realignments are reflected in partisan politics. Rural townships have traditionally been Republican strongholds, whereas the larger villages or small cities have generally had Democratic majorities. With growth occurring mostly in the population centers, at the same time that agricultural influence subsides and rural areas remain sparsely populated, the larger villages and small cities are gaining political ascendancy; with this, Democrats are gaining ground in rural county governments. As the 1988 and 1989 elections approached, some Republican county legislators predicted they would lose districts they had traditionally held, and this was indeed the case in some counties, but not everywhere. The connection of local partisan politics to state party politics is somewhat loose, however. Some politically active Democrats in rural counties reported that they feel quite distant from "big-city Democratic power." One rural township supervisor, a Democrat with particular interest in social issues, reported that he feels rural social needs are ignored by both "downstate Democrats who think the only places with social problems are big cities" and "upstate Republicans who are concerned with rural areas, but not with social issues."

NEW AND DOMINATING ISSUES
FOR LOCAL GOVERNMENTS:
CHANGES IN THE WHAT

The issues and problems that occupy county, township, and village governments have been changing for decades, but with increasing speed in recent years. Some of the issues now closely parallel those that occupy suburban or even city governments. Other issues are old ones, perennially rural preoccupations, though now cast in new terms or bearing new urgency. Most local governments are dealing with several of these issues at once.

Solid Waste Disposal

In many upstate New York counties, as around the nation, the number-one issue now is waste disposal, the inadequacy of existing sanitary landfills and the need to finance and construct new facilities that meet new standards. The high costs of designing, constructing, operating, and closing a landfill are only in small measure covered by increasing tipping fees and state aid; the rest comes from—and strains—local budgets. For example, one rural county with an annual budget of $22 million is wrestling with a proposal to build a $14 million facility for solid waste resource recovery that will cost $10 million annually to operate and will require costly ancillary facilities such as transfer stations and state-mandated recycling programs. Some of the more rural townships that participate in a county landfill particularly resent being assigned a share of its operating cost that they feel is excessive: For example, a remote township of 800 residents was assessed $13,000 per year, even though residents contribute little household garbage and there are no commercial waste generators in the township. Some intercounty cooperative efforts have been undertaken to reduce costs, but political problems, technical problems, or both may limit their success.

> In one creative solution, two adjacent counties agreed to pool facilities. They placed a trash incinerator owned and operated by one county in a village in the second county, and disposed of the incinerator ash in the landfill of the second county. Revenue was generated by selling steam from the incinerator to a nearby dairy products plant. After more than four years of working to implement this solution, the landfill opened in summer 1987, cited as an exemplary case of collaboration. Soon, however, concern arose that the ash disposal system might be polluting nearby groundwater. Then the incinerator system caused unacceptable levels of air pollution. For the county where both the incinerator and the dump are located, "what had been the politicians' dream has now become the county's nightmare."

At least as difficult as the financing is finding a site for a new landfill, a problem that becomes monumental in the face of opposition from any selected locality, even if geologically and geographically appropriate. Site selection pits town against town, jeopardizing intermunicipal coop-eration that for other purposes and in other arenas may have been carefully nurtured. When a landfill is finally constructed, environmental or space concerns lead to restrictions and extra fees for certain items, such as tires and "white goods" (refrigerators, stoves, and washing machines). These items are now increasingly discarded instead along roadsides in remote rural areas. Another problem is that when a county opens a good state-of-the-art landfill with excess capacity for the future, it may be wooed by neighboring counties who would like to pay to get rid of their solid waste in someone else's landfill.

> As one county legislator said, "A landfill is like a bomb shelter: The problem is not what happens to you, but what do you do about your neighbors. Counties on the west, east, and north of us want to use ours, now that it's open. . . . The landfill was paid for with local monies, and I don't feel as though we should let others use it because our county will have to live with it."

In the various concerns and expenses of getting rid of trash in an environmentally sound manner, rural areas face exactly the same problems that more densely populated areas do. Despite their large land area and their sparse population, rural areas cannot find enough places that are both geologically safe and socially or politically acceptable to get rid of solid wastes. The problem comes as a particular shock to rural sensibilities, however, for it strikes many rural people as a new one. Dumping the garbage has never before required much outlay from local governments or much thought from rural residents.

Welfare Costs and Other Mandated Social Service Spending

The continuing high cost of various social service programs is another major concern of county governments and generally makes up about half of a rural county's budget. As unemployment declined in the late 1980s in rural New York, the number of rural AFDC and Home Relief cases also declined in some counties, giving much satisfaction to county budget personnel. County social services spending, however, did not drop as dramatically as unemployment, for the low wages that some former welfare clients now earn mean that they may still need and qualify for medicaid and other programs partially supported by county funds. In some counties, welfare rolls were already growing again at the end of the decade.

New York is one of the few states that require a local input for welfare programs. On average, the local share amounts to about one-quarter of the cost of every case in the total range of programs provided by a county's department of social services. Although some parts of the program, such as AFDC, require a lesser local input, others require more. To a large extent, the state Department of Social Services determines which programs will be offered, how they will be run, and how funded, giving counties little control over these mandated expenditures. Continued high levels of local spending for social service programs presents a particular problem to many local governments not only because of their current fiscal stress but also because it clashes with a traditional preference for spending on infrastructure rather than human services (Lifton 1988).

Roads and Bridges

Roads and bridges compose another major segment of rural government budgets, personnel, equipment, decisionmaking, and authority. Because half of the state's entire road mileage is township roads (whereas 18.5 percent is county roads and only 14.8 percent state), maintenance of roads is a particularly important activity of townships. Road maintenance and construction occupy most of a town's employees and generally between 50 and 80 percent of its budget. More than that, roads have long been symbolically important in the social structure and political maneuvering of township life (Vidich and Bensman 1958, p. 158), and thus the allocation of time and funds for roads is part of the ongoing sociopolitical negotiation within the township. At the county level, where roads take up a smaller share of the budget, road expenditure is nevertheless among the faster-growing budget items.

Presently, attention is especially focused on bridges. The collapse of a New York thruway bridge in 1987 brought bridge safety to the attention of all levels of government but has placed special strain on localities that have a great many bridges but only limited revenues to devote to them. With decreasing or discontinued state assistance for local bridge replacement, some counties have worked out a cost-sharing to help townships and villages cover the local portion of repairing their bridges. Behind the "crisis" is the fact that regular preventive maintenance has been inadequate in recent years of tight budgets and that old bridges on town and county roads are being assaulted with heavier vehicles and higher volumes of traffic and are corroding from de-icing salt.

> In Allegany County there are 364 bridges. Recent state inspections rated 40 percent of the 120 county-owned bridges deficient; 70 percent of the 225 township bridges were found deficient. To put all of them back in satisfactory condition is estimated to cost about $30 million, and to repair even a small village bridge may cost $1 million.

The bridge issue has special urgency because of the importance of truck traffic in rural areas. If a deteriorating bridge needs to be "posted" to restrict the weight of vehicles crossing, the impact on a nearby factory that uses the route for shipping and receiving could be considerable. Bridges on minor roads must also be maintained adequately to carry school buses, milk tank trucks, and fire trucks as well as normal residential vehicles. And even the small bridges on gravel roads leading up to weekend cabins of nonresidents must be kept safe enough to prevent accidents that might result in lawsuits. Some of these smaller bridges may require expenditures out of proportion to the use they get or the tax revenues generated by scattered vacation homes along back roads.

> One recent development that may help localities replace some small bridges is the encouragement by the state's Office of Local Government Affairs and by grants from the U.S. Forest Service for using local hardwood timbers rather than the more expensive metal structures to carry short-span local roads over small streams.

Even though rural communities have no particular responsibility for and little influence over state-owned roads, the quality and maintenance of state roads is critical for rural communities. It is the state highway system, after all, that enables the long-distance trucking that is so essential to the survival of rural economies and that allows rural people to commute to urban jobs, which more of them are having to do. The high caliber of most state roads in rural New York is widely praised by local officials and residents.

Water and Sewer

Old, failing, and inadequate water and sewer infrastructure is a problem especially affecting village governments. In New York State as a whole, it is estimated that 90 percent of existing water and wastewater problems are in small communities with under 5,000 people. Despite considerable federal funding in the 1970s, only a small portion of rural communities were helped. Problems not addressed then may now be acute and cannot be ignored much longer, but there is little federal assistance available now, and local governments are too pressed fiscally to do anything more than emergency repairs.

An added difficulty in addressing the problem of crumbling infra-structure is that these problems may bring to light the fragile social structures of some communities. Except in clear cases of emergency, preferences and expectations about the quality of infrastructure may differ widely within a community, leaving the community polarized in adversarial factions.

One hamlet has recently been stirred up over its long-standing water problem. Old pipes, some of them too small for modern methods of cleaning, have to be flushed at least four times a year to eliminate buildup of iron deposits and iron bacteria that cause odors, off color, and stains on residents' laundry. After each flushing and after any other flow surge, such as use of village fire hydrants, water appearance is particularly bad. Most long-time residents have utilized a variety of strategies to put up with the problem, and consider the cost of improving the old water system prohibitive. However, some residents are pushing for further investigation of the water problem, and have openly expressed distrust of village officials and health department water tests that indicate the water is safe to drink. The water problem has been cast as a dispute of "newcomers" versus "people born and raised here," and it became the issue through which a subtle tension was openly acknowledged. As one long-term resident pointed out, though, the split is also based on economic differences: "A lot of us come from families where we didn't have a lot. We've learned to make do with what we've got. If you can't afford it, you don't get it. Maybe people who want services and conditions the rest of us don't want and can't afford should go elsewhere."

Land-Use Planning

Another issue that towns and counties are increasingly becoming involved with, one that is often divisive socially and politically, is land-use planning. New York State law gives land-use planning authority to governments nearest the people, particularly township and village gov-ernments, with a much smaller role for counties. Traditionally rural governments have resolutely opposed doing anything at all to institute planning or zoning. In one county the president of a family-owned feed company remembers that back in the years immediately after World War II, his father was in local government and tried to get planning instituted, "but every time he got up and started saying something about planning he was cowbelled down." One county official said, "There is still strong resistance in this county to land-use planning of any sort. People here see planning as a euphemism for zoning, as an infringement on their rights." Antagonism to land-use planning is also connected to perceptions of socioeconomic class differences.

> Formerly urban people who have moved to a rural area seeking "a better place to live and to bring up the kids" have generally been in the forefront of favoring land-use controls so that the rural haven they had come for might be preserved. But this may bring them into opposition with longer-term residents. As one town supervisor commented, "City people are moving in. They're welcome to come as long as they don't try to change things here to make it like where they came from. For example, they want the poor residents to get tidied up, get rid of the junk cars in their yards. A few of these city people want me to enforce ordinances—or want new ones. And many of them want zoning. I'm very against it. People in rural areas need to be unrestricted. For example, someone might need to open up a little hair shop."

In some regions where there is little land development or population growth, the traditional rural reluctance for any sort of controls over land use has prevailed. Some counties have halfway measures, such as an appointed planning board and a professional staff that serves in an advisory role only, as consultants to local townships. In growth regions, however, many township governments are now overcoming their traditional aversion to land-use regulation, as they try to fend off an avalanche of land development, to protect groundwater quality, and to hold down taxes.

> The people of the Tug Hill area had typically regarded land-use planning as anathema, citing the problems that tight regulations had brought to Adirondack Park residents. Then came the announcement of the expansion of the adjacent Fort Drum military base, and with it an overwhelming rush on the part of many localities to protect the local quality of life through regulating building densities and drafting other common land-use planning strategies.

EMERGING ISSUES OF FINANCE AND STRUCTURE: CHANGES IN THE HOW

Taxation and Finance

No matter what the specific issue facing a local government may be, or what the resolution on the table, the underlying concern is the budget. Finance is the silent agenda, underlying the disposition of most issues. The preeminence of finance shows up in that the most powerful committees and positions on legislative boards are usually in budget and finance and in that a county fiscal officer may essentially be serving as a county administrator. A county budget is not simply a spending plan but a policy document.

As local governments deal with the central issue of funding, the overriding question is how to pay for the wanted and needed local services. But the inevitable qualifier is "without raising local taxes." In general a tacit assumption prevails that nothing will be done by local governments that would unduly raise taxes—or, conversely, that everything will be done to try to prevent or limit local tax increases. As one local leader said, "Our county board is taxpayer oriented, and its goal is the bare-bones budget." Because most locally generated revenue comes from real property taxes, property assessments and tax rates are a major preoccupation. Other taxes, such as a sales tax, can be added at local discretion, on top of the state's 4 percent sales tax; and if some localities use sales tax as a way to avoid increasing property-tax rates, in other localities the opposition to increasing taxes may extend to sales tax, too.

The contribution of farmland to the local property-tax base may be over 50 percent still, even where many dairy farms have recently gone out of business, but the proportion has been falling in recent years. By state law, land that is actively being farmed and lies within a duly constituted agricultural district is assessed separately as agricultural land rather than in terms of its potential market value for housing or industrial uses. Where demand for residential or recreational land is strong, the agricultural districts help preserve agricultural viability and protect farmland from speculation. The special agricultural districts have generally been regarded as, in one county official's pun, "sacred cows." However, in a period when local governments are "fiscally stressed" and where populations and political strength are in flux, there are indications that the local political commitment to agricultural districts is not as firm as it formerly was, particularly in the case of absentee ownership of farmland. As one county's real property tax officer said, "The ag districts have a negative effect on town highways, the town general tax, the county tax, and the school tax. It impacts on all those who pay taxes—and while it helps farmers in the ag districts, it impacts everybody else negatively."

For some rural townships, especially in the Adirondacks, but elsewhere, too, the tax-base problem is exacerbated by the fact that 40 to 50 percent or more of the land is owned by the state of New York as state park or state forests. Although the state makes contributions to localities in lieu of taxes, some local officials feel these are inadequate. More significant are the recreational lands held by nonresident individuals, as there may be a shortfall between tax revenues on these parcels, especially if undeveloped, and service costs.

In one county, with new levels of fiscal stress and new computer feasibility, officials studied the tax structure of all townships. Juxtaposing tax-exempt property with percentages and dollar value of nonresident ownership, county officials raised new questions about local tax policies. A communication to town supervisors (who are also county legislators) and town assessors states, "the numbers are significant enough to give many towns food for thought in regard to land use policies, demand on services and the changing demographics of your tax base."

In Delaware County, with its high percentage of absentee-owned recreational parcels, a recent survey showed that about half of these lots were undeveloped, yet township roads leading to them required regular maintenance (Warren and Banks 1988). The county planning office is trying to document its contention that weekend and vacation homes and even retirement residences may actually cost the town more in maintenance, services, and equipment than the town gains in tax revenue on these properties. Many hidden costs had not previously been figured in, such as wear and tear on roads and bridges over which developers' heavy equipment travels. If a town has to purchase a new snowplow truck in order to do all the added plowing in a timely fashion, the cost will be $70,000 to $80,000—with trade.

In the northern townships of Allegany County, public expense for vacation properties with low tax contributions is growing. In an attempt to tackle this problem, one township broke its traditional stance and passed a simple zoning regulation requiring minimum 5-acre lots as a way of being able to collect sufficient taxes on small cabins to offset the cost of services to them.

Reduction of Federal and State Assistance

The catalyst forcing local governments to rethink taxing policies has been the major reduction in federal and state financial support for local government operations. The general trend in the 1980s has shifted the financing burden from federal to state and from state to localities, and in so doing has shifted revenue generation for local functions from income taxes collected by federal and state government to property taxes collected by counties, townships, cities, and school districts. More than half of all local budget dollars, including those for school districts as well as governments, are now raised locally. Although it is nothing new for local governments to be concerned over budget problems, local officials generally agree that the "fiscal stress" has become much greater recently. Required by law to have balanced budgets and limited by state law in their borrowing capacity, local governments must carefully watch expenses.

Reductions in categorical federal funding for various social welfare programs were particularly hard on counties with a significant low-income population, especially because the cuts came just when rural areas, along with the rest of the nation, were deep in recession. Federal block grants and extra money from the state were inadequate to cushion the shock. Later, while rural economies slowly climbed out of the recession, local governments were hit again by termination of the federal revenue-sharing program. Though gradual and anticipated, the demise of federal revenue sharing is blamed by local officials and agencies for much of their current fiscal plight.

State funding for local government operations has also decreased recently. During the 1989 and 1990 state budget negotiations, localities bitterly protested reduced state assistance as the state tried to deal with its own serious budget problems. The fiscal problem for localities grows tighter because not only is funding diminishing but required expenses are increasing. The chairman of one county legislature pointed out that out of his entire budget of nearly $50 million, only 20 percent is fully at local discretion: All the rest is mandated spending to comply with various federal and state programs and requirements, although there is some room for local spending decisions within the mandates. Despite a $.5 million decrease in state funding for this county in 1989, there was no reduction in the state's mandates for programs that counties must provide or administer, and there were some additional fees passed on to localities, for instance, permit fees for sewage treatment plants.

As direct federal assistance was cut back, more of the remaining federal funding was switched to competitive grants. However, people in rural governments claim that small communities have lost ground as grants have replaced categorical funding and the federal revenue-sharing program. Because they lack the grant-writing capacity, either in in-house expertise or in funds to hire a grantsman on staff or to contract with a consultant, they feel unable to compete with the sophisticated public-relations-type grant-application packages submitted by more experienced outfits.

> "We only need small grants here because we're a small county and our problems are small—compared to an urban area. But the time it takes to write a small grant proposal, say for $40,000, is as much as for a large grant, like a million and a half—and we have two people and a secretary to do those grants—as well as everything else we do. . . . A $5,000 grant gives you $20,000 worth of paperwork."

The problem of small places being less able to compete for grants has been addressed, though not adequately rectified, by allocating some grants specifically for smaller places or dividing applicants into different categories so that small places are not competing against larger ones. Additionally, assistance from regional and state programs has helped to redress the imbalance, and there have been some qualified rural victories.

> One of the special services of the Tug Hill Commission is its regional "circuit riders," who are at the disposal of local governments to provide grant-writing help and technical assistance where and when requested. The new Office of Rural Affairs, in the state's executive branch, instituted a computer network that helps local individuals, agencies, and governments access information about the entire range of grants and state financial and technical assistance programs.

> Essex County in the North Country won a major rural Economic Development Zone grant from HUD in 1988 that included business development, housing,

and rural water systems—but Allegany County at the opposite side of the state did not get one.

In Chenango County, a Farmers' Home Administration housing grant represented the effort of a concerned and dedicated planning office to make at least a start in tackling a long-standing problem of serious substandard housing in three of the poorest townships in the county. In one township the supervisor was very active in advertising the grant to his constituents and encouraging and helping them through the application process. Ten houses in this desperately poor township got their first running water or a septic system where they had previously had only an open sewer pond. But even this grant had only limited success in meeting rural renovation needs because it contained restrictions inappropriate to rural situations and because the most needy residents were too poor to qualify.

Emerging Structural and Operational Issues

One of the most significant changes in the operation of rural government has been the transformation from policy-oriented, decisionmaking bodies that shaped the course of local events to administrative bodies with very limited decisionmaking roles. Boards that are elected and constituted as legislative bodies are in fact largely becoming executive or administrative, responsible for running programs and keeping track of large amounts of money. Although they delegate and contract many functions to nonprofit organizations, county legislatures still run many governmental offices and agencies of their own, as well as overseeing the contractual arrangements with private agencies. Some rural counties have hired administrators or managers recently or have loaded managerial responsibility onto a county fiscal officer or an administrative assistant. More rural counties are now considering moving to an administrator or even to a county executive form of government. Nonetheless, in many counties management functions still rest largely in a legislative body. The problem, affecting all levels of local government, was referred to as "a structural problem of local government." One legislator asked, "Are local governments up to the management functions that have been thrust upon them?"

This county legislator explained, "With so much that is mandated, county government is more a pass-through for federal and state money. This is an executive and management operation, yet the management function that counties do is done not by professional managers, but by part-time legislators. . . . It is a county government based overall on nineteenth-century ideas and realities. To some extent the structure of county government is now outmoded. Will it be able to take us into the twenty-first century?"

Even though some of the more urbanized and affluent rural municipalities have been able to meet increasing technical and operating standards by contracting with specialized consultants, for many rural communities this is neither possible nor desired. For townships or villages with few people, the carrying out of ordinary local government business now involves much more state regulation and paperwork than in the past—and more than some rural officials feel is warranted. And some time-honored rural ways of doing business are no longer considered acceptable.

> A township with only about 800 residents must file affirmative action reports every two months concerning its sixteen employees, fourteen men and two women. The supervisor of this township suggested that perhaps adding a third classification for really small towns would help.

> A town clerk is not supposed to operate out of her kitchen table any more; a town highway superintendent can no longer record the work hours of his employees by simply writing them down on a wall calendar in the town highway garage. However, some local officials feel that what should really count is performance standards: "If you keep records on the calendar or on the kitchen table, as long as they're good records, the state should not be telling you how to do it."

Another structural issue in local governments is the relationship between the various county, township, and village and city governments in the provision of services to residents. Cooperation between municipalities in offering services and sharing programs or expertise ranges from minimal to very effective, depending on the locality, the people, and the issue. Cooperation is usually most acceptable and effective in the form of ad hoc, single-function agreements rather than formal consolidation of services. But a few villages with a small population and a dwindling tax base have recently contemplated joining the ranks of the few dozen rural villages that have dissolved themselves over the last years, allowing their functions to be taken over by their surrounding township.

TENSIONS BETWEEN CENTER AND PERIPHERY

In some rural counties, political shifts reflect growing dominance of a central place over the more rural areas. The county's largest village or its only city, combined with the built-up area in the township surrounding it, may account for anywhere from one-fifth of the county's population (as in Allegany and Delaware) to more than one-third (as in Clinton and Franklin). Tension appears to be growing between the more rural people—not necessarily farming people, though—and the people of the larger villages or small cities. This dichotomy is apt to appear as the "fault line" in more and more county government decisions and intermunicipal relationships in coming years, and it may retard efforts at intermunicipal cooperation within counties. Fissure and disagreement in county politics may increase along center-periphery or city-rural lines. Leaders in some of the smaller villages and hamlets complain sometimes that "the city" (meaning the county seat, which may actually contain under 10,000 people) "dominates and controls everything." "That place is a little New York City. It's acting like a big city. They're gaining power over rural areas, and the division will be heightened."

Some of the more rural residents perceive a "service discrimination" that shortchanges the more distant and sparsely populated areas. The implications of differential county services in such matters as highway maintenance is not merely a matter of inconvenience and potholes, however: It is also a harbinger of future widening of the economic disparity between center and periphery, between the growing economies of the larger villages and the stagnating economies of the more rural parts of the county. Without adequate roads and other infrastructure, such as up-to-date electric and phone service, the more remote areas cannot possibly hope to support modernized agriculture and industry, much less to entice any new job-providing industries. It seems likely that even within counties that are basically rural, there will be an increasing urban-rural split, with "urban" winning out. In a microcosm of what happens at state and federal levels, then, the rural parts of rural counties will be losing both political power and economic ground relative to the population centers.

> One rural supervisor spoke with strong feeling: "The county's economic planners, grants writers, and so forth all work for the interests of the businesses in the county center. For our remote area they suggest only wood chipping plants. They'll find companies who will come in and grind up the woods— hiring our people at minimum wage. But we don't need minimum-wage jobs. And we don't want our woods ground up while people in town get high-tech industries."

One center-periphery issue that will become increasingly significant involves land-use regulatory power, which, if utilized differently by different local entities, has the potential to create inequities and strained relationships among neighboring municipalities. An obvious example is in differing regulation of mobile homes. In many townships where housing values are high and residents affluent, mobile-home ordinances have been enacted that are quite restrictive, virtually banning any additional trailers (Geisler and Mitsuda 1987). The result is that adjacent townships that do not have such ordinances may find a steady increase of mobile homes within their borders, both on individual lots in the open country and in mobile-home parks. Displacement of moderate- and low-wage earners from central towns by adding exclusionary mobile-home restrictions to price mechanisms already operating in the housing market may have an increasingly negative fiscal impact on outlying townships, adding to expenditures more than tax revenues and creating social instability as well.

Although assessment levels for mobile homes range from a few thousand dollars on up to $40,000, low assessments on small, older trailers generate little property-tax revenues for local schools and town highways. According to one county official, a modest trailer set on land that would not otherwise be buildable would help the local tax structure, but the same trailer placed on a 5-acre lot will bring far less in property taxes than would a new conventional house. The rural township with growing numbers of mobile homes finds increasing difficulty paying for schools and roads for its growing population.

The displacement may also undermine social and economic institutions of the rural township or hamlet where trailer parks are rapidly growing. Rural trailer dwellers may spend their paychecks in the shopping malls closer to their place of work. And mobile-home dwellers pushed to the periphery may have neither the time nor the energy to participate in community activities at the elementary school, the church, or the town hall.

The mobile home issue is an intermunicipal equity issue that may become increasingly divisive. The advantages continue to accrue to the central place and the disadvantages to the more rural community. The question then arises, as several rural supervisors and town planning board members have asked: "Can this rural township continue to allow unregulated growth of mobile homes?" The broader question in this issue would be: "Should the more populated and affluent localities be allowed to enact restrictive zoning that forces its lower-wage workers to live in trailers in distant places?" The equity issues, similar to those involving the placement of public housing in suburban areas, no longer escapes rural town leaders, local people who want to keep their township affordable but who resent the actions of their more affluent neighbors.

At all levels of local government, this is a time of rethinking old patterns of governance and renegotiating old sociopolitical alliances, a time when mismatch between the structural design of local governments and the fiscal and operational realities of contemporary rural communities has become great enough to demand attention.

CHAPTER THIRTEEN

New Governmental Interactions Around a New Environmental Problem

Environmental problems now mingle with natural beauty in rural America; global, national, and regional environmental degradation affects many rural places. Some of the problems cross state lines and must be addressed by interstate and federal action. But even on the local level, rural governments are increasingly involved in environmental problems and issues that only recently have come onto their agendas. Local officials and staff now devote considerable time, attention, and paperwork to assessing and controlling environmental impacts of existing, proposed, and future activities. The problems with which they deal, the "threats to our beautiful rural environment," come not only from the outside and from the future, however: They are also homegrown and from the past. For example, many rural governments are presently involved, and more soon will be, in addressing and mitigating the problem of chemical contamination of groundwater. Where groundwater contamination affects local drinking water supplies, the problem must be assessed and addressed promptly, and this inevitably leads to new and increasing interactions of rural communities and their governments with agencies of state and federal government.

GROUNDWATER CONTAMINATION: A RURAL PROBLEM WITH STATE AND FEDERAL DIMENSIONS

Groundwater contamination is preeminently a rural problem, for whereas about half of all Americans depend on groundwater for their drinking water supply, virtually all rural Americans use groundwater to supply their household needs, whether they have individual private wells or municipal wells that feed public water systems. The critical issue for rural people using groundwater, as many have now become aware, is that in most cases no alternative water sources are readily available. The irony of groundwater pollution is that during the 1960s and 1970s, when the country was becoming increasingly aware of the problems of contaminated rivers and lakes, many communities drilled into underground aquifers to tap "pristine," "limitless," and "uncontaminated" water for domestic needs. Only subsequently was it discovered that groundwater, too, is vulnerable to contamination and that contamination in an aquifer eventually reaches a drinking water supply.

Rectifying the presently known instances of groundwater contamination poses a monumental problem, but the problem will grow still larger in the future as more aquifers are found to be contaminated. Even if no more chemical contaminants were added to the ground from now on, which is an unlikely supposition, the number of cases of groundwater contamination requiring attention and remediation would increase anyway, as contaminants already in the ground and traveling slowly through it will eventually get into aquifers and reach the wells that supply drinking water. Additionally, with increasingly stringent state and federal drinking water standards and more testing of drinking water supplies, using increasingly sophisticated technology, more existing contamination will be brought to attention. (New York State, for example, has recently moved from a 50 parts per billion "advisory" limit for organic compounds, such as trichloroethylene, to a mandatory limit of 5 parts per billion.) Treating the water drawn from a contaminated aquifer so that it can be used in a public water supply is a costly procedure, but cleaning up the aquifer itself usually requires millions of dollars and takes as long as ten years or more. Merely tracking where the chemicals are and predicting where and how fast they will move through a gravel or bedrock aquifer is a highly technical matter, and each situation is unique. Contaminants may show up in one well but not in the wells of next-door neighbors, and levels of contaminants may fluctuate over time.

The difficulty of responding to a groundwater contamination case is compounded, however, by the complex institutional arrangements among local, state, and federal agencies and private engineering firms that may become involved. The state's Department of Environmental Conservation (DEC) and Department of Health (DOH) become involved in groundwater contamination cases because of the state's role in enforcing drinking water standards for public water systems. Where pollution situations pose an imminent health hazard, the federal Environmental Protection Agency (EPA) may become involved. Several different engineering firms may be contracted for different parts of a cleanup, and several different "responsible parties" or "presumed polluters" may be involved. To an unfortunate extent, relationships among these various actors in a groundwater case, and especially between them and the affected community, may be characterized by poor communication, lack of effective coordination, and, often, distrust. Although new, less costly technological remedies for purifying water and cleansing aquifers are urgently needed, observations of a dozen groundwater contamination cases in rural communities in New York revealed that an equally great need exists for better institutional response patterns.

In rural New York, many small towns and villages may have a looming groundwater pollution problem resulting from past practices when underground aquifers were thought to be "naturally safe" from contamination and restrictions to protect them were virtually nonexistent. This chapter describes in some detail three separate cases where drinking water was affected by groundwater contamination, each from a common but different cause. These particular cases were selected because they illustrate important points about the interface between local communities and state or federal agencies in the resolution of a groundwater problem (Fitchen 1987b).

EXAMPLES OF GROUNDWATER PROBLEMS ARISING IN RURAL COMMUNITIES

Sources of groundwater contamination are varied. In the densely populated Northeast, the most common occurrence of groundwater contamination is from "point source" contaminations, where chemicals enter the ground in one limited spot, from one incident or a series of operations over time. Storage and disposal facilities of all sorts, including chemical and petroleum storage sites, industrial lagoons, impoundments, settling ponds, old-fashioned dumps, and even some "sanitary landfills," may cause contamination in the aquifer below. Most such disposal places were located in land areas that people were not interested in for other purposes, for example in swamps, lowlands, and natural "low places" that were considered wasteland "unusable" for residential or industrial development, cheap land that no one wanted for any other purpose. Ironically, however, the very places that were used for storing or dumping have often turned out to be the most sensitive areas for groundwater contamination because such sites are often right on top of aquifer recharge areas, where surface water—and whatever is suspended or dissolved in it—percolates downward into the aquifer. Suddenly, in 1978 with the Love Canal disaster near Niagara Falls and subsequent cases elsewhere, the time bomb of materials dumped in old canals, pits, dumps, and other facilities burst into national attention. Ever since then, toxic materials that had been disposed of and forgotten have come back to haunt nearby residents, in some places affecting drinking water. Even the highway departments' uncovered storage piles of de-icing salt can cause contamination of an aquifer. On a smaller scale, but serious in its consequences, the time-honored rural practice of pouring used engine oil down the nearest woodchuck hole—out of sight, out of mind—comes back to haunt rural residents.

Gasoline Leaking into Wells in a Small Hamlet

Leaking underground storage tanks for gasoline and for agricultural and industrial chemicals have become a serious problem. (Originally this problem was known as LUST, for leaking underground storage tanks, but the acronym more commonly used now is simply UST.) A prevalent potential for groundwater contamination involves gasoline tanks at the hundreds of small filling stations that exist or used to exist in small communities. In the past there was little monitoring of the underground apparatus at these filling stations while they were in operation, when they changed hands, or when they closed down. Any leaks that developed in aging or unused tanks, valves, and pipes might continue undetected for years—until one day residents began smelling something bad in their water. It has been estimated that there are about 70,000 buried gasoline tanks in New York state that are now leaking, and more than half of all tanks will be in the "failure mode" by the mid-1990s. In small communities where there is no municipal water system, the consequences of leaking gasoline tanks may be particularly devastating.

A poignant example of gasoline contamination involves a small hamlet in a semirural county in the Southern Tier. In 1979, fifteen private wells in this community of about sixty homes were found to contain gasoline products. Four of the homes that were tested, as well as the gas station itself, had particularly high levels of the gasoline substances benzene (a known human carcinogen), toluene, and xylene, all at levels far exceeding the state's safe drinking water guidelines. One additional well was questionable, and the others had traces but were below guideline levels. Mobil Oil Corporation, which had franchised the gas station for years, eventually found small leaks in the valves and pipe leading from the tank, and although replacement and routine monitoring of tanks has prevented more gasoline from leaking into the ground, the gasoline that had already leaked out in the past was slowly making its way through the soil and migrating in the groundwater to reach private wells nearby. (Groundwater locally was estimated to "flow" at a rate of about 75 feet a year, but the contaminants were thought to be moving much more slowly than that.) Some people had already drilled new wells but still found contaminants. Some households reported respiratory distress and other unexplained health problems. In 1985 Mobil supplied four houses with filters, but residents of those homes were not convinced that filtering and monitoring was adequate. Even with filters, these families drank bottled water, "not the filtered water—hell no!"

Friction developed within the community over the water situation, based on different experiences and on differing perceptions of how serious the problem was and what should be done about it. There was no concerted community-wide outcry demanding action, and no hamlet-level government to deal with the problem. Residents with affected wells felt that they were both ignored and resented by their unaffected neighbors. According to one of the residents with an affected well, "A lot of people in the hamlet think everything is OK because the county health department said *their* water is fine." "No one cares as long as it's not *their* problem."

As these affected residents began to agitate for more permanent solution, they turned to the county health department, the state DEC, and the town government, which became active in their behalf. Other state agencies were also involved, including the DOH and the Department of Transportation, which at that time was in charge of petroleum problems, such as oil spills and gas leaks. Part of the residents' difficulty in getting action was that no particular body or agency seemed to feel the problem was within its mandate to address. For example, county health departments, which are frequently involved with contamination of public water supplies, rarely get involved where private wells are affected. In describing their years of dealings with these various agencies, the most common word used by affected residents was "frustration." People reported that most agencies had given them "the runaround," that "we get buried in paper bureaucracy," and "you can't *get* directly to the authorities." Some agencies were reported to be "concerned but busy," whereas others were reported to be "impossible to get to." One resident emphatically stated, "Individuals might as well talk to a wall as try talking to the state agencies." One exasperated resident said, "The county health department tells us to contact Mobil, but how can you do that? Did you ever try contacting a major oil company?" Another said, "Everybody bounces us around. By one we're told 'We don't know' and by another we're told 'It's not our responsibility.' So, in the end, you get nowhere."

Affected residents were skeptical of answers they received from governmental agencies about their wells, about contaminant levels, and about the health risks or the effectiveness of filtering. Most troubling were the contradictory statements of experts. From a health department official they heard both, "Personally, I wouldn't drink it," and "Professionally, I would say it's OK to drink it." They were told that "this is not a major health hazard," but they saw interagency memos that labeled the local problem "one of the worst situations in the state."

The combination of frustration and distrust heightened anxiety that some residents felt over the water problem as it dragged on into its seventh year. One resident, whose home was pervaded by an odor coming from the filtration system, wrote in a letter to the editor of the nearby newspaper, "As the years go by and nothing is done, I feel myself becoming more depressed and distressed. Think of the stress upon my family that I feel. How would you like to smell gasoline when you wash your family's dishes and clothes. How would it feel to be afraid to take a shower? Brush your teeth? Would you like to live in constant fear of a time bomb in the future called 'Cancer'?" In another house, as a couple recounted their years of living with the problem, the frustration, fear, and strain it had caused became apparent. After the interview, the husband quietly confided, "My wife didn't tell you, but there was a time there when she'd cry at the drop of a hat."

Nearly a decade after contamination had been discovered, resolution—of a sort—occurred. Various efforts by the town board to develop a community water supply for the hamlet, or just for the affected homes within it, had failed. Test wells drilled near the hamlet came up with a variety of chemical contaminants. The remainder of the township, including unaffected residents in the hamlet, voted down a town water district that would bring water in from another village several miles away. Finally, under threat of litigation brought by the state DEC, the oil company reached settlement with the most severely affected homeowners, agreeing to purchase the affected houses, as no adequate substitute water supply could be found. According to the announced settlement, the houses were to be demolished. And so in this case "solution" of the problem meant tearing down a string of houses in the center of the hamlet—the outcome of ten years of frustration and effort, all caused by a few tiny holes hardly bigger than the head of a pin.

Because this hamlet lacked a municipal water supply and because the majority of unaffected residents of the township appeared only minimally concerned with the contamination problems of a few homeowners, resolution of the problem took a great deal of time, even though the source was known and the spread of contaminants limited. Failure to reach a community-wide solution involving the creation of some sort of municipal water supply under the aegis of township government leaves other hamlet residents still vulnerable to any further spread of the plume of contamination.

Agricultural Chemicals Seeping into Wells in a Small Hamlet

Residues of agricultural chemicals may enter aquifers as a result of application of fertilizers, herbicides, and insecticides on farmland, and this "nonpoint source" contamination has become a problem in some areas where there is heavy use of agricultural chemicals. But penetration of these chemicals through the soil into underground aquifers can also come from accidents, such as train derailments, truck accidents, explosions or fires, or from regular procedures in which agricultural chemicals are handled in such a way that a certain amount of the substance routinely is spilled over onto the ground. Again, recent regulations, safeguards, and hazardous spill cleanup procedures should reduce the risk of such problems occurring and the risk to human health when they do occur. However, some spills from earlier periods, as well as accidents or customary procedures that had not previously warranted concern, may only now be starting to cause contamination of aquifers, or may have caused drinking water contamination that is only now being remedied. A case in point is the tiny hamlet in a rural county outside the Albany region, where routine practices in handling agricultural chemicals at a supplier's facility eventually contaminated the aquifer and local residents' wells.

This hamlet is a rather poor, somewhat run-down community of about forty families, with most residents commuting out to blue-collar jobs in nearby or distant towns and cities, or else retired. There is no village government. For many years an agricultural supply firm, Agway, ran a facility in the hamlet where pesticides and fertilizers were stored and where chemicals were mixed for custom application elsewhere. As routine procedure, the spray trucks were hosed out behind the facility, and the wash water was poured on the ground behind the building, a standard practice at the time. Unbeknown to local residents, these agricultural chemicals were working their way toward residents' shallow wells. More chemicals were spilled onto the ground when a fertilizer storage building caught fire.

In 1979 a county health department technician who was conducting routine testing of private wells for coliform bacteria found nitrates, from fertilizers, at levels of concentration that he described as "off the top of the charts." Assuming that if nitrates were so high, maybe other, more toxic contaminants might also be present, the technician took the initiative to have the water more systematically tested for a whole variety of toxins known to be part of the particular agricultural chemicals handled at the facility. Indeed, atrazine, alachlor, and metolachlor did show up at high levels in several wells. Suddenly, the persistent undiagnosed headaches, diarrhea, and skin irritations that some residents suffered began to make sense to them. When informed of the presence of these contaminants in their water and told not to drink it any more, people began hauling in drinking water from relatives or places of work, and their health problems cleared up. Through its insurance company, Agway acted quickly to provide new deep wells for ten affected homes in 1980, and these families resumed drinking their own water with no noticeable health effects. Even the odor in laundry and wet dishrags was no longer a problem. After a careful cleanup of the ground around and under the burned-out building, the company ceased operations in the village.

But a problem that was "solved" came unsolved again as the chemicals began to penetrate down farther into the deeper aquifer from which the new wells drew their water. Headaches and nausea began to return, and skin irritations, too. The state Department of Health and the attorney general's office became involved in 1985 and ordered Agway to conduct new monitoring tests, which confirmed that contaminant levels in the new wells were increasing, although fluctuating. Residents were told that the water was "acceptable" because no tests showed contaminants in excess of state guidelines in effect at·the time. Nonetheless, some families reverted to hauling in water from elsewhere and found their symptoms disappeared again.

Reactions by individual families and residents varied considerably. From the start, those whose wells were contaminated felt that other residents paid little attention to the problem. Even among those with contaminated wells, there was no single voice, no concerted action; rather, each family responded and reacted according to its own particular water situation, its physical symptoms and perceptions. Some residents tried to get information and to bring action, but there was no group effort. Fear and confusion, anxiety and distrust characterized the stories from most affected households. One resident pointed to a label from a container of a pesticide: "The warning on the label tells you to burn your clothing after working with these chemicals. But the [state] health department says we can drink water that has these chemicals in it, that it is 'unlikely' to cause health effects at this level. . . . Who should I believe?" This resident had obtained a copy of a letter the same health department sent to the state attorney general's office, which said, "continued exposure to alachlor represents an increased health risk to the individual consuming the water. Based on all the available information, I would rec-ommend that measures be taken to eliminate exposure to alachlor . . . to the maximum extent feasible." Again, this resident asks "Who are we to believe?" "How serious is it?" One family has a filter but continues to bring in drinking water from elsewhere. The homeowner says, "If the filter takes out 90 percent of the contaminants, you still have 10 percent remaining. Ten percent of something bad is still something bad! I won't let my family drink the water from this well, even if it is filtered."

A full decade after the first, inadvertent discovery of toxic chemicals, the problem is not yet totally resolved. The toxins have dissipated somewhat with the passage of time. Some residents now have too little contaminant for official action but, they believe, too much for their own well-being. The official in the state Department of Health, who has been especially helpful in the case since its onset, sums up the dilemma as follows: "We would like to get filters put on there, but our case is too weak to take to court, and the trace level of contaminants is too low to involve either the state or the federal Superfund."

The protracted nature of this case is not unusual, but as in the first case described, the problem here was especially difficult to resolve because the community had no alternative water supply to replace contaminated water, neither a municipal supply that could be offered to affected households nor a public water supply in a nearby community that could be extended into this community. The physical infrastructure simply did not exist. But the problem also lay in inadequacy of institutional infrastructure for dealing with the problem, as there was no village government to develop and push for a solution, and the township government had little authority or desire to act for such a limited problem. No official or even unofficial community action was possible because there really was no community in the formal, institutional sense, and only a very weak community in the informal, social sense.

Industrial Chemicals Contaminating
a Small City's Water Supply

In earlier years disposal of used industrial chemicals, such as solvents, degreasers, and cleaning fluids, was only minimally regulated. As standard practice, manufacturing firms often—and legally—dumped chemical wastes out behind the building, perhaps storing them in barrels that gradually filled up low places on the property, perhaps spreading the chemicals on the ground, where they also served to keep the weeds down.

In a rural county in the southwestern part of the state, a small city has spent nearly a decade struggling with a groundwater contamination problem from industrial chemicals that leached from these dumping places behind factories (Fitchen et al. 1987). In late 1980, trichloroethylene (TCE), a volatile organic chemical commonly used in industry as a degreaser, was detected in the new city water supply wells. TCE is a suspected carcinogen in humans and is known to cause damage to lungs, heart, and central nervous system. In this case a city government was involved, as well as town and county governments, but difficult relationships between local government officials and state and federal agencies became a problem that often loomed larger than the contamination itself (Fitchen et al. 1987).

This city, over the last few decades shrinking to under 18,000 people, is the manufacturing, retail, and service center of its county. In a forward-looking action in the late 1970s, the city had decided to replace its public water supply that used river water, heavy chlorination, and an antiquated filtration plant with wells sunk into groundwater that everyone assumed was safe from contamination. Soon after the new wells came into service, the county health engineer thought it would be prudent to test the wells for TCE, as it had been used in nearby factories and routinely dumped on the ground behind the buildings. The tests detected the colorless, odorless, tasteless chemical in the water supply at a level three times the state's suggested guidelines. Residents were immediately warned to boil their drinking water. After further testing and consultation with the state Department of Health, and because residents were tired of boiling their water, it was decided to close the affected new wells, even though the contaminant level was not high enough to make closing mandatory and despite the absence of health complaints. The city reverted to using river water and its old filtration system. That was in the very beginning of 1981.

Public concern was minimal, for residents had adequate substitute water and felt that their city Department of Public Works and county health department were acting responsibly in the matter and watching out for the public's health. Even when contaminants were detected in nearby private wells and the levels in them subsequently soared, there was still little public stir: Affected residents hauled jugs of water from relatives or friends nearby in the city and assumed the problem would soon be resolved. Few citizens attended informational meetings on the problem, and hardly anyone complained in public or in the press about either the situation or the health threat it might have posed or might still be posing for some residents with private wells. People had confidence that their public officials could solve the problem.

Nonetheless, as the contaminant seemed to be spreading and reaching higher concentrations, local government officials felt they had to turn to higher levels of government for technical and financial assistance. They appealed to the state DEC and to the federal Environmental Protection Agency (EPA), which subsequently designated the wellfield as a federal Superfund site (under CERCLA, the Comprehensive Environmental Response, Liability, and Compensation Act). Over the next several years, the EPA directed the overall "response" while the New York State DEC oversaw local operations. Several engineering firms were brought in to investigate the nature and extent of the problem, to determine its sources, and to establish "potentially responsible parties" so that the costs of remediation could be recovered. Some nearby companies, which in the meantime had been purchased by outside ownership, had already openly admitted that they had been the source of the chemicals and expressed willingness to cooperate with the city in devising a solution. However, the EPA required thorough investigation to establish legal claims, and so there were more investigations, and then more. The only remedial action in those years was EPA's provision of several dozen carbon filters for private wells with high contaminant levels in cases where homeowners wanted them.

By 1984, elected officials, and leaders of business and community institutions had become frustrated over the slow process of investigations. In a community that prides itself on its manufacturing history, a product has more appeal than lengthy studies. The city mayor, addressing a modestly attended public informational meeting at the start of 1985, stated with feeling, "Here we are, four years later and $1 million spent on studies! And we're still at least two years away from a permanent solution. I'm frustrated!" He turned to the ten representatives of DEC and EPA seated on the platform and pleaded, "Please help us out. . . . We have a problem. We can't wait until 1986. I'm completely frustrated."

Meanwhile, the public paid little attention. People assumed that their officials and leaders were doing what they could to provide safe water and resigned themselves to a long, slow bureaucratic process. For citizens, as for their local officials, a major concern was the cost of all the studies, for they fully realized that the bill sent to the polluting companies would reflect the full series of lengthy investigations—most of which seemed to local people to be totally unnecessary. The community's official anger over what appeared to them as EPA's excessive concern with finger-pointing was even communicated to the media.

By 1986, with no solution in sight yet, all of the investigations had finally closed in on three firms as "potentially responsible parties"—the same three firms that had long since openly admitted that they were the source of the chemicals, the same three that had long since agreed to doing or funding their share of the cleanup and had been working cooperatively and quietly with city officials to try to arrange and pay for safe drinking water. Then came a period of protracted discussions of who would pay for what, still with city and company officials feeling that their suggestions were being ignored or dismissed out of hand by the EPA, and that this was delaying the solution still farther. Eventually, a settlement was reached whereby the companies agreed to pay $1.1 million of the $2 million investigation costs and $1.9 million for the air strippers (towers packed with small plastic pieces, in which water is pumped in at the top and flows down while air is forced upward through the column, so that as the water travels downward it discharges its volatile contaminants into the air). A water district was set up and water lines constructed so that when clean well water became available, the people who had had contaminated private wells would also be served by the city system. Finally, in spring 1989, construction for the air strippers started; the new water system finally came on line in early 1990.

In this case, the difficult relationship between interacting agencies and levels of government added institutional complications to the already difficult problem of tracking and remedying the seepage of discarded chemicals. Because of the way it was handled, the case was redefined in local minds from an environmental issue to a governmental issue. Somewhere in the long process of investigations local people began to feel that "the problem" was no longer the TCE, but the EPA. Although the EPA saw the local factories as "villains," local people saw these same manufacturing plants as "victims" of "adversarial finger-pointing by the government." It was a strange drama in which villains and victims had traded places. But as one member of the county legislature said, it was really "a nondrama," for so little happened, and it happened so slowly.

Once the Superfund process was initiated, it continued inexorably, whether or not local citizens were satisfied, and without their input. Local leaders in this case sometimes expressed privately that they wished they could "tell the EPA to stop, to go away now and leave us alone to solve our own problem." In a situation that seemed scripted out of "The Sorcerer's Apprentice," there was simply no way that the community, having asked for help in the first place, could now tell the EPA, "Stop!"

LOCAL ROLES IN
RURAL ENVIRONMENTAL PROBLEMS

Local communities and their governments will find themselves dealing with more groundwater contamination problems in the future and also debating measures to prevent further contamination. Given the diversity not only of aquifers and chemicals and water systems but also of communities, both response and protection will need to be tailored to the local situation and therefore should maximize the use of local capabilities.

Rural Preferences Versus Urban
Agencies and Urban Solutions

Despite good will, best intentions, and honest attempts on the part of the individual actors in such a case, friction can easily arise because of differing institutionalized worldviews. For example, government agencies seek some standardization in approaches and solutions from one case to another, but rural people who believe that their community is unique may not trust a solution that was designed for some other community's problem somewhere else.

Frustration and misunderstanding may result from differences in attitude, perception, and customary modes of operation between local governments and state and federal agencies. Rural people would like state and federal agencies to behave as local governments do. When they call the agency office in Albany, they want to talk not with "the agency" but with a certain person, preferably the same person they talked with last week. Local people want a contact person, someone who actually knows their community and is familiar with its problem. One of the comments that surfaced repeatedly in communities with water problems was, "Those people in that agency don't even know our community, so how can we feel confident that they will really do what is best for us?" But because of the characteristic ways bureaucracies operate, the cast of characters sent out by the agencies to work at the local level frequently changes. As residents of several communities complained, "Just when we were getting to the point where we could work well with and trust that guy from the central office, he leaves and they send in a new one." Another institutional factor impeding the kind of personal relationship rural people want is that a large agency such as the DEC or EPA has many different regions, branches, offices, and programs, with each subdivision having its own responsibilities, expertise, and personnel. This complex institutional structure often leaves locals wondering, "Who are we supposed to be talking to about this?"

The locally perceived dichotomy between "us" and "them," between "small-town and rural residents" and "agency people" has its trivial aspects: Rural residents poke fun at the clothing styles, such as fancy shoes, that prevent a government official from actually walking through snow or mud to the contamination site. People who know the rural landscape like the back of their hand delight in hearing that "the people from Washington" got lost on the back roads somewhere in the remote regions of the county. But the trivial complaints and embellished anecdotes derive from a deeper feeling on the part of local residents that "the Albany people" and "the Washington group" really have little respect for rural officials, and do not like spending time in areas they call "the boondocks." Rural residents feel that government agencies are only familiar with urban solutions and will try to solve a rural problem with an urban solution, an inappropriate approach that does not fit the rural scene or the rural pocketbook.

Local Input and Local Control Versus Agency Solution Under Agency Control

In the first two cases presented in this chapter, the absence of a local village government left an institutional vacuum that was partially filled by a township government in the first case and by a county health department in the second. In both, however, because there was no local government at the level where the problem existed, affected residents were left more on their own, with no formal support from the community and to some extent, in fact, with resistance from unaffected neighbors. Resolution of both the gasoline case and the agricultural chemical case was hampered by the lack of local leadership, cohesion, and institutional structure that could take initiative, and so action was left, by default, to outside authorities. Many similar hamlets throughout the state may lack the institutional framework for handling such problems, and yet these places are as prone as any to serious and costly groundwater contamination. In the absence of village or city government, greater effort will be needed by the next higher levels of government, the township or county, and by the agencies that are supposed to oversee the health of the populace and the well-being of the environment, to be responsive to and inclusive of local people.

The lack of local government in the first two cases only serves to emphasize the irony of the third case, in which a local government *was* in place and where that government had demonstrated capability to look out for its own people and held the trust of its residents—and yet was systematically excluded from the process of responding to its own environmental problem. The Superfund process described in this case brings out strongly the issue of struggle for control of the response to an environmental problem. The adversarial nature and restricted access to information required by the federal legislation are frustrating to local leaders; essentially they result in a "de-powerment" of local governments.

In the case described here, much of the friction between local officials and personnel of the state and federal agencies was over the issue of what role the local community might play in addressing the problem. Once the U.S. EPA was involved, the community had virtually no role to play at all, except that in the end the community was left to operate whatever purification system had been installed, a system about which local people had been allowed no input. In cases like this, where there are local governments in place, with competence and an interest in participating in the process and with technical staff who would be quite capable of carrying out some of the investigation and monitoring procedures, to ignore these local resources is not only to forgo considerable cost savings but also to incur considerable local resistance.

Ignoring local expertise and restricting local input has another negative consequence: The community learns very little about how to take care of its own environmental problems or how to prevent similar problems in the future. Additionally, where local communities are shut out of the action and consequently dissatisfied with it, their discontent travels to other communities. This city's "problem with the EPA" became a well-known story in many other communities. Apparently, the lesson other communities learned was *not* how important it is to take good care of your groundwater or what to do when contamination is discovered, but instead that "whatever else happens, *never* turn to the EPA for help!"

The institutional interactions triggered by discovery of groundwater contamination or other forms of environmental pollution could go more smoothly. Building on and utilizing local common sense and expertise, taking advantage of the existence of local governments, and capitalizing on the trust that many residents have in their local officials would all make a difference. In fact, New York State's Office of Local Government Services has been working to promote just these approaches. Its local government self-help approach, tailored to the needs and capabilities of rural communities, could be built into the mandate of state and federal environmental agencies, encouraging them to play a more enabling, proactive, and educational role with respect to local governments, rather than concentrating solely on regulation and enforcement.

Local Cooperation in Preventing
Future Environmental Problems

In groundwater contamination situations, and also in other environmental problems, an ounce of prevention is probably worth many hundreds of pounds of cure. Although many contaminations are already on the way because of past practices and events, the number of future contaminations could be reduced by immediate measures to protect groundwater, particularly by restricting activities around well heads and in the sensitive aquifer recharge areas. But prevention will not come easily, for it will threaten a traditional rural bias against land-use regulation, and it will probably require unprecedented cooperation among local governments. However, in counties with a great many towns and villages (such as Allegany, with its 50,000 people divided among twenty-nine townships and ten villages), the need for protecting the water supply could serve as a framework for intermunicipal cooperation that could then be used toward other goals as well.

The sheer necessity of aquifer protection for rural people who have no other water source can become the vehicle for penetrating the old attitudes against restricting what individuals can do on their own property. The freedom of any landowner to do more or less whatever he or she wants on privately owned land will increasingly be seen as subordinant to the need of the community to have clean, safe drinking water. The penalty for not safeguarding groundwater is so severe as to make the limited trade-off of individual land-use rights more palatable.

> The state's Temporary Commission on Tug Hill, for example, has helped many communities in that area to realize the absolute importance of protecting the aquifer on which they all draw and also to realize that aquifer protection need not lead to zoning or even to a fight over whether to zone or not to zone. The Tug Hill Commission has fostered intermunicipal cooperation in groundwater protection, so that villages and townships that all share the aquifer can work smoothly toward a strategy for protection that is equitable and mutually acceptable. For obtaining the required intermunicipal cooperation, the focus has been centered on the needs of the entire area for safe water, not on the rights of separate municipal entities.

In the process of considering such trade-offs, certain fissures within the community may develop or be opened up: splits between antiplanning and proplanning advocates, between growth and no-growth factions, between those who favor regulation to prevent spoiling the landscape and those who see regulation as the agent of ruin, and between "old-timers" and "newcomers." But all these people together require safe drinking water, and carefully planned community discussion and negotiation could be used in preventing the issue from overly polarizing a community. Involvement of all segments of the community and awareness that the common good of the community as a whole is a critical benefit to its individual residents will help bring many communities to more effective environmental protection for their future.

PART SEVEN

New Uses for Rural Lands: Dumping Ground for Society

CHAPTER FOURTEEN

Prisons in the Wilderness: The New Growth Industry of Rural New York

A significant recent development in rural New York is the construction of many new prisons to hold the state's rapidly rising incarcerated population. Perhaps nothing demonstrates the close ties between rural and urban America better than the state prisons, largely filled with urban inmates but mostly located in rural places, where populations are sparse and land is available. Although some rural communities are opposed to or ambivalent about having a prison situated in their midst, many communities and their governments are eagerly offering their land and their community as a prison site. In fact, the recent flurry of prison-seeking activity in upstate New York could be dubbed "the Great Prison Competition of 1989."

The prison phenomenon also illustrates starkly some of the economic and social problems now facing many rural communities. The energy that some rural communities devote to obtaining a new state prison dramatizes the depth of their economic plight and the fiscal stress of their governments. The debate engendered by the question of whether to seek a prison also brings out or intensifies latent social and attitudinal schisms between different segments of the local population. Prison debates display the range of attitudes about the community and images of rural life as well as differing attitudes toward and images of prisons.

Observations and interviews in communities where a possible prison bid was being discussed and where a prison has been built reveal reasons why some rural people and communities are seeking prisons, why others are not, and what the advent of a prison does for and to a small community.

RURAL PRISONS FOR URBAN INMATES

Across the nation, from the highly urbanized Northeast all the way to the West Coast, rapidly rising crime rates have overwhelmed existing prison facilities. The drug epidemic and the federal war on drugs have greatly swelled the number of individuals incarcerated in state prisons. In virtually every state and major city, this dramatic increase, which is projected to continue its rapid rise, has exacerbated already overcrowded prison conditions and has propelled urgent prison construction programs. Finding available and affordable urban locations for more prisons is hardly possible, and building a prison in a residential suburban area may be prevented by strong local opposition, as is the case in a celebrated antiprison battle in suburban Newtown, Connecticut (Kirk Johnson 1989b). Consequently, many states and cities, too, are increasingly turning to rural areas for incarceration of convicted criminals. In 1989 the District of Columbia was considering sites in rural West Virginia (Bates 1989); New York City opened a 700-man jail on the banks of the St. Lawrence River in northern New York, to which it flies overflow prisoners from its urban facilities on a DC-9 (Ravo 1988).

Rural prisons for urban inmates are not a new phenomenon in the nation or in New York State. In New York's most extreme northeastern county, Clinton Correctional Facility was established in the town of Dannemora in 1845, followed by other prisons; in the western part of the state, the Attica Correctional Facility was established at the end of the Depression. In the 1980s, as the population of prisoners soared, the state undertook a major prison construction program. But the state's inmate population kept growing, increasing by 8,000 prisoners in 1989 alone, to bring the total above 50,000, which was 20 percent above the combined capacity of its sixty facilities. The state announced that several more prisons would be built and ready for occupancy in 1990, with subsequent appropriations enabling the building of still more facilities. Although the growing inmate population is a burden for the state correctional system and the taxpayers, the issue of finding a site on which to build a new prison presents much less of a problem. In fact, the early 1989 announcement that the state would construct more new prisons touched off an intense competition among more than a dozen rural communities, each of which wanted to be "given" a state prison.

A 750-bed medium-security facility, the main type being constructed, typically contains a male inmate population representing the full range of felony offenses, with four years or less remaining on their sentences. The brochures of the state Department of Correctional Services reveal why these facilities are sought by many localities. Such a facility entails a construction expenditure of $65 million, and an annual payroll of $13 million for a staff of 380 to 400 (New York State Department of Correctional Services n.d.). The smaller, 250-bed "shock incarceration camps" entail a proportionately smaller construction expenditure, payroll, and staff. Once a community's governing body has filed the official resolution requesting consideration as a site for a correctional facility, representatives of the Department of Correctional Services personally inspect the suggested parcels of land. To be considered, a proposed site must meet the general specifications set by the department.

Specifications for a 750-bed medium security facility include at least 100 acres of land, preferably gently sloping, with sandy soil rather than heavy rock or forestation or protected wetlands; access to county or state highways suitable for large truck and bus transport; access to municipal water and sewer as well as fire-fighting and hospital services; and compatibility with local land-use and planning objectives.

These specifications make it more than likely that an ideal space for a prison would be a farm that had gone out of business, located at the edge of a small village. And indeed, a number of the sites recently selected fit this pattern.

With at least three serious contenders for every prison to be built, competition was intense. Local governments in many rural places mounted energetic lobbying campaigns, and local citizens deluged their state representatives and the governor with letters and postcards proclaiming their desire for a prison. The final decision is made by the state legislature and the governor and may therefore involve various political factors, but only communities that have officially requested it will be considered, and only knowing-and-willing sellers of land are approached.

TWO SIDES OF THE PRISON DEBATE IN RURAL COMMUNITIES

Local attitudes about seeking a state prison vary between communities and among residents of any given community, but the benefits and drawbacks cited by local governments and residents appear remarkably similar around the nation. Many communities in rural America are definitely not interested in having a prison; others eagerly seek one. In eastern Kentucky residents of one county claim their new prison is "as good as a Toyota plant for the jobs, money and hope it's brought to their chronically depressed area" (Bruno 1990, p. 57). In Oregon it was reported that "some communities welcomed prisons, some were ambivalent, and a good number were horrified by the idea" (Bruno 1990, p. 64).

Pro-Prison: Needed Economic Development

In upstate New York, as on the tip of Washington State and everywhere in between, the prison-seeking community is apt to be small, has lost a significant number of jobs in recent years, and has suffered a significant loss of population, particularly young adults. For example, in northern California, an area badly hit by a slump in the timber industry and in tourism, Crescent City officials sought and welcomed a 4,000-bed maximum security facility (Bruno 1990, p. 64). Although the official request for a prison may describe the prison-seeking community in glowing terms, the real situation is that these communities have gone through enough years of economic decline and population loss to get to the point where they are reduced to begging state authorities to "give us something. . . . Give us a prison." Each time a town is selected, its jubilation for having "won" in this competition seems to spur other communities to enter the next round. In one New York township that just landed a prison, the supervisor stated to the press with obvious elation that the prison would bring "a sense of security." He added, "This is going to change the pattern around here; you're going to see some good things happening. . . . It could very well turn the economic picture around" (Cox 1989). For local government politicians and officials, "winning a prison" is viewed as enhancing reputations, their own and that of their community.

The words and images that local prison promoters use when referring to the desired prison often run to hyperbole. County economic development directors routinely refer to a prison as "a clean industry," with "no smokestacks and no environmental pollution." They tout a prison as a "safe industry" that is "recession-proof," is not subject to foreign competition, and will not "pull up stakes and leave town." It "stabilizes local employment." Physically, the new prisons are usually quite attractive and unobtrusive, except for the high level of light at night. According to one local description, however, the buildings will be "invisible," meaning that they would be back from the road and not generally within view of the town, and several public statements described the buildings as "a campus setting." The educational metaphor is often extended to the staff, activities, and inmates as well: The top official in a prison is no longer called a "warden" but a "superintendent"; promoters described one proposed facility as having "a junior-college setting," in which inmates would reside in "dorms, rather than cells" and emphasis would be on "vocational training." Despite the state's fact sheet describing medium-security inmates' crimes as "a full range of felony offenses," the most common of which are listed as "robbery, burglary and drug offenses, non-violent type of offenses," some eager town officials emphasize only the "nonviolent" term. One local official claimed that the inmates "will typically be non-violent, white-collar criminals, burglars, etc."

> One prison official, delivering a testimonial about the benefits of his prison to its host community, told a county planning board in a neighboring county that the prison inmates include considerable talent and educational level. He concluded his remarks with the statement that "it's a crime that some of these people are in jail" (Ross 1989).

Underneath the hyperbole though, the overriding reasons for seeking prisons, the arguments that silence the opposition, are almost entirely economic: "The three leading reasons why we want a prison here are jobs, jobs, and jobs." Employment gain, either directly on the prison payroll or indirectly through growth in local business, is the major enticement and still carries widespread appeal, despite recent declines in rural unemployment rates. Memory of past layoffs and factory closings remains sharp, and fear of future employment shrinkage makes the jobs a prison brings especially attractive because they are not subject to cutbacks and layoffs caused by competition and because "the market"—the number of incarcerated persons—is expected to grow. In contrast to recent growth of part-time, low-wage jobs in the lower echelons of the service sector, prison jobs are mostly full time; they pay well and include desirable state health and retirement benefits. In local discussion of prisons, at public meetings, and in letters to the editors of local newspapers, it is also claimed that a prison will reduce the welfare rolls, a possibility that persuades many local taxpayers.

A special aspect of a prison's appeal is that the jobs it brings may stem the tide of out-migration of the community's youth and may even be the means to lure back some of the local sons and daughters who have left town to seek jobs elsewhere. In some communities, as the state announced future prison-building commitments, young-to-middle-aged adults have immediately signed up, taken the civil service exam, and been willing to "serve time" on the prison payroll in distant parts of the state, hoping that they could later put in their name for transfer back to their hometown. In communities that have received prisons, the number of local men and women who can utilize this strategy may be quite small, limited to those who have "the ability to pass the tests and the mobility to move to other parts of the state for a while." But the successful cases may carry a significance for the community that outweighs their relatively small number: The important point is, as one woman phrased it, that "Hometown boys are coming home." Other communities would like to be able to achieve the same.

Other economic benefits that make a prison desirable include an anticipated local real estate and construction boom, including not only the prison itself but new homes and upgraded older ones for incoming prison employees. Local businesses eagerly await a profitable role in supplying goods and services to a prison. Although some commodities "must be purchased centrally through Statewide contracts," the Department of Correctional Services says that the prison system has "a policy that favors the local purchase of goods and services": An estimated $.5 million might be spent locally each year for a 250-bed facility. Restaurants and small retail shops also anticipate increases in customers, both during the construction period and even more when the prison is open, from people who move to town with prison jobs and from relatives and friends of inmates who come to town for visiting.

For the municipality, the advantage foreseen is an increase in the local tax base, largely through the housing boom, which would stem the recent trend of rising local property taxes. In some cases, local officials voice the hope that the prison, with its needs for adequate water and sewer systems, will contribute to upgrading the local infrastructure. All these business and municipal advantages, amounting to a veritable boom in a small, declining community, drive a coalition of business and political interests to proclaim officially, "We want a prison."

Anti-Prison: Unwanted Social Change

Despite the anticipated economic benefits and a strong pro-prison stand by a local government, individual residents may privately express hesitation about inviting a prison to their community. Many residents are ambivalent; they recognize the economic benefits a prison could bring, but not really wanting one in their town, they take no stand for or against a prison. Other residents are staunchly opposed to the idea from the start; still others who are mildly opposed only become galvanized into action after the decision has already been made to request a prison.

Residents who oppose the prison do so for a variety of personal or philosophical reasons, most of them difficult to argue persuasively without sounding overly emotional. They do not counter the employment argument but raise reservations and voice fears about some of the social or "quality of life" changes they foresee. Concerns may range from realistic to quite far-fetched, and they reflect firmly held feelings about the community itself as well as about prisons, feelings that may in turn rest on idealized images of rural life and stereotyped images of prisons.

Some of the more frequently expressed anti-prison anxieties relate to the inmates themselves: Some locals fear escapes and prison riots, with the potential for violence to community residents and their property. One man indicated that he would not feel safe about leaving his wife home alone while he went to his night-shift job. He perceives inmates as potentially very violent and locals as totally "innocent" and inexperienced in dealing with "dangerous people." Some residents worry that AIDS and drugs would infiltrate the community, either through prison escapes or by prisoners who are released on parole after having completed their sentence or by visitors to the inmates. Even without drugs and AIDS, there is concern that a prison attracts what are referred to in some localities as "an undesirable element." A particular concern is that visitors will come by busloads for visiting, perhaps spending the weekend in town, and that families of some prisoners may move to the community to be near inmates. Although few people talk openly in racial or ethnic terms, residents are well aware that the inmate population, and the friends and families of inmates, are mostly black and Hispanic. In private conversations and in interviews, residents reveal considerable anxiety on this issue, though they deny that racism plays a role in their fears. The same racial imbalance and potential for racially based opposition surfaced in prison discussions elsewhere, as in the case of a proposal for locating a Washington, D.C., facility in rural West Virginia (Bates 1989) and in southern Oregon (Bruno 1990).

Some opponents also voice concern over what a prison would do to a community's image, fearing that a prison brings a stigma. Others oppose a prison mostly on the grounds that the state and nation ought to be putting more money into prevention and rehabilitation and into alleviating poverty as a more effective attack on the drug involvement that drives many to crime. Still others report that what troubles them most is the likelihood of major change in their small town. Their concerns center not on inmates but on the assumption that many new people will be moving into town as prison employees, most of them with "city ways." There will be new faces on the street, and rush-hour traffic jams, situations that jar the time-honored perception of a slow-paced life in a town where "everyone knows everyone."

Such amorphous concerns do not hold much sway against economic incentives for seeking a prison. Because of the employment benefits it offers, many small towns compete for something they do not really want. Obtaining a prison is perceived as the only available means toward a strongly desired end: community survival.

PRISON EFFECTS: SOME BENEFITS AND SOME DISAPPOINTMENTS

After a prison is established in a community, local perceptions of its effects vary considerably, depending on a person's niche in and perspective on the local community, as well as on prior attitudes about the prison. Community leaders, politicians, and some businesspeople who worked to get a prison have been quick to voice their enthusiasm: "Great!"

As one exuberant official said in an interview, "Overall, the effect has been *very, very* positive—but then, we did have a long ways to come up."

However, the impact may fall short of desired expectations in some respects and may be qualitatively different in other respects. Many local businesses do report increased volume, though some complain that it is less than had been anticipated. Because many prison employees commute to work rather than moving to live near it, they may not do much of their shopping locally. Some local businesspeople report that competitive bidding in procurement of prison foods and supplies goes mostly to large outside firms, often in distant cities.

Employment effects, though positive and welcomed, may fail to measure up to prior expectations. A 750-bed medium-security facility does generally employ about 400 people, with an annual payroll in excess of $12 million. But the jobs and payroll are not just for people already living in the community before the prison came to town. The state indicates that about 20 percent of the 400 jobs will be filled by local residents; but within the local hirings, only certain types of jobs go to locals. Top-level jobs, the administrative positions, usually go to people already in the prison system and well up its career ladder, people who are almost always from other parts of the state, including metropolitan areas. Similarly, many of the positions for corrections officers are filled by people already in the system, transferring from elsewhere in the state. The jobs that tend to open up to local people are more in the line of skilled service workers and clerical and personnel jobs, including keyboard specialists, secretaries, data processors, receptionists, nurses, social workers, educators, and lower-echelon administrators. In fact, one of the most significant—and usually unanticipated—effects of prison openings is to create an unprecedented raid on employees of the community's institutions: local hospitals, doctors' offices, social service departments, business offices, law enforcement and corrections departments, and educational institutions all report that they lose employees who are attracted to prison employment by considerable gains in salary and benefits. In one case, an intake interviewer from a local employment office obtain a $7,000 pay raise by taking a similar job with the prison. Senior staff at some human service agencies report some critical staff losses: "We've been wiped out here."

The direct impact of the prison in providing jobs for people on welfare, however, appears minimal. Most prison jobs have qualifications much too high to take local people off the welfare rolls. The low-skill jobs that the prison adds to the community are usually fewer in number than had been hoped for, partly because much of the menial work is performed by prison inmates. "Corrections hiring," one official said, "is not coming out of the ranks of the unemployed." Indirectly, though, people on welfare may realize employment advantages from the prison. Lower-skill workers can "backfill," as one employment director referred to it, the gaps left by others who vacated local jobs to take prison jobs. For some, this may represent a better job with better pay. Or they can get the "spin-off jobs," new jobs in local businesses such as restaurants that are hiring a larger work force to meet an increased volume of trade. Increased employment of people formerly on welfare, whether through backfilling or spin-off, however, is not guaranteed or automatic. It seems most effective where an aggressive local training agency works with low-income clients to enable them to make the upward move successfully. Some counties have reported that there are also new welfare costs connected with the prison.

> Occasionally, visitors to inmates have become stranded in the community without a workable car or without sufficient bus money for the trip home and require a night of shelter or a return bus ticket. In some cases, families of inmates may temporarily move to the community for the remainder of the period of incarceration, and because not all of them may be able to get work, some may turn to welfare. With the state's system of counties paying a local share of welfare costs, the local county may be left with increased expenditures, although this has not been a significant problem thus far.

The economic effect of a prison, then, is usually positive but far more complex than had been envisioned in community deliberations and projections. With the prison attracting workers from other jobs, local employers, including county agencies and departments whose wages are set by local legislatures, may be forced to improve their wage and benefit packages in order to retain or replace employees. Even the fast-food restaurants and the malls may be caught with a labor shortage that can be met only by increasing wages and benefits. Thus, a prison may result in a general ratcheting-up of the local employment situation and local economy, even though the dreams of falling welfare rolls and steady employment for all may not fully materialize.

On the down side, however, there are reports of social and personal costs associated with having a prison. Some families have found that using the prison as a strategy to get a good local job has drawbacks in its effects on family functioning. Some local men who get prison guard jobs have to serve two or three years in a distant facility, coming home only during time off, before they are transferred to a prison near their hometowns and can rejoin their families.

> A corrections officer's wife, who had been in favor of seeking a prison for the community, admits, "It's hard on me and hard on the kids—on him, too. I'm just like all the single mothers I know, trying to manage a job and to be both father and mother to the kids all the time. Thank God I have my mother nearby, and also my husband's sister and her husband."

Additional family effects, reported by some local mental health workers, include interpersonal stress, alcoholism, and domestic violence within prison-employee families. Being a corrections officer creates stresses that it may not resolve—and that may consequently be acted out at home. From other local residents, there are also reports of minor changes in everyday living that may carry more significance than would be apparent on the face of it. In one town where a prison has come in, some residents reported that they feel less free to go out in the evening and that they lock their houses and their cars overnight, little behavioral changes that can have subtle but unsettling impacts.

One negative impact of prisons may be that they cause hardship for some lower-income residents because of increased housing costs. Especially for single women heads of households, their welfare payment or employment income has not kept pace with the rising rents generated by population influx connected with the prisons. Some of the cheap apartments are upgraded, with the rent raised accordingly.

It is too soon to tell whether other negative effects, such as rise of AIDS and drug use, that are feared by some local prison opponents will materialize in the community. There have been only minor instances of rioting in the new facilities, and media reports of prison violence elsewhere have not dissuaded local prison advocates.

ESTABLISHING REALISTIC EXPECTATIONS: LEARNING FROM OTHER COMMUNITIES

With more prisons required in coming years, more rural communities will be considering whether to seek a prison and more will be adjusting to the presence of a prison in their midst. In several communities that have recently debated whether or not to seek a prison, some residents expressed frustration that they simply do not know what to expect; they feel that their decision on seeking a prison is being made without a sufficient information base. Lacking adequate information, the discussion may become more polarized than might otherwise be the case, splitting the community between those who want to preserve the rural attributes they cherish and those who see prison-related economic development as the only way they can remain in the rural community. This is potentially another split between long-term and less affluent residents and others, especially retirees and suburban professionals who have been in the community for a shorter time, although the alignment is not necessarily this clear. Some opponents protest that a prison will "spoil the beautiful landscape and peaceful life," but prison advocates retort, "You can't *eat* scenery! We need *jobs!*" Judging from experience thus far, the landscape will not be "ruined," but the job situation won't be "cured" either. Information about prison effects elsewhere, particularly in communities of roughly comparable size and where other parameters are similar, would help residents consider benefits and drawbacks ahead of time and develop realistic expectations and effective adjustments should they get a prison.

One of the few in-depth studies of community attitudes and effects, conducted in the state of Washington, helps clarify the mixture of benefits and negative impacts and seems applicable to the new prison communities in upstate New York. In Clallam Bay, Washington, employment was a major reason why a small and shrinking town of 1,000 residents in a very rural and economically depressed area worked hard to get a prison (Carlson 1988a), despite "a substantial but less well organized opposition" (Carlson 1989, p. 2). In some ways the community's early perceptions of the prison's impacts centered not on the prisoners but on the prison itself as a new local institution, and on the new prison-employee population it brought to town.

> Among guards as well as other employees hired for this prison, a rather low percentage is local or formerly local people. In fact, relatively few locals applied for prison jobs. Sixty percent of workers commute to their prison jobs from other area towns, indicating that fewer employees than predicted decided to settle in the immediate community. As a result, there was less local homebuilding and less local purchasing of household goods and services than had been anticipated. The prison employees who did move to town are characterized by limited participation in community affairs, dissatisfaction with the community, and an expectation that they will not stay long. In fact, there is a high turnover rate among prison employees who move in from elsewhere. Those without rural living in their background complain of the town's remote location and its lack of amenities, activities, and services, and see life in this little community as "boring." On the other side, there is only lukewarm acceptance of these newcomers by longer-term community residents, who refer to them as "prison people."

From increased elementary school populations, improved school performance, and growth of the community volunteer labor pool on the positive side to such negative effects as shortage of rental housing and fears about prison escapes shaping new practices of locking doors and cars, the impacts of the prison on the small Washington community were mixed. Employment figures were indeed up, the volume of business in local stores was up, and there was a much-appreciated new supermarket. But in less countable, less obvious ways, local residents appeared to perceive a loss in their "quality of life." Also resented was that despite its promises not to do so, the state chose the community's own name for the prison, thus merging the community's identity with that of the correctional facility.

Perhaps the biggest difficulty in making a wise decision in seeking a prison and adapting to its impacts is the development of unrealistic expectations ahead of time, either positive expectations about jobs, commercial benefits, welfare decrease, and community development or negative expectations about crime in the streets and unwanted settlement of prisoners' families in the community. In the community debates, exaggerations and unrealistic hopes and fears often dominate the dialogue and shape expectations. In the final analysis, the overall effect of a prison, on the Northwest Coast or in rural New York, is mixed, not a total panacea, but not as bad as some had feared.

As the Washington study points out, "In considering and weighing these impacts, it is important to note that without a prison, [this community] was a community at risk. With a prison [it] may have to live with other dangers and disadvantages, but it will survive" (Carlson 1988b).

Economic survival may thus be ensured, but with social changes that may be less than welcome. In one New York county that has several correctional facilities, two comments written by residents on a county-wide needs assessment survey indicate the range of local feelings and experiences (Compass 1988).

"Last year at this time we were struggling dairy farmers. We had a very rough time of it. My husband now has a good job as a corrections officer. We sold the farm and our lives now are much easier."

"It's sad that the area's economy is tied to the number of prisons here. There must be a better way to develop our local economy."

While states commit further funds to building yet more prisons in rural areas, some communities will mount a unified campaign to get a prison, others will undergo heated debate, and in others the idea will not even surface publicly. Although rural areas may have the space for state prisons, not all rural residents want their community to be the place where such a facility is located.

CHAPTER FIFTEEN
Waste Disposal:
LLRW and Other LULUs

For the nation as a whole, rural lands present a convenient dumping ground. In many areas rural lands are being redefined by powerful nonrural interests as suitable sites for the cast-off, unwanted by-products of society, thus creating an urban-to-rural effluent flow of unknown magnitude. For rural residents, however, the commodities they are asked to store usually represent an unwanted intrusion. From low-level radioactive waste (LLRW) to a variety of other locally unwanted land uses (LULUs), many rural American communities are now threatened with the prospect that their landscape will become what one resident termed "a rural solution for urban pollution."

From eastern coastal communities in Maine, through upstate New York, through the rural South, Midwest, and far West, a number of rural areas are becoming the ultimate service industry of our times— the receptacle for the unwanted refuse of a waste-generating society. Some localities are now undergoing a change from being a place where agricultural and manufactured goods were produced and resources extracted to becoming a repository where wastes are stored. Rural lands vulnerable to this conversion include those where large expanses of space are available, where activities upon the land are returning only small profits, where land prices are relatively low, and where the population is small. Proximity to major transportation arteries further increases vulnerability.

In the highly urbanized Northeast, some of the remaining remote areas have a great deal of overgrown, abandoned farmland and wooded areas that are only sparsely inhabited. Until recently, only in areas where scenic or recreational amenities and proximity to metropolitan centers have promoted vacation-home development has anyone expressed interest in using such land. Market value and property taxes on these marginally productive lands have remained low. Now, however, the enormous differential in land prices between metropolitan and rural areas, coupled with the huge differential in population density, makes these more remote rural areas very attractive as places to discard commodities that metropolitan areas do not want and can no longer dispose of locally.

A MAJOR UNWANTED LAND USE:
OTHER PEOPLE'S GARBAGE

As more densely populated areas have run out of space for their wastes, both the public and private sector are turning to distant rural areas for a variety of waste disposal needs, from landfilling household garbage and construction debris to burying incinerator ash. Almost everywhere in rural America, such wastes are "invading" rural places. And almost everywhere, storing other people's garbage is a LULU.

Although the problem of solid waste disposal troubles rural as well as suburban people, in many rural communities residents have a sense of trust that their municipal authorities can operate and manage the proposed landfill professionally and safely, and so resistance to a new landfill may be relatively short-lived (Furuseth and Johnson 1988, p. 137). Much greater public resistance arises in cases of exogenous wastes, wastes carted in from elsewhere, whether ordinary municipal garbage, construction debris, or the even-less-wanted toxic chemicals. Leaving aside the undocumented problem of illegal dumping and its connections to graft and crime, even the authorized, institutionally sanctioned dumping by private firms and governmental authorities from distant places poses a looming problem for rural communities where land is available and population sparse. Pressure on rural parts of the crowded northeastern states will increase as more rural states in other regions step up their resistance to the out-of-state wastes they currently receive. Each state will become more responsible for wastes generated within its borders; for New York this means more wastes—of all kinds—destined for its rural communities.

Some rural communities have had the experience of awakening one day to read in their local newspaper that land in their county is being purchased by an out-of-town private firm that plans to create a state-of-the-art landfill for the purpose of disposing of wastes from a large surrounding region—as a commercial, profit-making venture. Such a private, regional landfill may be especially resisted because it will have a much greater volume of wastes coming into it than what would be generated locally. Furthermore, it will not be as easily scrutinized, regulated, and monitored as a local municipal landfill would be and thus may get away with undetected environmental pollution. There is also a cultural basis to this resistance: Material brought in will be "foreign" garbage, "other people's wastes," that are usually perceived as being more dangerous, perhaps with good reason. The "foreignness" of the waste makes it even more unwanted because it comes from an "outside" that is generally looked down upon as the opposite of all that is good, the opposite of rural. No matter how well managed in a state-of-the-art "sanitary landfill," urban wastes are unwanted: Conceptually, they represent urban pollution invading the rural environment.

Even if an outside firm proposing a landfill promises a state-of-the-art facility that will be responsibly run, routinely monitored, and, when full, carefully closed according to all environmental regulations, a regional disposal site for exogenous wastes is apt to stir strong local resistance. In one township plagued by poverty and unemployment, even the jobs that were promised in construction and operation of a regional landfill were not enough to seduce residents into allowing the destruction of a beautiful upland area where many locals fish, hunt, and camp. Such disposal facilities, it is argued, are insidious: "Once you have one in your county, other firms and municipalities consider your land already spoiled. They assume that you don't care about what happens to your land, and they will seek to place another facility near the first, then another, and another." For many rural residents, the presence of a large, cut-open hillside disposal site to store wastes generated elsewhere represents a major dissonance with the image they have of rural life and rural environment.

A relatively new—and heated—waste disposal issue is that of incineration of municipal garbage, and particularly the problem of what to do with the ash produced by incineration. In the mid-1970s, incineration was thought to be the wave of the future for landfill-crowded metropolitan areas. Densely populated Connecticut led the way in converting to incineration for over half of its household trash, and other northeastern states also moved in this direction. After incineration, the remaining ash has routinely been transported to municipal landfills and disposed of along with ordinary wastes. However, it is now understood that the incineration of such commodities as styrofoam and batteries produces an ash with toxic chemicals, including dioxins, lead, and cadmium, that may escape from the landfill as "fugitive dust" or leachate. Ironically, stricter air pollution controls now required on incinerators have made the incinerator ash even more toxic, to the point where it is no longer regarded as safe for ordinary municipal landfills, although technically and legally it is still not classified as toxic. New landfills designed specifically for ash are needed, both to provide safely for ash burial and to relieve the rapid rate at which ordinary municipal landfills are filling up.

Not surprisingly, rural areas with small populations are being sought as potential sites for ash landfills. In spring 1989 the state of Connecticut was attempting to establish thirteen new landfills to take ash from incinerators throughout the state (Kirk Johnson 1989a). After considering various possibilities, the Department of Environmental Protection came up with a list of sites deemed suitable in terms of geological and hydrogeological factors. It came as no surprise to the people of the northeastern corner of the state, the "least populous and least affluent area" that nearly half of the sites were located there. A similar situation developed in Maine in spring 1989. The easternmost county along the coast, one of the poorest in the state and very rural, was the site of hearings on a proposed ash landfill for two large incinerators. Local government officials had already formally declared their opposition and public sentiment against it came out strongly at the hearings. Residents were "incensed about their area becoming the permanent home to all that waste they had no part in creating" (Kreis 1989, p. 21). A member of the state's Board of Environmental Protection received "a hearty ovation" when she suggested that perhaps an area already environmentally spoiled, such as the Portland Maine Mall area, might make a better dump site.

In New York State, incinerator capacity and land for ash burial is greater than in Connecticut, so there is not yet a statewide ash crisis. Nonetheless, current and proposed regional incinerators and ash landfills represent a looming problem for several rural localities, ranging from suburban and semirural counties on Long Island and downstate to the North Country, and including one small township in western New York.

A private company recently proposed building a large incinerator-ash landfill in the center of Allegany County. This landfill, or "ash monofill," would not only take the county's ash but would be large enough to accept ash from a number of incinerators throughout the Northeast. The site for this proposed private operation is on farmland, just a few miles from the present county landfill.

Limited opposition began with the first announcement. Some residents in a small village nearby hoped that the permitting review by the state DEC would either deny the proposal or slow it down while local opposition mounted. Meanwhile, the proposing company mounted a videotaped promotion campaign and promised that the facility would create fifteen new jobs and spend $1 million locally each year. In addition, the company would pay the community $.25 million annually. To some residents, this package of incentives seemed irresistible, but for others the potential risks to environment and health, or to their satisfaction with rural life, loomed larger. While the ash dump proposal was undergoing lengthy review procedures in Albany, however, a local debate on the subject was suddenly eclipsed by an issue of much greater and more unifying public concern: Some land just a few miles away was identified by the state as a possible site for storage of all of New York's low-level radioactive wastes.

LLRW—LOW-LEVEL RADIOACTIVE WASTES

The phrase "low-level radioactive waste" hardly existed in the public lexicon of rural New York or any other rural areas of the nation until very recent years. Suddenly, in the late 1980s, radioactive waste disposal burst into rural attention, and many rural communities around the nation found themselves caught up in a new issue that has totally dominated certain rural communities in New York and elsewhere.

Background

Until the present, the nation's nuclear wastes have either been stored where generated or shipped to facilities in the rural areas of three states, Washington, Nevada, and South Carolina. (Three other sites in Kentucky, Illinois, and western New York had been closed about 1975 because of leakage, and most of New York's radioactive wastes subsequently went to South Carolina.) In 1980 the federal government shifted much of the responsibility for radioactive wastes to the states: The Low-Level Radioactive Waste Policy Act declared that the federal government would oversee the disposal of "high-level" radioactive wastes at a single site to be built and operated by the federal government, and that each state would "take responsibility for all low-level" radioactive wastes generated within its borders.

Low-level radioactive waste is officially defined by the federal government only in terms of what it is not, as "everything that isn't high-level radioactive waste." "High-level" radioactive waste (labeled "Class D") is defined as waste that exceeds acceptable standards for shallow land burial or that is "generally not acceptable for disposal at a low level waste site" (New York State Department of Health 1988), and it includes spent fuel rods from nuclear power plants, wastes from reprocessing spent fuel rods, tailings from mining or milling of uranium, and waste produced by federal defense and research installations. Most other radioactive materials are classified as "low-level" wastes and subdivided by level of radioactivity and length of half-life, from C (highest) to A (lowest). In terms of materials, low-level waste includes dry trash, paper, plastics, glass, clothing, discarded equipment and tools, sludges, and liquids contaminated with radioactivity. The largest proportion of "low-level" wastes, both in volume and in level of radioactivity, comes from power plants. (In 1989 power plants in the state produced 60 percent of the volume and 95 percent of the radioactivity, whereas in 1988 the figures were 69 percent of the volume and 78 percent of the radioactivity.) Low-level waste would include the core shroud that directs the flow of coolant through the core of a nuclear reactor; it is Class C material, requiring packaging designed to last 500 years. Another major source of LLRW, contributing significantly to the volume and radioactivity of Class B wastes, is a private firm located downstate that is the major U.S. producer of radionuclides for use in medicine and scientific research.

The federal radioactive waste legislation, amended in 1985 to include a timetable and fines for noncompliance, triggered a series of actions by state governments. In most cases, neighboring states banded together in interstate compacts to set up a joint facility; some progressed well, but others faltered. By 1990, progress in selecting sites was mixed. California had found a site in the desert, and in Illinois two towns that already have nuclear power generators were reported in competition to get the dump, while Texas was on hold because of the proximity of its chosen site to an international border. In Pennsylvania, the designated host state in a four-state compact, a private nuclear systems firm from South Carolina was engaged in selecting a site. Some compacts surmounted disagreement over which state would get the dump only to meet resistance from potential sites within the selected host state. From Riga, Michigan, which was selected but then disqualified for technical unsuitability, to Nora, Nebraska, small communities have offered strong resistance. New York was one of the few states that did not enter into a compact because its authorities feared that as the nation's sixth-largest producer it would very likely become the repository for neighboring states that produce less radioactive waste.

In New York a 1986 act of the legislature, the Low-Level Radioactive Waste Management Act, was hastily passed, with minimal public awareness, during a session that began after midnight just before a holiday recess. The legislation set up a special siting commission, its five members to be appointed by the governor, with an operating budget of $15 million, paid for by the generators of nuclear waste. The commission was authorized to hire technical staff and contract with expert consultants and to select and acquire a site, by condemnation if necessary. The early work of the commission was conducted quietly and out of public view, as technical staff studied existing data to determine areas of the state that might merit further consideration. In the very end of 1988, the commission burst into public attention with announcement of the results of its early screening.

Chronology of Events

Just before Christmas 1988, parts of ten counties in rural New York suddenly learned that they were on the list of "candidate areas" for an LLRW facility. Within each of these areas, further examination of geological and other technical data already available would be conducted to generate a short list of four to six potential sites, which would later be narrowed still further before final selection of one place to "host" the facility. In the ten counties where such candidate areas had been named, the news came as a real shock; people were stunned, caught right at holiday time with a major and unwanted issue, an issue so new to them and so complex they hardly knew where to turn for information. A protest sign in one community facetiously wished residents "MERRY XMAS AND A HAPPY NUCLEAR."

Within a month, public opinion in these rural areas had crystallized into a strong opposition, many citizen groups formed, and many local governments made official statements against the dump. In some counties an "antidump coordinator" was hired to lead the official and citizen opposition; in other counties a loose coalition of citizen groups carried the opposition with help from some local officials. When members of the siting commission held a series of information meetings in each of the named counties, local residents turned out by the thousands, with loud voices and strong opposition. In March the state Department of

Health visited each of the candidate areas to hold public "informational meetings." In the central part of the state, close to three candidate areas, the information meeting drew a large, two-county crowd.

The school's entrance and gym were festooned in posters and signs created at community "poster parties" and by children in school. A "Dump Da Dump" message, computer printed on a long paper banner, contained signatures of many high school students. One poster urged "Be Active, Not Radioactive"; another insisted "Not Here, Not Now, Not Ever"; another asked "Year of the Child?" referring ironically to a special, just-completed year proclaimed by the governor. Several posters, playing up the rural character of the county, featured cows, barns, milk products, and maple syrup. One poster proclaimed "We Want Farms, Not Dumps!" The day-glow orange signs with a black skull and crossbones saying "Posted, No Dumping" that had begun to appear on trees and fenceposts along many local highways and in front yards and windows were being sold in the gym lobby, along with buttons, t-shirts and sweat shirts, and piles of photocopied technical material on LLRW. Women were signing up volunteers to organize and contribute to bake sales to raise money for the resistance campaign. One table staffed by two DOH people offered official publications of information about LLRW. As the crowd came in on this wintry night, a half dozen or so state troopers wandered around outside and in, their presence quite obvious in the lobby and the gym.

The evening's program began with very knowledgeable experts from the Department of Health explaining to a very dubious audience all about rems and millirems, risk studies, and engineering plans, trying to state convincingly that they believed it possible to construct a facility that would not exceed the 25-millirem emission limit. However, the audience did not seem persuaded. One resident said into the microphone, "You in public health tell us to eat well, to exercise, don't smoke, and all that. Yet you want to put this here?" She added, "You're dealing in theory; we're dealing in reality." A member of the audience commented afterward, "They can present all the technical information they want to—but we don't believe them. It won't be safe. They can't guarantee our safety."

During late winter and early spring, local opposition groups in each of the ten candidate areas were becoming better organized, starting up new chapters and branches, attempting to get neighboring towns and counties into the opposition, and networking with other candidate sites. Local groups calling themselves "Concerned Citizens," "Citizens Against Radioactive Dumping," and "Public Action Committee" banded together to form a statewide coalition group, "Don't Waste New York," which not only served as a clearinghouse of information and strategies but also attempted to call statewide attention to the issue, through such events as a mock funeral march held in the state capital in April. Through letter-writing campaigns, hundreds of telephone calls to the siting commission's toll-free hotline, and pressure on state legislators and representatives in Washington, people in all candidate areas sought to argue that their locality would be "unfit to host a nuclear dump." No locality in New York was tempted by the state's vague proposal of an incentive package for the host community. The specter of four tractor-trailer loads a week delivering radioactive wastes to their land was not appealing.

The next step in the site selection process was the narrowing of the list of ten candidate areas to "four to six" specific "potential sites" to be further investigated and "pre-characterized" over the course of a year by various technical teams doing on-site soil and geological testing.

One County's Struggle Against the LLRW Dump

Allegany County was one of the ten counties on the original list announced in late 1988.

When Allegany residents had first learned, on December 20, that their county contained a candidate area (actually a combination of two contiguous areas), there were a few days of confusion and a week or two in which some residents and even a few politicians expressed a "wait-and-see" attitude. But very quickly public opinion crystallized into strong opposition. With just a few brief exceptions, any people who were not opposed to the dump simply kept quiet.

By early spring, Allegany County had earned a reputation as the most unified, organized, active, and perhaps most feisty antidump county in the state. The main source of this reputation was the public meeting held in the county by the siting commission in late January. Allegany produced the largest turnout of any area: 5,000 people, fully 10 percent of the total county population. It was the largest public gathering in anyone's memory. The overflow crowd from the auditorium crammed into the gym, classrooms, and the bus garage to watch the proceedings on closed-circuit television, and still 1,000 people stood outdoors in the cold night. The meeting lasted over six hours, with a coordinated local response, including a mixture of emotional pleas and technical statements or questions. There was a good deal of audience applause and cheering, but the audience was neither unruly nor excessively rude or abusive.

This public meeting gave rise to a sense of euphoria that swept the county in the period immediately afterward: little Allegany County produced not only the biggest opposition crowd of all but also the best-behaved crowd. The day after that meeting, the county seemed to be bursting with pride, a pride that made many people optimistic that Allegany could indeed fend off the dump if people continued their efforts. Surely, it was felt, the state would not put such an "evil facility" in such a "good community." Newspaper accounts of the meeting, as well as individuals' comments, exuded a sense that the county was at its most important moment in history and that it was up to the challenge. "Allegany may be a poor, out-of-the-way rural county, but it is prepared to fight a nuclear waste facility by mounting an organized, informed campaign." "We may be rural and few in number, but we're not dumb." "Little David will eventually triumph over Goliath." "The forces of nature and beauty and rural goodness will win over the forces of evil, defeating the dangerous wastes of a society gone wrong." The meeting, commemorated on its anniversary a year later, was remembered as "an unprecedented celebration of Allegany County . . . a shining moment in the county's history."

Through the next half year, local groups sprang up in every section of the county, even in hamlets and neighborhoods more distant from the candidate areas, and all coordinated under a county-wide "Concerned Citizens" framework. Most of the county's twenty-nine townships and eleven villages came out with statements against the dump and money to help in the fight—even as little as $250 from a tight township budget was symbolically significant. The county government, with a long history of trying to keep expenses and taxes as low as possible, had spent $35,000 in the first four months and then appropriated $9,000 more, mostly covering extra staff for its Soil and Water Conservation District experts who diligently compiled detailed information for overlay maps depicting the county's physical, hydrologic, and climatological characteristics. These specialists pointed out to the state siting commission that some of its information was out of date and wrong and should not be used in making siting decisions. For example, they found more active and abandoned oil and gas wells near the sites than the state had counted, and they found that the state's consultant had "missed or misplaced part of our aquifer," which locals insisted passes near one site. Additionally, a geological fault stretching into the county had not been considered by the commission.

The LLRW issue has had high local visibility. Throughout the county, many existing groups, having widely divergent purposes and memberships, all took a stand against the dump. Volunteer fire companies and ambulance squads, schoolteacher groups, and fraternal organizations came out against the dump and pledged support in the fight. In this county, where summertime celebrations are numerous, the 1989 homecoming days in villages and hamlets, the county fair, a balloon launch, and many special days celebrating virtually every possible locality and famous local citizen all became centered on opposing "the dump." In addition to the many meetings, public statements, and public discussions, each thoroughly covered in the local press, there were also marches, rallies, bake sales, dances, and demonstrations. The quantity of newspaper coverage was impressive: More than three pounds of clippings on the LLRW issue from twelve months in the county's local daily paper, which hardly missed a single day without one or more articles, photographs, editorials, columns, and letters on the issue. A plethora of antidump signs all over the county kept the issue in the forefront of people's minds, reminding them of the county's potential risk and its determination to fight and also of their membership in a special community, Allegany County.

Then in September the next blow came. In a bungled announcement that leaked out of the siting commission a few days ahead of schedule, Allegany County learned that it was designated as having *three* potential sites, all within its single candidate area, out of the state's short list of five potential sites. The other two sites were both in Cortland County, in the central part of the state. Allegany was also listed as containing the majority of alternative backup sites, should all five of the originally selected potential sites prove infeasible. Suddenly the odds had shifted from having one of ten candidate areas, to having three out of five potential sites. Although there was renewed commitment, rededication of effort, reorientation and redirection of strategies, there was also some sense of resignation: "We will fight like hell to protect ourselves, our county, our children—but we may be doomed, as the state will probably put it here anyway." A nonviolent action group put on a strong demonstration of resistance when state technical experts first came to town, and the group recruited more people who would be prepared to go to jail or to support those who would go to jail, provided training, and established an effective network of communication among themselves. Local residents with well-organized communication networks were driving the back dirt roads in the potential site areas, notifying each other of any out-of-county cars and strangers in the area, stopping motorists to ask their business, and running a campsite of observers on the potential sites to obstruct technical investigators sent by the state siting commission whenver they should arrive. Vigils, demonstrations, and a "night of rage" were held on adjacent farmland along a narrow dirt road, where normally only a few deer hunters wander. Through the record-breaking cold of December 1989, one year after the first announcement had been made, the watches on the hilltop camps continued, and forays by siting commission members and staff to inspect the three potential sites were headed off or detained by human blockades.

As "year one" of the LLRW issue came to an end, local resisters expected that nearly another year would pass while the state investigated all five sites, with still more time before the actual site selection would be made. Strategists planned for the long run and tried to maintain the high level of public interest and generate even wider support in the county, in Rochester and Buffalo, and in adjacent Pennsylvania, where nearby rural counties were under consideration for that state's LLRW facility. Meanwhile, some moves were being made in Albany and Washington to urge reconsideration of the LLRW legislation. Both state and federal lawmakers, citing a report by the federal Office of Technology Assessment, argued that the legislation would create more sites than necessary because production of radioactive wastes had decreased recently.

As 1990 began, no significant resolution was in sight. The state initiated a lawsuit challenging the constitutionality of the federal legislation requiring states to "take title" to wastes generated by private firms. Locally, more Alleganians were taking days off from work and evenings away from home to protest the dump and the siting process. More of them were arrested for blocking inspection tours of siting commission members and their contracted specialists. An injunction was issued against further protests, but more people protested and arrests rose to over 125 people. In early April some site inspectors were rebuffed by local protesters, among them a phalanx of masked horseback riders and a "grandparents' brigade," including an eighty-eight-year-old woman college professor, who handcuffed themselves to a chain stretched across a bridge leading to one site. After that protest, the governor temporarily suspended site visits and moved to slightly revamp the siting commission and its process. But the issue has not gone away, and the states currently receiving New York's radioactive wastes warned that they would begin to activate penalties for the state's failure to meet timetable deadlines.

UNDERSTANDING RESISTANCE TO THE LLRW FACILITY

The siting-centered approach, established in the federal and state LLRW legislation, has had two crucial consequences. First, the issue of selection of a site was allowed to take precedence in the public dialogue, and perhaps in planning as well, over the more general issue of disposal, and this has diverted attention away from complex and important public safety questions, for example, what maximum levels of radioactivity should be included and whether low-level radioactive wastes actually present only a low level of risk. When the issue is only where to put an unwanted facility, the larger problem of disposal of wastes from nuclear energy production commands little public attention from society at large. Second, the entire process has centered on which place might get the facility, the possible sites fighting against it while residents of the rest of the state, believing they have nothing at stake, barely noticed or cared. In New York the struggle has almost entirely been between agents of the state and the citizens of the rural localities under consideration.

To a great extent, the vocal and angry reaction of citizens living near potential sites has not been taken seriously by residents of nondesignated localities or by government officials. Resistance has been belittled as driven by ignorance of "the real facts" about radioactive wastes and by selfishness. Closer observation in the two counties where potential sites are under scrutiny, revealed more complex reasons behind local resistance.

Citizens' "Emotionalism" or Ineffective State "Education" Efforts?

The most obvious explanation for heightened emotions in these LLRW cases is that the subject matter itself *is* scary. Radioactive wastes generate not only radioactivity but also fear. As protesters in the potential dump sites expressed their fear, they were no different from the general U.S. population in their assessment of the risks from nuclear facilities. For example, although death records show that people are more likely to die from riding in a canoe than from living next to a nuclear power plant, research subjects consistently rank the latter as having a much higher risk of death (Slovic, Fischoff, and Lichtenstein 1979). In the public's thinking, even the mere term "radioactivity" carries with it an overload of connotations about atomic bombs, nuclear weapons, Three Mile Island and Chernobyl, and birth defects for generations into the future. There is a ready vocabulary of words and images ("nuke," "nuke site," "nuke war," the mushroom-shaped atomic cloud, and the stylized skull and crossbones) all easily adaptable to the "fight" at hand. If the public's use of the fear-inducing and war-connected terms for the radioactive emission from a waste facility might be considered technically inappropriate, it was ideologically inevitable: The day-glow, spray-painted words on abandoned buildings and forest trees near the proposed sites scream "No Nukes," "Nuke War," or simply "War."

On the premise that providing "the facts" would calm people down, reduce their fears, and lead them to a "more rational" approach, the siting commission, the Department of Health, and other official bodies held public information meetings. But in this case as in other situations of environmental risks, no matter how attractively packaged or carefully presented the technical information may be, it is not effective in overriding opposition or calming fears, especially if provided after people have already formed their opinions. Additionally, because much of the information was controlled by state authorities, it was perceived locally as either biased or intentionally incomplete, although unclarity in the factual information was not so much the fault of the presenters, such as DOH personnel, as it was inherent in the way radioactive wastes are classified by the federal government, with no specific radioactivity levels assigned to the several classes of materials. Furthermore, the many unknowns, uncertainties, and unknowables in a complex environmental issue such as LLRW give rise to confusion and frustration. As an exasperated coordinator of one county's resistance effort exclaimed, "This whole thing is a pile of uncertainties." Further reducing the effectiveness of technical information is that different expert sources sometimes present conflicting or contradictory "factual" material. For example, in answer to the question of what proportion of the radioactivity in the "low-level" stream is of the more dangerous Class C, the DOH brochure distributed at its informational meetings gives a figure of only 0.04 percent, but printed material distributed by the state's Energy Research and Development Authority that will operate the facility says 66 percent of the radioactivity comes from Class C wastes. The magnitude of such a discrepancy in "factual" material presented by two state agencies, both of which hope to convince residents that the facility will be safe, makes citizens doubt both experts and leaves them even more convinced that the facility will *not* be safe.

"NIMBY" Syndrome in Chosen Sites
or Reverse NIMBY Elsewhere?

Citizens struggling to fight off an unwanted land use, whether a new highway, a power-generating plant, a landfill, ash burial, or a toxic or nuclear waste dump are often accused by others of displaying "NIMBY," meaning the "not-in-my-backyard" syndrome. NIMBY refers to the presumedly selfish position of residents who, although they may favor such a facility in principle, will resist having it located near them. In the LLRW case, though, practically no one in the selected rural "candidate site" locations is in favor of the general concepts of a LLRW dump as currently proposed. They oppose such a facility in *anyone's* backyard, not just their own. Neither Cortland nor Allegany people have ever suggested that the other county should have the dump. As a result of their own self-education efforts, residents of both counties question whether the items placed by bureaucratic and legislative fiat into the category labeled "low" are actually low in radioactivity or in potential harm to humans and the environment.

In fact, this LLRW case points up another side of NIMBY that is often ignored: The majority of the population, and of the political power as well, is at least as guilty of a reverse-NIMBY syndrome as the people living near the designated sites are of NIMBY itself. People whose backyards are not threatened seem to feel that the threat itself is intrinsically minimal and tend to pay very little attention to the potential health and environmental effects that concern the resisters: "As long as it's *not* in *my* backyard, then it's *not* a problem or threat."

Rural residents are particularly sensitive to the question of equity, or fairness, in the distribution of risks and benefits in this issue. Although many agree that a nuclear waste dump should not be put where population is high, they feel that certain rural areas are being required to take all the risks for benefits that mostly go to other people. As Michael Edelstein has said in his book entitled *Contaminated Communities*, "Siting thus becomes a modern ceremony for selecting victims for sacrifice" (Edelstein 1988, p. 195). It should not be surprising, then, that most rural communities resist such a facility: Indeed, the opposition may be a sign of their collective social health.

Fundamental Rural Distrust of Government

A major element fueling the rural LLRW resistance is distrust of state and federal government. Because official definitions and categories of radioactive waste are bureaucratic and institutional in nature rather than based on radioactivity levels, citizens fear that the government or industry could change the rules to allow the inclusion of yet higher levels of radioactive materials in the facility, such as a special class called GTCC (greater-than-Class-C) wastes, which is not necessarily included under federal responsibility, and the "mixed wastes" category containing hazardous chemicals along with radioactive wastes. Air pollution standards could also be changed at the federal level, and this would allow more venting of radioactive gases into the air than the state currently says would be allowed.

In Allegany County distrust of state government hangs like the morning fog. But distrust doesn't burn off at midday. As one candidate for political office said while looking for votes, "I have a basic mistrust of governmental agencies. . . . They are extremely hard to sue for mistakes." Residents point out that it is probably no coincidence that their district's assemblyman lives in a town further away from Albany than any other assemblyman. They also point to the fact that virtually all of the LLRW candidate areas were represented by "Albany's minority party," Republicans. It is not just that the county is largely Republican and the governor Democratic, however; it is also that Albany is perceived as controlled by "big-city interests," and that it cannot always be trusted to follow through on promises made to distant rural places.

These negative feelings about the state and its urban domination compound negative feelings about the waste facility itself. Not trusting the state, locals are unlikely to believe information the state provides, and, in circular fashion, not having information that they believe is full and honest, they develop further distrust of the state. This distrust adds more emotional fear and more determined resistance.

Related to lack of trust is fear of control by the state. Rural residents, and their official bodies and spokespeople, resent and frequently rail against the state for imposing excessive mandates, for meddling in the conduct of local affairs, for telling rural people how they should live, what they should do, and what they should not do—even in their own communities and on their own private property.

One Allegany County farmer complained in exasperation at a public meeting, "The state is on my case about my manure that might sometimes be running off into the creek—and at the same time the state is proposing to come in here and put that thing [LLRW facility] right in the middle of an agricultural county where cows and people live, where we produce milk and maple syrup and crops . . . that will be irradiated."

At public meetings a common statement is, "The state is coming in and against our will imposing something on our land that we don't want and that is not good for the environment or for us." Another county resident summed up the control issue as follows: "The state tries to control us, requiring us to do this or not to do that, but we cannot control the state."

The crux of the matter in the case of LLRW is that local people simply do not believe the state authorities when they say, in effect, "Trust us. We can design, build, and operate a facility that will be safe. We will look out for your health." Such assurances offered by state officials or their representatives in the public meetings generated more catcalls and boos from the audience than any other statements.

This request for trust falls on especially unlistening ears in Allegany County, for residents can easily point to their neighboring county to the west, where the West Valley facility, one of the federal government's original six radioactive waste facilities, was finally closed after nearby residents complained for years about health effects. Federal authorities, though not assigning credibility to neighbors' health complaints, finally admitted that there was a problem with the storage facility: Water had seeped past the earthen barriers, into the site, and out again, carrying radiation with it. With that experience next door, Allegany residents ask incredulously, "You expect us to trust you to protect us, to build something that doesn't leak, and to inform us in the event that it does leak?"

In Allegany County, as elsewhere in communities fighting off an LLRW facility, people see the issue as a rural equity issue and as an issue in which they have little say in what happens in their own communities. The phrase "No radiation without representation!" becomes a battle cry in a war that also features tricornered hats and other Revolutionary War symbols. These rural people feel that they are being asked to take a disproportionately large share of risks resulting from nuclear operations, when they only receive a small share of the benefits. Suddenly, there is a huge penalty for being rural.

FROM FARMLAND TO DUMP SITE: AN UNNATURAL SUCCESSION

Through many decades of the past, as farms have gone out of business and marginal farmland has been abandoned, a natural succession has taken place on the landscape of rural New York. After a couple of years, a former hayfield or pasture grows thick with goldenrod and milkweed, then thorny bushes and trees; gradually it grows up in white pines, swamp maple, and poplars, which later give way to sugar maple, oak, and other hardwoods.Now, however, due to the economics of land values in the entire region and the lack of available land closer to metropolitan centers, a new *un*natural succession is occurring on the rural landscape: The effluent of the larger society is increasingly spreading over lands that were formerly farmed. As the waste dumping in rural areas grows and spreads, rural lands are no longer providing foods and other goods but space in which to discard the nation's wastes. Although rural people certainly participate in the activities and buy the products that contribute to the total society's waste stream, the majority of the wastes, like the majority of the state's people, are not from rural areas.

Disposal of society's wastes, whether solid waste, incinerator ash, or radioactive wastes, is most likely to occur in areas that are not only rural but poor as well. Thus in 1989 the county in rural New York that had just won bottom place on the state's ranking of per capita income, Allegany County, was actively fighting off a radioactive waste dump, was facing a proposal for a regional incinerator-ash dump, and, at the

This cartoon originally appeared in the Cuba (New York) *Patriot and Free Press*. Reprinted by permission of Christina Arden-Hopkins.

same time, was lured by the prospect of jobs to press the state to bring it a prison, which, indeed, it was awarded in 1990. For the 50,000 residents of one of the state's poorest counties, with one of the smallest populations and weakest political representations, the events of 1989 epitomized the vulnerability of remote and less affluent rural places to becoming redefined to meet the disposal needs of an urbanized society. "We were picked," stated an antidump activist, "precisely because we're poor, rural, and have no clout in the legislature."

PART EIGHT

Rural Identity and Survival

CHAPTER SIXTEEN

What Then Is Rural?
Challenges to Rural
and Community Identity

During the 1980s it has become less clear what rural really means and what the rural community is. As the pace of farm failures and farm consolidations quickened, residents of rural communities expressed a sense that what was happening was not only the loss of individual farms but the loss of farming as the basis of their own social and ideological identity. Similarly, the closing of a prominent local factory or the construction of a new residential or vacation-home development also had the effect of calling people's attention to their community. In a more dramatic way, discovering toxic contamination of a water supply or deciding whether to seek a prison or fighting off a radioactive waste dump commanded local attention and focused it on feelings about the nature of rural life and rural community. Each of these incidents and issues has served as a stage on which residents openly acted out their implicit assumptions about space and place, about the way life ought to be. Played out on each stage is a dramatization of incredible richness for the anthropological researcher: People repeat time-honored phrases and try to make sense of new dilemmas and competing views of the future. The issues are presented through spoken lines and suggestive props and backdrops, but much of the interpretation is left to the observer.

A dominant emerging theme in these local dramas has been identity—"who and what we are"—phrased both as statement and as question. People have recently been pensive and unusually verbal about feelings that are generally not discussed because everyone knows them. They grope for words to talk about topics that are hardly even discussable because there are few words that adequately express people's assumptions about their rural communities. As residents of New York's rural communities expressed their questions and musings, they were giving voice to feelings that are expressed in many small communities across the nation, picked up in local press coverage, and occasionally reported and analyzed in the social science literature (Greenhouse 1986, 1988; Engel 1984, 1987). Although they may be surprised to hear it, rural New Yorkers are verbalizing concerns that are not unique to each separate community but are part of a pattern that is apparent all across the state's rural areas and in much of the rest of rural America as well.

The cumulative effects of the changes described throughout earlier chapters of this book have created a triple challenge to identity, calling into question each one of the three terms commonly joined in the phrase "rural community life." The age-old conceptualization of "rural" in terms of its being the polar opposite of urban was beginning to break down: With urban areas seeming no longer quite so distant or distinct, the concept of rural became ungrounded and vague. Gradually, also, "community" was challenged as a result of demographic and social changes that reached a level at which belief in the traditional images of a small cohesive community with a strong, clear identity were less tenable. Additionally, "rural life-style" or rural pattern of living was also undergoing significant change: Residents of rural places imported more mass-society patterns of employment, leisure, dressing, eating, and shopping; they grew increasingly subject to the influences of mass media— while at the same time the urban centers stepped up their level of exports, both human and material, to rural places.

By the end of the 1980s, some rural residents sensed and talked about a growing identity problem. In the new order, old meanings and referents of rural identity had become problematic. As the changes progressed and the gap between small-town, isolated, and agrarian images and the postagrarian realities grew more apparent, rural residents were left with a sense of uneasiness resulting from an unclear self-image. This lack of clarity, in turn, heightened people's anxiety about the changes.

RURAL DEFINED

Rural America's problem in defining who and what is rural may be growing particularly acute in the densely populated Northeast, where numerous metropolitan areas and smaller regional centers push outward into the countryside. If at the same time a number of farms are being squeezed out, the image problem becomes even more troublesome. But the definition problem is by no means confined to the rural Northeast, for "rural" is nowhere well defined, not even in a quintessentially rural place (whatever that may be: Montana? Idaho? South Dakota? Iowa? Texas? Mississippi?). The considerable diversity within rural America, even within one region or a single state, defies an easy definition of what rural means in the contemporary American context. About the only common generalization is that it is easier to say what a rural area is not than to say what it is. In the official definitions and the unofficial, "folk" or local definitions, rural is identified in terms of what it is not.

Official Definitions of Rural Places

The official definition assigned to rural America is a definition by exclusion: Essentially, that which is not metropolitan America is rural America. According to the U.S. Bureau of the Census, a "metropolitan statistical area" is a central city of at least 50,000 people or an urbanized area consisting of 50,000 or more people in a city (or cities) and the surrounding counties that are economically tied to it. "Nonmetropolitan" America is all that which is not included in such metropolitan statistical areas; whereas "rural" technically refers to "the population outside incorporated or unincorporated places with more than 2,500 people and/ or outside urbanized areas" (Fuguitt, Brown, and Beale 1989, p. 6). In general, however, "rural" is used interchangeably with "nonmetropolitan," and all the United States is thus divided into "metropolitan" and "nonmetropolitan," or "metro" and "nonmetro." Rural America, then, is officially just a residual from urban or metropolitan, leaving it less than clear what rural really is. The very existence of a rural America is thus contingent upon an urban America.

The lack of clarity in the official definition of rural is further compounded by the currency of still other, slightly differing official definitions, such as those used by the Office of Management and Budget, the Farmers' Home Administration, and the Department of Housing and Urban Development, several of which define rural somewhat differently from the U. S. Department of Agriculture. Then, too, states delineate their own rural areas and count their rural populations according to their own definitions. In New York the legislature has designated forty-four counties, out of the total of sixty-two, as rural counties. The 3 million people who live in these rural counties compose 17 percent of the state's population. However, according to the federal Census Bureau definition, only 9.5 percent of New Yorkers are rural. Thus, differences between federal and state definitions leave 1.3 million people and many localities in limbo, either rural or not rural, depending on which official designation is being used at the moment.

Defining rural only in demographic terms and only as a residual category has real drawbacks for knowing what rural really is and has real consequences for rural people. The population designated as rural can be made to shrink just by choosing or inventing a different definition, or just by allowing more smaller urbanized areas to join the expanded definition of metropolitan statistical areas (Beale 1984). When a rural population shrinks—on paper—as a result of such reclassification, just as much as if residents actually moved away, rural communities lose programs, funding, and political representation. As a rural New York publication stated, "Counties outside MSAs [Metropolitan Statistical Areas] . . . are labeled 'non-metropolitan' and they qualify for . . . a nondescript second-class status as though they hardly exist" (*Rural Futures*, January 1989, p. 1). To define a group of people in terms of what they are not is a nondefinition, an invidious definition, an opening for all sorts of disparaging comparisons (Gearing 1970). It is possible to think that the prevailing forms of definition might be otherwise. We could consider starting with rural America, for historically America was first rural: By this approach, all the rest of the population would become "nonrural people," which would relegate them to residual status, almost

"Remember when they used to send us poverty programs! . . . "

Doug Marlette

Reprinted by permission of Doug Marlette.

as nonpeople. But because more than three-quarters of the nation's population is now urban or suburban and because there is really no single definition around which the diverse millions of rural Americans could coalesce, rural America continues to be a residual category.

The problem with such evasive official definitions is that rural America is also treated as a residual place. Rural America, the residual space of the nation, is increasingly becoming the place for the minor and low-paid manufacturing enterprises, for the prisons, the landfills, incinerator ash, and nuclear waste. The "rural as residue" problem hurts rural places, then, not just in the funding that they don't receive but also in the "goods" that they are asked to accept.

"Folk" Definitions of Rural

In much of rural New York, farming remains the basis for residents' conceptualization of their ruralness. Even if most residents are not commercial farmers or don't even know a commercial farmer, farming holds a major importance in the physical and social landscapes that surround their lives. Thus, as we saw earlier, the dairy farm crisis loomed large in those areas where many farms went out of business. The loss of specific farms, even if agriculture as a whole survived, threatened a basic plank in local collective identity. Future farm losses may further erode rural identity and self-image. The demise of small farms and consolidation into large farms will mean not only fewer farms but a diminished visibility and social presence of farming in rural areas. Increasingly, the cows will not be distributed in pastures all over the landscape; they'll be concentrated in a few places only. Furthermore, although there may still be as many cows, perhaps even more cows, they'll not be as visible because of changes in farm practices: In the more modern and larger operations cows are often kept inside or close to "loafing barns" and "milking parlors" and are rarely out in pastures where they could reassure rural residents of their own rurality.

Residents of rural areas cling to agriculture as a basis of identity, even where farming has declined, in part because other components of the "folk" definitions they use to claim their ruralness have recently become more vague. Although people are "sure" that they *are* "rural residents," that they *live in* a "rural place," and that they *lead* a "rural life-style," they are less certain that they can define what "rural" means in these instances. Two important components of the folk definition of rural include, on the one hand, "a high quality of life" and, on the other, a set of "sacrifices" and "difficulties" that mean that "you have to live with less." What people mean by that is not really a contradiction, however, as quality of life is nonmaterial, whereas standard of living is material. Another component of ruralness is the speed of life—or, rather, lack of speed: "It's a little slower way of life." All three of these components are undergoing change.

The folk conceptualization of what it means to be rural is most clear when juxtaposed against its presumed opposite, "the city." Defining rural by opposition to urban, a dualistic conceptualization that parallels closely the nature of official definitions, has long provided basic assumptions upon which to build a sureness about what is rural. In the traditional rural ideology that poses rural and urban as paired opposites, there is also a moral ranking, in which rural equals good and urban stands for evil. Rural residents have thus been provided with a simple mechanism for categorizing and judging themselves and others. The loss of this traditional dichotomous scheme is a direct result of the movement of ideas, behavioral patterns, people, and goods between urban areas and rural areas. Though in many places fewer people migrate from urban places to rural than from rural to urban, the balance of ideas, goods, and behavior may be a net *in*flow to rural communities. As the boundary between rural and nonrural becomes more permeable and permeated, the binary opposition becomes fuzzy, and the concept of rural loses some of its clarity and its symbolic effectiveness.

As the city-versus-country dichotomy has become less tenable, it has been somewhat revised in some people's thinking, moving toward a continuum model in which there now is something between rural and urban; there is suburban. By inserting this middle band into the continuum, the rural identity and "goodness" vis-à-vis the city stands intact because suburban is distinct from city, assigned a more neutral valence, and not defined as evil. By this new construction, if patterns of living of rural people come to resemble those of people in suburban areas, it does not cause rural residents to question their own goodness or the goodness of rural living. This change from a dualistic system of opposites to a conceptual continuum also allows the concept of rural to slide toward the middle a bit: "Traditional rural" may be out at one end of the continuum, but there is also room for a "modern rural" somewhat in from the end, somewhat closer to the suburban range. A few people are beginning to question openly whether indeed "rural" is an appropriate self-definition any more. One small-town resident thoughtfully pondered, "Maybe we should stop thinking of ourselves as rural. Sure, there are still wide-open areas and woodlands. But we are not a rural psyche like my grandparents, who have spent all their lives here. Most of us, even if we've grown up here, are rural in name only. Maybe we have more of a suburban mentality."

Many small-town and even open-country residents are aware of the diminished distinctiveness of their daily lives. One person remarked, "We live in the country, but I'm not sure you could call us rural people." They eat in fast-food restaurants, wear designer running shoes as they jog along country roads, spend Friday nights shopping in the mall, watch the same network TV programs and rented videos, and commute out to work. But they still identify themselves as living in and "being from" a different kind of place, a rural place.

LAND AS THE SPATIAL BASIS
OF RURAL IDENTITY

People who identify themselves as rural are often quite happy to engage in conversation about the landscape that surrounds them. Residents of rural New York can wax poetic in their descriptions of the mountain scenery, the beautiful sunrises, the open spaces, the river edged in ice, the cows grazing in pastures or deer running through woods. Moving from describing specific landscapes to making general statements, people invoke words such as "peaceful," "pristine," "natural," and "unspoiled"; thus, description of the physical landscape elides into a statement of socially valued attributes of the space in which they live.

The land that makes up rural space includes not only one's privately owned land but the entire landscape that surrounds people, including land owned by neighbors, by the farmer across the valley, and by the state, whether a few thousands acres in a state reforestation area or 6 million acres in the Adirondack Park. The hills and valleys, the streams and lakes, the fields and woods, are all part of what residents see every day, what children ride through on the school bus, what adults drive through on their way to work or shop, and what they think of as "the place where I live." The landscape is a constant space in which people operate, a backdrop against which the activities of daily living are carried out, a space that is both setting and symbol of rural life. And this space has the power to modify activities that take place within it, to transform essentially mass-society activities and objects into "rural life."

The land is also the space in which social relationships are grounded: It is inhabited not just by individual people but by families and groups of related families, and by people tied together as neighbors in the same village or hamlet, in the same valley or along the same road. The spatial "surround" is held together by marriages and sibling bonds, by ties to cousins and grandparents; and these social relationships, in turn, are anchored in the land. An overgrown hillside pasture is still known locally as part of "the Northrup place" long after no Northrups live there. Local roads and rural cemetery markers bear local family names. The space as a whole, as well as each individual parcel of land, has a social history known and referenced by local people, and the very term "locals" or "local people" is a way of affixing people in relationship to space.

Rural land is also the space in which certain activities with particular sociocultural importance take place. For example, deer hunting, though it provides a seasonal tourist boom, is above all a local cultural activity rooted in rural space. "Deer season" is an annual ritual, part of the annual cycle of seasons and events, that helps proclaim "who we are" and "what we do here" and that defines "the kind of life we lead in this rural county." Deer hunting is also a male ritual, a rite of passage promoting boys into manhood, though many women hunt, too. The first day of deer season is surrounded by anticipatory social events, opening-day breakfasts, and community camaraderie; it is an undeclared holiday from work and an undeclared social competition, with the trophy hung on display in the front yard. As such, deer hunting is an activity that proclaims and reaffirms the relationship of people and land.

Even land that is not being actively used for commercial agriculture or forestry production, including the thousands of acres of abandoned fields and of scrub-forested hills, plays an active role in the social and symbolic construction of rural life. The low population density and limited economic contribution of these lands is perceived not as a negative trait but a positive one. Residents see not an absence of people and production but an absence of crowding and exploitation. Residents consider their overgrown land amply inhabited by the few people who live on it, and by the deer, wild turkeys, beavers, and other species. In the rural lexicon, this land is neither "unused" nor "underdeveloped," but simply "undeveloped," and in rural values "undeveloped" is the way it ought to be.

For generations, farmland and forest together have provided a buffer space for local residents, a buffer that was not only physical but also ideological, protecting the good life (meaning rural life) from the influences of evil (the city). As one resident said, "Our rural lands have protected us, kept us safe from all the things we didn't like and don't want, giving us isolation from the cities, an opportunity to live life as we wanted to and at our own pace." In the current period of change, the ability of rural space to serve this buffering function is no longer certain. The land is still there in the physical sense, and the landscape is still there, with the scenery not yet changed all that much in most areas of rural New York. In many areas, in fact, the landscape has actually become more "wild" and "natural" as more marginal farmland regenerates into brush and forest. Additionally, the state's protection on lands it holds, combined with the "wilderness" preferences of vacation-cabin owners who hide their man-made constructions deep within the woods, helps retard visible alteration of the landscape. In other places, though, the landscape is changing and the changes are obvious: Individual houses and major housing developments stand prominently in former pastures; large landfills gouge the curve of a hillside; and malls, factories, or prisons intrude where cows once grazed. The buffer is being nibbled away—and just when its necessity is more keenly felt. As the city-country separation is increasingly breached and rural people's patterns of living become less distinct, the land itself may become even more cherished as necessary to supporting a separate rural identity.

These symbolic meanings augment the environmental and health concerns underlying efforts to protect rural lands. For local residents, the threat of dumps and landfills represents a double pollution: Not only the possibility of chemical or radioactive pollution but also a symbolic pollution in terms of contaminating something that residents hold sacred, the space that defines them, with objects that are clearly both profane and polluting. Though residents do not put this anthropological interpretation on what is happening, their comments and actions reveal a diffuse, unverbalized sense of defilement of a special space, and hence of self.

The symbolic function of rural space in supporting rural identity also explains why rural residents are troubled by seeing the pastures and woodlands sold and parceled out among people they do not know. As long as the vacation homes in the hills are not particularly visible, and as long as local people still have access to most of their surrounding lands for hiking, hunting, or watching birds and deer, then the "wild" terrain may still be considered "public" space. But at some point the growing number of "POSTED" signs appearing on tree trunks around the perimeter of many newly purchased parcels breaks through the barrier of local consciousness. The signs are not only orange squares that proclaim that no hunting is allowed: Their deeper effect is to force the realization that local people have lost some of their communal setting, the space that protects and defines them. Even though many individual rural residents have themselves been the willing sellers of separate parcels of land, at the aggregate level of community the symbolic effect is that some of the collective space—"our space"—no longer serves the common good. In a sense, this is a version of the "tragedy of the commons" (Hardin 1968), in which the individual benefits from the sale of land, but the cumulative effect of land sales by a number of individuals is damaging to the interests of the commonweal—and hence damaging to each individual. A lifelong North Country resident commented thoughtfully, "We have always been so isolated, so protected. Maybe we have become selfish, but we'd like to keep the mountains to ourselves."

COMMUNITY AS THE SOCIAL/SYMBOLIC BASIS OF RURAL IDENTITY

Social scientists have researched, written, and debated for decades about what the terms "community" and "rural community" mean, but the people who live in rural places have generally not had much trouble understanding that they do in fact live in and belong to a community. If they cannot satisfactorily define what they mean by community, they nonetheless go about their business believing in its existence and certain of their own social existence within it. In a sense, without being told that they should, they do just what the social scientists say they do: "People construct community symbolically, making it a resource and repository of meaning, a referent of their identity" (Cohen 1985, p. 118). In terms of locality, the rural community can be variously determined to be a small hamlet, a village or small city, an open-country neighborhood, or even an entire county; but the social community may or may not be coterminous. However, the deeper meaning of community, while locality-connected, is of the mind: the ideational or symbolic sense of community, of belonging not only *to* a place but *in* its institutions and *with* its people.

Not being troubled by imprecise definitions, rural residents can and do talk about and describe their communities. Physical boundaries, political jurisdictions, as well as the various institutions of production-distribution-consumption, socialization, social control, social participation, and mutual support (Warren 1963, pp. 9–10) may all be alluded to or included. The primary descriptors, however, are the qualities or characteristics that people attribute to their communities. Rural communities are presumed by their members to have individual identities, each different from the next. Uniqueness is an article of faith, an untested assumption, in fact, an assumption that should not be questioned or tested. The ingredients of uniqueness are not always clear, yet people just "know" that their community is unique. A common expression of the uniqueness assumption is the phrase "We're different here," although usually there is no comparative reference point cited and little specification of what the difference might be.

Invidious comparison with other communities is, in fact, essential to people's definition of their own, for in describing the negative characteristics of the other community, the positive character of one's own and the communal values "we" hold are revealed. Other places are often described as "too large" and "unfriendly." Conversely, among the attributes people most frequently mention about their community, qualities that need no measurement or proof in local minds, are that it is "small" and "friendly"; it is a place of knowing and being known. These qualities reflect enduring rural values, captured in the mid-1950s in the classic "Springdale" study (Vidich and Bensman 1958, pp. 30–37) and revealed in most rural community studies since then (Engel 1984, Greenhouse 1986). An elderly man, a lifelong resident of a small upstate New York village put it this way: "Everybody knows everybody here. They speak when they're on the street—they say 'good morning' and they mean it."

Another important plank in the collective representation is closely related: The rural community is an egalitarian place where "we're all the same here" and "we're all ordinary people here, just common folk, each of us pretty much the same as everyone else." This, too, is an old and widespread conceptualization reported in most classic studies of rural communities (MacLeish and Young 1942, West 1945, Vidich and Bensman 1958), and it still undergirds communities in rural New York, even where significant socioeconomic differences exist. If some people are poorer than the rest of the community, they are usually explained as aberrations, individuals who have "fallen on hard times," and they may be assisted by networks of neighbors and church "to get back on their feet," or they may be left to manage on their own as best they can with their dignity and pride intact. Or, as frequently happens, they are assigned to a group that is conceptually placed outside the social structure, thereby allowing the basic conceptualization that "everybody is equal" to stand unquestioned.

Yet another plank in local identity is the connection between community and family, often expressed as "this community is a family place." Actually, this conceptualization has two somewhat different meanings. First, the community is a place for and of families, a place with "a healthy family atmosphere." Second, the community is seen as composed of families, as an aggregate of its constituent families. Community, thus, is the projection of the family order into the next level of social organization, or the family writ large: "We're all family here," "This community is like my family to me," and "This place is one big family." Although "family" in these phrases often means nuclear family, it also has a broader reference to "relatives," and includes one's "own relatives" and also one's "in-laws," which in turn may include the relatives of one's immediate in-laws. This extended sense of family is commonly phrased as "everyone here is related to almost everyone else," and "we're all related here" (see Bryant 1981). Even a full-grown adult is known as "the neighbor's kid, son of so-and-so and what's his name's cousin." Even a person not born in the community can nonetheless be *of* the community if he or she "has relatives here." The extended family ties are both known and acted upon, connecting political leaders to each other and to the farm or business "community," connecting children in school, prompting networks of telephone conversations, and enacted every weekend in the clusters of "family" people who go to a regional shopping mall together and in holiday meals and individual birthdays, graduations, anniversaries, and funerals.

Another aspect of the credo of rural community is that it is a chosen place. If the predominant population trend for a century may have been an exodus, from the point of view of residents who remain in small towns, their present location represents a decision not to leave but to stay. They have chosen to remain even though others left or have chosen to return after sampling life elsewhere or have chosen to come here from elsewhere. And they claim that more would have chosen to stay had there been jobs available that would effectively utilize their education. And so the collective representation of a chosen place remains intact despite loss of many members. As people quickly add, the choice is not without penalties, in that good jobs are scarce, salaries are low, the general standard of living is lower, movie theaters are few, distance to specialized medical facilities is greater, and in some ways "life is just a little harder." But it is their choice. "People in this area make sacrifices," said one small-town resident who had returned home from several years of a high-paid job in a big city. "But for the most part, they do so because they choose to be here." Another resident affirmed, "I have lived here for thirty years [the speaker's entire life] and have watched my friends and family move away. I have chosen to stay."

Yet another touchstone of community is security, the security of a known and stable social surround and the security of physical safety within it. This is most commonly expressed in the stock sentence, "This is the kind of place where you never have to lock your doors." This sense of physical security also has its symbolic aspect: The remark refers not only to unlocked doors but also to the *kind of place where* locking is unnecessary. In villages and small cities in all regions of rural New York, never locking one's doors is less a statement about behavior than about what it means to live in a rural community.

CHANGES IN RURAL REALITIES; CHALLENGES TO COMMUNITY IDENTITY

But change has come to many rural communities, causing a divergence between reality and ideology and forcing an adjustment in conceptualization of the community. To the above aphorism about not locking doors, many people add an update: "Well, we *didn't use to* have to lock our doors." One person lamented, "I have to lock my doors at night now. And *even the church* has to lock its doors now." The perceived necessity of locking house doors, barn doors, car doors, and locking

churches and tractors, too, seems to be a turning point in local consciousness, its full impact only understandable in the context of people's
earlier definition of their community as the kind of place where locking
was unnecessary and almost unsocial. The locked door now stands as
symptom and symbol of a disturbing change that has come to rural
communities, a loss of both physical and social security, a deterioration
not only in actual behavior but also in the conceptualization of the
rural community.

Part of that disturbing change, people now realize, is that actually
they do *not* know everyone they see on the streets of the town, nor
even every family along their county roads, and, what is worse, not all
of the residents know or even recognize them. In some communities
more than others, the socially integrated face-to-face community where
"everybody knows everybody" is no longer operable as a description
of or guide to the present, although it is still held as a description of
"the way it used to be here."

When the gap between traditional assumptions and current social
realities can no longer be denied, one strategy for keeping intact the
collective vision of the community as a close-knit, homogeneous place
is to compartmentalize local residents (Greenhouse 1986, p. 131). Unknown or unfamiliar people are lumped into generic social types under
terms that essentially keep them separated from "bona fide members"
of the community. Year-round residents who have recently purchased
village homes or moved into new housing tracts are termed "newcomers";
vacation people are called "outsiders"; and low-income renters in the
apartments and trailer parks are referred to as "transients," or sometimes
"foreigners." Although the valuation attached to these categories is a
gradation downward, all of the people thus categorized are externalized
rather that folded into the community. Residing within the locality, they
are nonetheless conceptually marginalized and kept as social nonmembers.
Labeled as "outsiders" or "transients," or even as "newcomers," their
presence becomes less of a challenge to traditional assumptions and
identity.

The distancing of unwanted or unfamiliar "elements" within the local
population allows longer-term residents to continue making their traditional claim that everyone in the community knows everyone—for the
unknown people have been defined out of the social community. The
mechanism of distancing also provides a reason not to feel obligated to
get to know the unknown people who live within the physical borders
of the community. As a class, "newcomers" may be kept at bay for
years or decades, usually to their consternation and dismay, even though
as individuals they may be cordially received. As a class, "outsiders"
may receive rather unfriendly treatment, and "transients" may be written
off as not likely to stay and therefore not a population with which one
invests time or social interaction. By these distancing mechanisms, no
changes are called for in community social behavior or community

institutions. The distancing of unknown populations also sets up the framework for scapegoating. Unwanted changes and unwanted items entering the community can be blamed on these externalized populations: "It's the newcomers that are changing this place." "The drugs are coming in here because of all the people moving in from the city." Even having to lock the doors now is routinely blamed on these distanced populations.

Externalization of unknown residents is also a mechanism for dealing with the growing perception that the wealth distribution no longer matches, if it ever did, the egalitarian ideology that "we're all the same here." The wealth—or lack of it—of newer residents is a topic of considerable interest to community residents. Long-time residents cite the lines of people whom they don't know standing at the post office to pick up food stamps on the first of the month. They also gasp and gossip about the very expensive houses some new residents are building. New residents are generally thought to have significantly less or more wealth than the "average people" who live in the community, a supposition that may or may not be correct. "Locals" can maintain their belief in an egalitarian community, however, because they assign these people at the lower and upper ends of the economic spectrum to the category of nonmembers of the community.

Significant society-wide changes in family patterns and household configurations pose yet another challenge to the collective perception of the rural community, to its essence as "a family place." Especially in communities closer to urbanized areas, growing numbers of households are not composed of standard nuclear families. Couples with no children, unmarried couples, and single women, whether without or with children, do not constitute a family in the traditional sense that many rural people still use that term. Furthermore, there are now more "people without family," meaning those who have no local relatives and who therefore "have to go out of town to see their family." When a significant number of households in a village is made up of people not locally recognized as constituting "families" or not embedded in extended families, it causes confusion in local minds (see also Greenhouse 1988, p. 694), and it challenges identity precisely because the community has, in the past, defined itself as "a family place."

Loss or alteration of some of the economically productive aspects of the community has also taken its toll on community identity. Until recently, many small villages had been centers of a farming hinterland, where the feed mill and implement dealer as well as the town hall, a church, and a main-street cafe were in-gathering places for farmers and where farm operators and village businesses enacted their mutual interdependence. Such a village could define its own identity in terms of farming. But now, many villages have become decoupled from local farming, in part because of loss of their agriculture-related businesses. As surrounding farm people begin to reorient toward a larger town, where they deal with merchants, take out bank loans, and attend field days, an agrarian identity for the small village becomes less tenable.

In similar ways major changes in rural manufacturing have also taken a toll on rural identity. Many communities were dominated by one or two factories, where many local residents worked, and where their parents before them had worked. This was the factory whose employees ate in the local diner on payday, the factory whose softball teams were featured in the summer championships, the factory whose whistle marked time for all village residents, not only employees. Local people knew and often boasted about the product made in "our plant" and everyone knew someone who worked there. With the shutdown of a large factory that had been at the center of the local economy, the social community, too, suffers a loss of cohesive identity. The several small replacement firms that may rent space in the old main-street building are each owned and managed by different corporations, each runs different shifts, makes different products or parts of products, and has a different, unfamiliar name. Where there had been one factory, there are now several, none of them large enough, strong enough, or permanent enough to form a basis of community identity.

To some extent and in some places, people in rural communities have themselves been the instigators of their own growth and their growing internal differences. As part of the strategy by which some rural communities have attempted to survive economically, to provide jobs for their residents, to keep their young people home, and to increase business activity for their shops and children for their classrooms, some rural communities in virtually every region of rural America have sought— not fought—an economic development scheme that, once in place, brought with it a snowballing of social changes within the community. Whether a Japanese automobile factory coming into central Kentucky (Kingsolver 1989 and forthcoming) or a large manufacturing plant owned by a multinational corporation moving into a rural Illinois town (Engel 1984, 1987), these large-scale economic enterprises were actively sought and happily won in these job-hungry rural places. But they brought with them significant and unanticipated changes in the local community, not only a marked increase in people, houses, and traffic, but a serious challenge to the assumptions of unity, homogeneity, and equality. Within rural New York in recent years, very few communities have been successful in "courting" large factories through their "smokestack-chasing" missions, and this strategy has been somewhat discredited. But other strategies for economic survival have been actively pursued by the leaders of many rural communities, for example, selling off major pieces of real estate for housing or recreational development, pressing for expansion of the military base, and campaigning to get a new state prison. In each case, the leadership and at least some segments of the general public felt that a major facility was necessary for economic survival and lobbied actively to aquire it. But in each case, too, the facility brought with it a demographic and social change that forced an identity change on the rural community.

UPDATING COMMUNITY IDEOLOGY AND IMAGE

These feelings and fears, surfacing in many phrases and conversations, in exhibits at a county fair, in letters to the newspaper, in public meetings, and in social interaction patterns, all indicate that the identity of rural communities is itself undergoing change.

The Present Distorting the Past, and the Past Distorting the Present

Living in a period of rapid change makes the past appear stable and unchanging by contrast. Seeing new and unfamiliar people on the sidewalk or in the supermarket now makes long-time residents believe that in the past everyone knew everyone. The presence of unfamiliar people is thus classified as a new phenomenon and, because of its presumed newness, unwelcome. Similarly, the complication of dealing with a new environmental problem, such as groundwater pollution, makes the past seem both simple and pure: Residents in communities with contamination problems talk about their precontamination community as an idyllic place, an ideal, flawless place, "It was a beautiful place to live, a beautiful community."

Conversely, these images of the past distort perception of the present. The image of the past as stable, unchanging, and pristine makes the present seem unsettled, dramatically changing, and polluted beyond all hope. Although the presumed unity and equality that are thought to have characterized the past may actually have hidden some dissension and inequality, believing in these characterizations makes the present social reality seem not only "new" and "unprecedented" but "wrong."

This mutual shaping of past and present perceptions is not merely a quaint rural custom or an idle cultural curiosity, however, for it has significant consequences as communities face and adapt to the changes that come their way. In some respects, the images of the past, if they are believed as still appropriate today, may make it harder for communities to come to terms with the present and future. In other respects, however, holding onto cherished identity and values may be the only way to enter the future with a claim to being distinctly rural and having a community identity. The problem, of course, is in knowing what to discard and what to keep, what to recategorize as the historical past and what to program into the community ideology of the future. Although rural residents do not want to become museum curiosities, many do want to preserve some of the differences they regard as their strengths. At the same time, they eagerly accept certain features of the modern mass society. Sometimes the making of these choices can become devisive within rural communities, and sometimes the choices that are made confound outside observers.

The Confusion of Form and Function

Effectively updating the rural community identity requires making a distinction between form and function, between outward physical appearances and underlying social meanings. Holding onto old forms simply because they are familiar, or rejecting new forms simply because they are unfamiliar, will not facilitate survival of either community operation or community identity. Rural places simply do not look the way they used to, and rural activities, too, have changed. For the most part, rural people have adjusted well. Most farmers, known more for pragmatism than romanticism, have long since relinquished the practice of shoveling manure or pitching hay by hand as new mechanisms came along to accomplish those chores. Rural schools have moved far from the image of the one-room schoolhouse with barefoot boys in the style of Winslow Homer running through the schoolyard: In today's rural schools, computer hookups and satellite receivers bring in specialized instructional material. In rural retailing, too, there are new forms, from drive-up automatic teller machines, to shopping malls, to franchised convenience marts, and these, too, have been embraced by rural people, even though they may be less personal and less picturesque.

But sometimes, a new form presents a community with inescapable evidence that it no longer has a totally unanimous opinion on just who constitutes "our community" or what constitutes "our rural way of life." Controversy has reached an acrimonious level in at least one village over a new form that some residents are eager to accept but others would like to have officially banned: a franchised convenience store on Main Street. Opponents, most of whom are relatively recent residents and have made their money elsewhere, object to the "visual pollution," the destruction of "this beautiful natural place of wildness," the "fake mansard roof" and factory-made architecture that does not "fit" with other buildings in the village. For long-term residents, on the other hand, this chain market has the lowest gas prices in the region, and gas prices win out over the desire for uniqueness. What is more, the place has become a new social gathering spot for them. According to a newspaper story, "The men come in for coffee in the morning. The ladies come in for lunch" (Halpern 1989). In this small community and in other rural towns scattered across rural New York, local people have quickly adapted the mini-mart form to fit their functional need for a community meeting place. News and gossip, warmth and a welcome are the social commodities available here. Even under a fake mansard roof mass produced in plastic in the late twentieth century, convenience stores serve as a modern-day functional equivalent of the old village general store. The ready acceptance of such an architectural aberration along the village streetscape and the willingness to suspend the traditional preference for not being like any other community do not mean, however, that residents in these communities have given up their rural heritage, that they don't value the scenery, or that they have no aesthetic sensibilities. Rather, they are trying to pick and choose their way in a changing world, modifying some of their time-honored preferences to meet their economic and social needs, adopting and adapting new forms to fit their own patterns, retaining rural meanings even while many of the patterns of their daily lives converge with the patterns of other people in other communities, nonrural as well as rural. In doing so, they will even accept some structures and land uses that are not especially scenic and that may be resisted by people who have been attracted to the community as a place to vacation, retire, or raise a family and who have their own ideas about protecting the scenery. As long-time residents welcome building or activities that newer residents consider visual pollution, it opens up controversy over the components of rural life and the interpretation of rural space. "Newcomers" may see the landscape primarily visually, as scenery; "local people" may perceive not only a visual but also a social landscape (Dubbink 1984, p. 415), with social ties coursing over the land. And although "old-timers" themselves are not entirely of one mind about development and not all pleased with what they get, in many instances "locals" favor development whereas "newcomers" oppose it. In any case, disputes over form, over aesthetic preferences, often involve deeper divisions over the meanings of rural life, and they may escalate to courtroom confrontations, becoming adversarial legal battles rather than local problems informally and locally resolved.

The Social Uses of Controversy

Controversy over a new retail facility runs in the same groove as controversy over growth (growth/slow growth/no growth) or whether or not to request a state prison. And like those controversies, it brings to conscious level the already existing but previously unspoken diversity within a community. It reveals that "we're *not* all the same here," and that what rural means depends on whom you ask. But acceptance of this diversity, quite apart from the particular development or growth issue that brought it to public awareness, is difficult for many rural communities. Open controversy within the community has traditionally been considered an unseemly denial of the way the community is supposed to be (Greenhouse 1986). If they could, leaders in many communities would totally avoid controversy within their ranks. In the traditional pattern of deliberation by local governing boards, no vote is actually taken until the chair is sure that the members have already reached sufficient consensus for a unanimous decision (Vidich and Bensman 1958, pp. 112–113), and in many local newspapers the editorial philosophy is not to publicize differences of opinion within the community but to reduce controversy (Kingsolver 1989, p. 11). Although there have probably always been disagreements within the community, they previously seemed small compared to the vast differences separating the rural community from the city. Now, as differences from "the outside other" are diminishing, differences *within* the rural community are growing to the point where they are undeniable and where many separate issues may develop into factionalized controversy that neither addresses the problem at hand nor builds community.

Overcoming traditional reluctance to acknowledge and accept internal differences of opinion could help communities select strategies for dealing with change. Willingness to admit and listen to controversy, in fact, may be one of the hallmarks of a rural community that will survive and adapt in a period of major change (Flora and Flora 1988, 1990). Differences of opinion concerning such matters as the physical appearance of buildings on Main Street, from historic structures to franchised fast-food look-alikes, will continue to surface. Disagreements and contests between farming interests and business or industrial interests, or between farmers and their nonfarm neighbors are likely to increase. Tight funding for local governments and schools, combined with reduced federal and state contributions, will surely provoke more controversies over what levels of service are desired and how to pay for them. Controversies are also apt to simmer over the balance in economic development, services, and political representation between the center and the periphery. For communities, it would be most healthy if such controversies could be openly discussed, with adherence to the issues rather than descent into individual animosities and group labeling, if they could be resolved informally rather than being turned over to the polarizing institutional path of lawyers and courts.

For addressing differences constructively, some communities already have a mechanism that could be put to greater community use. Local "community dispute resolution centers," where they exist, could expand from their present concentration on individual two-party disputes, such as marital, custody, consumer, and landlord-tenant disputes, to facilitating resolution of collective issues facing the community. At present, the only "community" aspect of most such centers is that they are located in, connected to, and sponsored by the locality. With added emphasis on *community*, however, existing and newly formed community dispute resolution centers could do much more to facilitate open discussion and debate. Dispute resolution processes that help people clarify and compromise would have a great deal to offer in getting residents to look at the substance of the issues that divide them, rather than conceptualizing local controversies in terms of individual personalities or social categories such as "locals versus newcomers," or "farmers versus businesspeople." A starting point is the knowledge, based on social science research, that "natives" and "newcomers" may not differ from each other as much as each group believes (Allen 1990). The resolution process could clarify the values people place on protection of their landscape and could mediate differences between people who want to look at "unspoiled scenery" and those wanting to sell their timber or those willing to accept plastic mansard roofs if the gas out front is cheap. Community dispute resolution could be helpful in issues surrounding village infrastructure, such as whether to replace an outdated public water system, a question that will become more common as these systems age further and as there are more residents using them. But addressing infrastructure problems will have to be done in the context of addressing the social structure weaknesses as well. Polarization among factions based on residential longevity will impede effective approaches to solving the pressing issues of the future.

Renegotiating a Rural Identity

A strong and positive identity can be a crucial ingredient in community survival. Nostalgia, however, will not suffice, and some of the attributes that traditionally anchored the identity of a community may have to be altered to reflect recent change and modern realities. If people believe that old-fashioned forms are the equivalent of rurality and rural identity, then adaptation to modern technological, economic, social, and political realities will be more difficult. The rural image needs to be modernized, in part so that people can sort out the differences between the real threats that loom and the spurious threats that are actually no more than threats to an outdated self-image.

The agrarian self-image, expressed as "This is an agricultural community," has been shown to be a somewhat vague basis for local identity in a period when agriculture is undergoing considerable change and in places where more farms are being lost. Nonetheless, agriculture is still vitally important economically, socially, and especially culturally, and it can still provide a substantial foundation as part of a larger composite rural identity. To update the agricultural identity and make it more effective than just a romantic, past-oriented nostalgia, it would be helpful if more rural residents were better acquainted with the contemporary local agriculture that does still exist. If the only interaction local residents have with agriculture is through Holstein cows they purchase on shirts, ash trays, and plywood yard ornaments, then real agriculture remains remote and hardly suffices as a basis for local identity. Even simple activities such as field trips to local farms could enhance residents' awareness of life on a dairy farm, crop farm, or orchard, and of the contribution farming makes to the local economy. Some agricultural leaders have attempted to utilize the county fair to reemphasize agriculture, raising its visibility above the honkey-tonk, flea-market aspect of the midway. In a more lasting vein, local identification with agriculture could be promoted through more encouragement of part-time and backyard farming. Taking hobby farmers seriously might work to the advantage not only of local agribusinesses but the community as a whole, in that farming could play more of an integrating role if more people at least have a small-scale sampling of what it is like. Providing an encouraging climate for hobby farmers would also serve to attract to the community more people who value some of the same rural attributes, including agriculture, that long-time residents do.

Similarly, although fewer of the old dominant manufacturing plants still exist to provide a collective image of a place and its product, more effort could be devoted to increasing a public sense of relationship to remaining factories. Management could be encouraged to facilitate community identity for the firm and to participate more in local affairs. Perhaps the signboard out front that identifies the plant as a division of such-and-such multinational corporation could also bear the name of the community.

Names may be a small issue, but for building community identity, such handles are important. Keeping the community name up front could help; some communities are now proudly erecting new signs at the village limits, individually designed and proclaiming who they are, when they were incorporated, how many residents they have, or whatever they want travelers to know. Names for new institutions could be more carefully selected. When two schools merge, children of two former identifiable school districts may end up attending a consolidated school with a generic name such as Valley Central School, unconnected to either local community, and they are thus deprived of any sense of place. On the other hand, when a prison or a radioactive dump comes to town, quite often the locality's own name is given to this new facility, which some residents consider a degradation of both their name and their community identity (Carlson 1986, p. 22). Boosterism has its limitations, of course, but coalescing around a shared and named identity can help hold people's attention. Community pride can translate into community action, and community action into solid institutions to sustain member individuals as they cope with future social and economic changes. Conversely, communities with no clear image may more easily sink into a negative, defeatist attitude, become fixated on the status quo ante, and develop an exaggerated fear of change. Such places will be less likely to adapt and survive.

Some rural communities, especially small ones, will be able to accommodate change only by giving up enough of their perceived uniqueness and separateness to be willing to learn from and cooperate with other nearby municipalities. Some will be innovative in creating such opportunities, as has been demonstrated by many instances of pooling professional expertise, joint purchasing, and cooperation in planning for service delivery or water and wastewater system improvements. Such communities discover that intermunicipal cooperation need not be a threat to community identity, although negotiated cooperation among municipalities must protect the interests of the smaller ones.

Local identity can be sharpened through open forums on community goals, such as have recently been sponsored by many individual communities and by regional groups in the Adirondack and Tug Hill areas. Another method of taking stock is through community surveys and self-studies, often conducted in conjunction with open public discussions. These are useful mechanisms for getting people to think about what their rural place means to them, what they feel are its strengths and its weaknesses, and what kinds of futures they envision. The process of conducting a "community needs assessment" contributes to a heightened sense of community and of the bonds among people and institutions that convert their physical space into a social place.

Residents can clarify and become more aware of a community identity through action. In working together to build a community playground and to put on a community day, residents of one village not only created a play space and organized parades, they also reminded themselves that they live in a small community, and rediscovered why they do. In such cases, the latent functions of building community identity, spirit, and awareness may be as valuable as the products created or activities produced. Surely this is a lesson from Allegany County as it has tried to fend off a radioactive waste facility. In the protest movement, Allegany was transformed from a loose collection of towns and villages sharing a reputation and self-image as one of the poorest places in the state to a cohesive county with a strident image. "Allegany's fight against LLRW" gained widespread attention, which in turn fostered a sense of pride and potential. If this dynamism could become harnessed toward a positive effort to gain something the community wants for its future, it could be extremely effective.

Negotiating a firmer, current identity that is better matched with present-day economic, demographic, and social realities can help communities adjust to and benefit from, rather than be engulfed in and swallowed by, this era of change in rural America.

CHAPTER SEVENTEEN
Ensuring the Survival
of Rural Places

The changes that took place in rural New York in the late 1980s all occurred at about the same time; they interacted with each other; and they affected not only individuals but also communities. Virtually no region in rural America will remain insulated from the combined effect of similar economic, demographic, and social changes, and in some places the effects will be profound (see Breimyer 1990). For rural places to endure economically and socially, local will and determination are necessary. In many cases these resources are already available and at work; in other places they need to be developed and nurtured. But local commitment and ingenuity will not be sufficient to ensure that rural places can endure. The broad-scale economic, social, and political forces behind the changes that endanger rural spaces are national, even international, in scope and thus beyond local control. The future of America's rural communities, then, demands national attention—and commitment.

FEDERAL AND STATE ROLES
IN ENDANGERING OR ENSURING SURVIVAL
OF RURAL COMMUNITIES

The general shift of funding for rural government, education, health care, and so forth from federal to state and to local revenues, primarily property taxes, reflects a series of separate federal and state decisions that, together, have had a cumulative and damaging effect on rural communities in the 1980s. Many rural government officials complain loudly about the way they are shortchanged by federal or state governments that "overmandate and underfund us." The money issue preempts most attention, especially because of the demise of federal revenue sharing and recent reductions in federal and state funding. However, there are other important facets of the relationship between rural localities and state and national government that also demand attention.

Limited Federal Recognition
of Rural Community Needs

The diversity among rural places and the nondefinition of "rural" makes it difficult to build a national constituency for rural issues or a national rural policy, and hard to defend federal spending for rural programs. The federal relationship to rural America is driven largely by the interests of production agriculture, as is indicated by the failure to establish a major governmental agency parallel to but outside of the U.S. Department of Agriculture (USDA) that would address rural community development issues and needs. In the absence of any other sense of what rural America is, it is widely assumed that rural and agriculture are synonymous and that, therefore, agricultural policy can stand in for rural policy. "Fixing the farm problem" is thought sufficient to take care of "the rural America problem."

The federal government has generally failed to perceive rural problems in their broader sense, beyond agriculture and beyond economic problems. It has not sufficiently realized that rural development must involve more than economic development. As former Secretary of Agriculture Bob Bergland has stated, "the revitalization of rural America must address social as well as economic concerns" (Bergland 1988, p. 32). Rural development, in its "community" sense, goes far beyond telecommunications systems or start-up loans for new entrepreneurial ventures, important as these are, to developing and enhancing the capacity of local social institutions, both formal and informal. Community development raises a community's ability to function in the multiple roles communities are supposed to perform for their residents, including adjustment to further societal change.

A number of specific federal policies cause or exacerbate problems in rural America. Federal health care reimbursement policies, deregulation of transportation, especially bus lines, and deregulation of banking all have the potential to erode further the quality of life in rural America. In locations where land development pressures are especially high, federal tax codes providing advantages for second homes give a bonus to developers and affluent outsiders while causing an artificially inflated pace of land development that leaves some rural places overwhelmed and some rural people "underhoused"—unable to afford a home in their own community.

Even those federal policies and programs that do address the non-agricultural aspects of rural America, however, quite often fail to address the special needs of small places. For example, although the Regulatory Flexibility Act of 1980 requires federal agencies to fit regulatory requirements to the scale of affected small governmental units, inappropriate regulations continue to pose a problem.

Some Recent Recognition at State Level

At the state level in New York, two recent creations, the Legislative Commission on Rural Resources and the Office of Rural Affairs in the executive branch have assumed an active role in coalescing rural concerns sufficiently to gain some political effectiveness, and thereby some legislative initiatives and access to funding not otherwise obtainable. The commission, for example, with its monthly publication, *Rural Futures*, serves as a clearinghouse and transmitter for information relevant to rural people and governments, as an educator of the state legislature, and as an overall advocate for rural New York. Pennsylvania has followed New York's example and set up the Center for Rural Pennsylvania to provide a focal point for rural policy development. On a smaller scale, seventeen rural counties of Pennsylvania are trying to wrest some political advantage by banding together into a Rural County Caucus. Through such mechanisms, states are becoming more aware of the special and different needs of rural communities, not just in agriculture but in many other spheres, including education, care of the elderly, and transportation.

Sometimes, however, the same hand that gives also takes away; the same government that fosters appropriate-level approaches in some activities may continue inappropriate regulations or programming in other activities. For example, although the New York State government is considering instituting income tax credits for volunteers in fire departments and rescue squads as a way to entice some badly needed volunteers into this service, the state Department of Labor and the federal Occupational Safety and Health Administration have adopted standards for uniforms and equipment that are beyond the funding capacity of many volunteer fire companies. In another example, both the state and federal governments operate some programs and provide some money to help rural people upgrade their substandard housing, but New York State has promulgated some housing requirements that add extra costs and may be inappropriate in most rural areas. New regulations restrict the use of used lumber in housing construction, require permits and inspections for alterations, and officially prohibit occupation of an unfinished house. Such regulations prevent rural residents from using their time-honored strategies of building and improving as they go along with whatever materials they can get, whenever they have the time. The resulting boost in the cash cost of rural housing is particularly difficult for lower-income people. Also in the housing sphere in New York, as in several other states from Maine and New Hampshire to Washington, new mechanisms are in place to help insulate trailer-park tenants from sudden displacement by market forces, giving them some legally protected tenancy rights. But the growing need for low-cost trailer-park space is itself partly a result of inadequate and insufficient federal and state activity in rural housing.

Some Negative Impacts of Governmental Inaction

Federal, state, and city *inaction in urban areas* can have a serious effect on rural communities. A particularly striking example of this is the impact that a shrinking supply of urban housing for low and moderate income people may have on some nearby rural areas. Very little new, low-cost rental housing was added in urban areas in the 1980s, and many metropolitan areas experienced a net loss due to upscaling and development. As metropolitan housing costs have escalated, more and more urban and suburban residents with limited incomes are turning to small towns to find housing they can afford. From the point of view of the receiving rural communities, however, becoming the solution to an unaddressed urban housing problem may pose a severe financial and social burden.

Rural communities that are becoming a safety valve for the cities are not receiving extra resources from the state or federal government to help them cope with the impact. If the state's low-income population is becoming more dispersed and more rural as a result of neglect of housing needs in the metropolitan areas, then, in the interests of equity and adequate services, funding formulas for the full range of educational and welfare programs, housing assistance, and other human service should be reexamined. Community services and the money to support them ought to follow people. Service-needy children who move with their parents to and among the inexpensive dwellings of a rural county should not be counted as this county's children, but as the children of the state of New York or of the nation. If families need subsidized day care so parents can work, if children need special education programs, or if they need coverage on AFDC or other programs, that programming, adequately funded, must be available wherever people with these needs are located. Thus, in addition to the long-proposed move to standardize welfare benefit levels nationwide, which would especially help rural poor residents in the South, it would seem necessary also to update the funding of public assistance in New York and a few other states by eliminating or adjusting the requirement of a local share, moving to a simple federal-state cost-sharing. Releasing local government from cost-sharing obligations in public assistance programs might also free up local social service departments to be more innovative and prevention-oriented in their work.

Dispersion of more poverty into rural areas and greater residential mobility of poor people within rural areas will require innovative responses in education, health care, and mental health, as well as basic public assistance. Traditional programs will fail to reach and serve a more mobile low-income population. One model that could be used is the state's migrant education programs for children of farmworkers, programs that provide educational assistance, expedite record transfers, and give the continuity of a personal tutor for the child as well as contacts and referrals for the family. These programs for migrant agricultural families should be copied and expanded to cover nonagricultural people of low income and high mobility as well.

The Penalty for Small Scale

Compared to urban problems, rural problems look so small that they attract neither public attention nor governmental commitment. For example, the numbers of cases of drug abuse, homelessness, or AIDS are much smaller in rural communities, and such problems are sometimes dismissed as negligible. But a problem that has only a small absolute incidence can be a major trouble spot in a small community. Just a dozen young adults unable to find and keep a place for themselves and their families to live is a big homeless population in a community of 200 families. Just a half dozen teenage pregnancies, although a minimal number in an urban high school, may represent a fifth of the girls in a senior class in a rural high school. And yet the small number of cases may work against obtaining funding to establish a special teen parents' program.

There is simply no way of getting around the fact that small and dispersed populations are costly to serve. However, continuation of the present dominance of the "cost-efficiency" model, on top of the "tyranny of numbers," will mean not only that the more rural populations will be more seriously underserved but also that the institutional potential of rural communities will be underutilized. If, on the other hand, extra outside funding is directed at providing adequate service to remote rural clients, pupils, and patients, rural institutions can use the funding effectively by modifying programs appropriately for dispersed populations. Fostering innovative service delivery in the rural periphery, including satellite and outreach services and creative patterns and hours of services, can help build or bolster community institutions as well as serve individuals.

When big, expensive solutions, funded by big, expensive grants, are the only solutions available, then small communities with smaller problems and smaller budgets are left out. For example, grants for community alcohol detoxification centers, for mental health programs for "at risk" teens, or for public sewer systems, are often too large in scale to fit the problems rural communities actually have. There have been some efforts to correct this bias against small communities and to help them cooperate with each other so that they can increase their chances for obtaining grants, but it remains an uphill battle for rural community governments and agencies to receive appropriate program support or to gain encouragement for developing their own solutions.

UTILIZING RURAL INITIATIVE, INSTITUTIONS, AND ENERGY

Putting the Scale Factor to Work and Resisting the Bigger-is-Better Ideology

The scale factor does also have its beneficial side. Many of the people who are active in their communities claim that one reason they are able to get results is the small size: The problems and projects they tackle are small, and they are working in a small community in which it is possible to spread information and assemble people. It is quite possible to round up a group of local leaders to meet at the coffee shop to plan strategy for a community improvement. It may also be easier to get things done in a small place because there is a base to start from, a commitment to community, and a network of relationships built over the years that still facilitates action.

Fostering Local Institutional Creativity and Community-building

Throughout these chapters, we have seen examples of individuals, groups, and institutions on the local level coming up with innovative strategies to carry out their obligations and missions in rural places. In some communities, networking among local institutions, including sharing of personnel and interaction of programs, has given local residents adequate services where otherwise there might be none. In a period of tight finances, there are many examples of pooling resources and clientele to make a sufficiently large program to gain funding or deliver services effectively. County Cooperative Extension staff can be especially effective in such endeavors because of their broad expertise in community development and because local Extension staff are apt to be well-connected in community networks. Trained Extension personnel can help a community's residents to consider options, form networks, and coalesce around the pursuit of common goals, from protecting groundwater supplies to organizing day care facilities. Community colleges and local schools can also be catalysts for local action.

Present problems in funding and delivering services in rural areas may bring renewed interest in a different approach to services, a community approach. Instead of concentrating only on serving the individual casualty cases caused by economic and social breakdown in rural communities, a community approach recognizes the problems that underlie the casualties and realizes that the economic deterioration that has plagued rural areas hurts not only individuals but community institutions as well. Policy and programs would, therefore, be directed at shoring up the community as a collectivity of institutions, so that the community itself can function more effectively to prevent and cushion the individual casualties. In "community-oriented social work," localism is favored over standardization, effectiveness is reinstated as a more important goal than efficiency, and the fragmentation, professionalization, and specialization of the more individually oriented social work is replaced by an approach that regards the members of the public and their informal social institutions as partners in a community enterprise (Martinez-Brawley 1989, 1990). In this approach, the process of designing and instituting a community-based service or program is considered as important as the product itself, for in meeting manifest needs, what happens along the way is the building or rebuilding of community.

From the community mental health field, too, there is a call for initiatives that treat the community itself, that foster community institutions as a means of providing a supportive social environment for individuals (e.g., Paulsen 1988, Wagenfeld 1988). As its first general conclusion, the National Action Commission on the Mental Health of Rural Americans affirmed that "the mental health problems of rural America affect not only individuals and families, but also entire communities—and the strain on the communities places further stress on the individuals who reside in them" (Bergland 1988, p. 32).

Also promising and closely related are community self-help approaches. The Tug Hill Commission (officially the Temporary State Commission on Tug Hill), facilitates community discussion of issues, helps communities come to decisions on desired futures, and through its circuit rider provides technical assistance for small governments in carrying out their required functions and applying for grants (see Dyballa, Raymond, and Hahn 1981). The state's Office of Local Government Services and the nonprofit Rensselaerville Institute also take an enabling role, providing information and some technical skills to enhance the capacity of local governments to tackle their own problems, which not only saves money and builds water or sewer systems but also builds community.

"OPTIONS" AND "FUTURES": ISSUES FOR SURVIVAL OF RURAL COMMUNITIES IN A CHANGED AND CHANGING WORLD

To borrow terms from the grain markets, many rural people are actively considering the kinds of investments and actions they should take today to bring desired returns in the future. The "options" and "futures" rural residents ponder and debate, however, are much broader than agricultural commodities, and with higher stakes even than the big dollars of the grain markets: The outcomes involve the survival and nature of their communities. To some extent this will require forging stronger economic and political linkages between rural hinterlands and urban centers (Harrison and Seib n.d.).

Crucial to the survival of rural communities, of course, is improved employment opportunities, either locally or within commuting distance. The critical need to raise the overall level of rural wages and incomes has been too lightly dismissed on the supposition that lower rural incomes, relative to metropolitan incomes, are offset by a correspondingly lower cost of living. In fact, while housing costs are lower in most rural areas, the difference is not large enough to offset the earnings differential, and the cost of other essentials such as utilities, transportation, food, clothing, and medical care is not significantly lower in rural than in metropolitan areas (Ghelfi 1988). Income improvement is therefore essential for individuals, families, and communities in general.

To improve rural incomes, more jobs and also better jobs are needed. Recent job growth in retail sales, tourism, and line work in some new assembly plants does fill an important niche in rural employment, allowing low-skill entry into the labor force, but it leaves workers' households financially poor and communities economically vulnerable. These weaknesses must be approached from two directions. First, there must be supplemental protection for the low-wage workers, such as extension of food stamps and child care assistance, and particularly health insurance. New York's recent extension of medicaid benefits to children under six in families earning incomes up to 33 percent above the poverty line will help, as will a new state-subsidized health insurance plan, similar to one in Minnesota, that extends at least partial coverage to children up to age thirteen with family incomes up to 85 percent above the poverty line. These programs will benefit rural areas where low wage scales and part-time and seasonal jobs leave many working families just enough above the poverty line to have been ineligible for medicaid and other assistance. Second, for longer-range rural economic development, the mix of jobs should be improved. Especially needed are more mid-level jobs with adequate wages and benefits, giving entry-level workers a chance to move up from the ranks of minimum wages without having to move out from their communities. Job growth targeted in this range should also be a priority because such jobs are essential for attracting new residents to invigorate community institutions.

The economic and demographic growth that occurs—or does not occur—in a given community is not usually just the result of community preference, action, or inaction but of forces outside the community in the wider national and global economy, and in the politics of allocating public resources. Communities that are larger to begin with, that are located closer to urban centers, or that already have some combination of economic and political strength will probably gain the most, whereas many smaller, more remote, and poorer communities will grow smaller, more isolated, and poorer still. The gap between winners and losers however, will not be as great in the densely settled Northeast as in the Midwest, where recent state government decisions and actions appear to reflect a "triage" approach of "promoting economic development in thriving towns and counties while permitting weaker ones to die" (Wilkerson 1990).

To write off small communities through triage or to consign sparsely populated rural areas to human abandonment may be issuing death certificates, prematurely—and may hasten their deaths. For communities that have been unable to gain the needed new jobs and people, either by luring jobs from elsewhere or through the "grow-your-own" approach, it is still too soon to give up. Other possibilities for community survival should also be pursued. One example is to use the graying of America, especially rural America, for positive community benefit. Elderly residents, whether in-migrants or those who have aged in place, can be "an economic asset for community economic development" (Summers and Hirschl 1988, p. 49). To gain this effect, local business and government leaders must work creatively to capture elderly consumer spending on goods and services, and to tap elderly residents' available investment capital for local business expansion (Summers and Hirschl 1988, pp. 51–54). The services required by elderly residents can create a range of needed local jobs that, in turn, could bring more residents to the community, creating even more demand for goods and services.

Toward Appropriate Growth and Development

Around the nation, in small towns and even in remote rural areas, one of the most common and most heated issues is growth and development. The issue divides people within communities and sharply differentiates communities from one another. Some communities are wrestling with too much growth too fast, whereas others are resigned to continued decline. Growth often brings with it the question of growth for whom—for whose benefit? For the benefit of local residents or the benefit of others who live far away, have money to invest, and see the rural spaces only as a better return on the dollar than the stock market or the grain market?

Embedded in growth and development controversies is the realization that the physical environment and the social environment are interconnected, that what a rural community does to protect or alter its surrounding space may have major implications for what kind of social place it will be in the future, whether it will be the kind of place residents want it to be. Increasingly, rural people in growth areas are realizing that planning for the future is not and need not be entirely an urban vision projected onto rural space, provided the planning is appropriate to the rural situation and sensitive to people's visions for their own community (King and Harris 1989). Some excellent regional and local planning organizations now have a rural focus and a commitment to doing planning with rather than for communities. The "circuit rider" approach to providing planning assistance, pioneered by the Tug Hill Commission, is an attractive model.

Planning cannot thoroughly tame market forces, however. For example, along the Maine coast, official designation of a harbor community as a "working waterfront" can help protect marine industry activities from excessive competition from the real estate and tourism forces of "vacationland." But it cannot ensure that local sons and daughters, civil servants, teachers, or businesspeople can afford to own homes along the water. On the other hand, planning and zoning should not be allowed to exacerbate market forces, which can happen when expensive and exclusionary regulations make it even harder for modest-income people to find adequate housing in their communities. In some places, especially the rural recreational hot spots, mechanisms to slow the pace of development, such as "antispeculation laws" that would heavily tax quick real estate turnarounds, may already be overdue, unless an early 1990s recession significantly slows real estate activity.

Where growing metropolitan centers abut rural agricultural areas, farmland preservation laws and farmland retention programs are becoming increasingly common. There is a growing awareness that pre-serving farmland is necessary for preserving not only farming but the space in which the community exists, its character, and its identity. Measures such as the purchase of development rights of farmland by state and local governments are now in place in most of New England and New Jersey, and Oregon has instituted mandatory statewide farm-land-use planning and zoning. Although agricultural districting is used as a tool in fewer than a dozen states, most states have some sort of tax relief that assesses farmland at its current agricultural use value rather than its market value. Most states have "right-to-farm" laws that protect farmers and ranchers from certain legal actions against normally accepted farming practices. But farmers also need protection of their right to sell land at a good price if they or their heirs do not want to continue farming. As a Farm Bureau president stated at a public meeting, "A farmer's pension is in his land, and he may need to sell it. He can't be chained to his land."

Incorporating Newcomers

Many small communities desperately need to have an influx of residents to balance out-migration and keep from shrinking further, to maintain and reinvigorate community institutions. Some communities are active in developing strategies to attract more people, as in the Iowa town that advertised a free lot and cash bounty to anyone who moves in and builds a house. By this strategy, in two years the town collected about seventy people from as far away as New Hampshire and California, boosting school enrollment by twenty children and increasing local population by 10 percent.

New residents enliven the local business district, not only as customers, though, but also as proprietors, as was found in a study in rural north Florida, where the majority of new businesses had been started or taken over by "outsiders" (Gladwin 1989). New residents may increase the demand for local educational institutions and the arts, and may provide the organizational abilities to expand these offerings locally. New retirees represent a potential source of energy, talent, and outside connections that could be devoted to community projects. Some of the younger retired people as well as new residents who are self-employed and working out of their homes, can staff the institutions, serve on boards, volunteer in the critical fire companies, or work part time in hospitals and day care centers. They can work with youth as mentors, enliven church congregations, address environmental issues, and add their political effectiveness for community purposes. The problem for many rural communities, however, it not just to attract new residents but to integrate them into the social and symbolic "we" of the community. Newer residents may be held apart by the labels that externalize them, and feared for the changes they might bring, although, as other research shows, population influx, even of boomtown proportions, does not necessarily lead to social breakdown (Krannich and Greider 1990).

Because it is likely that the population moving to many small towns in the future may be economically, racially, and ethnically more diverse than the population base already there, careful community strategies for incorporating new residents will be especially needed. Incorporation of a new and more diverse population will be made more difficult than it should be by an overly exaggerated impression of the homogeneity of the past, with everybody "the same" as everybody else. Collective misperceptions about the past need to be confronted and adjusted. Additionally, the common mechanisms of categorizing and externalizing those who are new or different make their incorporation unnecessarily difficult. Social and symbolic rejection of new residents may actually reduce the "holding power" of a community, to the extent that some newer residents with potential to make a contribution to the community soon move elsewhere (Knop and Jobes 1988). If people who have lived in the community a few years still find themselves socially and symbolically excluded, the result may be rapid turnover that will destabilize, rather than strengthen, the community.

To capture the opportunity that new residents offer requires getting them involved in local projects and task-oriented organizations. An organization such as a historical society, for example, could be a place where new residents can "learn to be local," for they can graft on a substitute for local roots, at the same time providing some service for the community in archiving and exhibiting its heritage, as was the case in a rapidly growing rural-suburban community in the South (Greenhouse 1986, p. 134). In instrumental tasks, such as designing a community hall, staffing an emergency food pantry, or helping with fund-raisers for a new ambulance, new residents can bridge the division between newer and longer-term residents, bringing them together for the benefit of their shared community. For incorporating new members into the community, an economic boom such as that engendered by the Fort Drum expansion can help a great deal. For solidifying disparate residents into a cohesive community, a common enemy such as a threatened radioactive waste dump can quickly produce solidarity. But only a few communities will get a boom, and virtually no communities would want to be thrust into the emotionally and financially draining position of trying to fight off a dump. More modest instrumental community-building tasks must be found.

Making a Bedroom Community into a Community

The economics of both employment and housing will further separate place of residence from place of work. Increasingly, rural residents will be unable to find adequate jobs near where they live and urban workers will be unable to find affordable housing near where they work. Hence, there may be a double source of increased commuting from rural communities to urban areas. In many parts of the nation already, some small communities are quite deserted during the workday, but for their very old and their young. This situation presents a tremendous challenge for making sure that the essential services, such as fire, ambulance, and health care, are available, but also that the formal institutional structure and the informal interaction of the community can survive.

The ability to become a bedroom community, of course, depends on having adequate jobs available within commuting distance, and this may not be within the power of the small community to influence. There are ways to enhance the "commutability" of a place, however, such as using political influence for ensuring that the roads connecting to the employment centers are well maintained and developing public transportation that could reduce the costs as well as the environmental pollution of commuting. Making a bedroom community into a community that is more than just a collection of places to sleep, however, is a challenge that may be both greater and more difficult. Having various community offices and services open evenings and weekends, from auto mechanics to recreation to veterinarians and village offices, could minimize the stress on families who must spend many of their daytime hours during the week away from the community. Child care facilities and after-school programs that meet the time needs of out-commuting parents, but preserve the small, known context of the community, can both facilitate commuting as an economic adaptation and build community. Retaining local businesses and increasing their volume of trade will also be important, partly just to keep some people in town in the daytime. But this will take a determination on the part of out-commuters that maintaining a base of local businesses and services is a "good" that they value sufficiently to offset the slightly higher prices of goods purchased locally.

Incorporating new out-commuters into local activities and holding the participation of longer-term residents who now commute out are as essential as maintaining good roads for people to travel to and from their work. It will take concerted planning to see that both types of commuters have sufficient attachment to the community to be involved in it during the hours that they are at home. Where a base of formal institutions and informal social patterns already exists, these institutions may need conscious shoring up to counteract the erosive effect of separation between residence and workplace. Where a local school still exists, even if only an elementary school, this can become the locus and focus of community-building. A community college, the public library, local governments, and churches will be important assets in the effort to maintain a functioning community.

There are indeed drawbacks to becoming a bedroom community, but again it is a case of survival: If enough people can continue to live in or can move to a rural community by virtue of the jobs to which they commute, then that rural community can survive. And if the resident population grows, that may even give rise to new local jobs and business opportunities. One potential dividend of the bedroom community adaptation is that some of those bedrooms could be occupied by the grown sons and daughters and the grandchildren of the community. If there is good transportation to get to adequate outside jobs, and solid schools and other social institutions, the commuting community could be a means to have children stay or return home.

WHY IT MATTERS

The extent to which the survival of rural America matters to nonrural America has diminished markedly since the time of William Jennings Bryan's fiery "Cross of Gold" speech to the Democratic National Convention of 1896 in which he warned that "the great cities rest upon these broad and fertile prairies. Burn down your cities and leave our farms, and your cities will spring up again as if by magic. But destroy our farms and the grass will grow in the streets of every city in this country."

In the 1980s, a farm crisis brought farms and farming to national attention. But after the farm crisis dropped out of the media limelight and the public's sympathy, rural America as a whole receded from public and political awareness. Very little public attention at all was paid to the severe recession in the nonfarm rural economy, which continued even after farm problems eased. Even less noticed was that the farm crisis and the nonfarm recession together took a toll on rural communities. Some scholars pointed out that the farm crisis was part of a larger "rural crisis" (e.g., Wilkinson 1988, Beaulieu 1988). A U.S. Senate subcommittee report concluded that communities, as well as individual farmers, were being affected and must not be neglected in this crisis: "Rural communities face unprecedented economic and social challenges as agriculture restructures and America enters its third century. The costs of assisting that transition pale when compared to those of ignoring it" (U.S. Senate 1986, p. 56). But in general, the recent problems of rural communities have escaped notice and publication.

In some places, especially in the Midwest, rural jobs, institutions, and populations have dwindled seriously, and some small communities are becoming virtual ghost towns (see Scheidt and Norris-Baker 1989). For the few people left behind, it's "like sitting there dying and waiting for someone to set the date for your funeral," as the mayor of a shrinking village in central North Dakota described it (Wilkerson 1990). The ability of these stressed communities to continue to provide a true community for their residents becomes doubtful, but the loss may not be realized until too late. It should not take a complete disaster, such as the flood on Buffalo Creek in West Virginia in 1972, in which people lost not only loved ones and houses but also community, to make it clear that "the preservation (or restoration) of communal forms of life must become a lasting concern, not only for those charged with healing the wounds of acute disaster but for those charged with planning a truly human future" (Erikson 1976, p. 259).

Nearly a century after William Jennings Bryan's speech, the question has to be asked whether as a nation we care about what happens to rural America. In the past, there was a federal commitment and there were federal programs "to overcome serious regional or territorial disadvantage" and to ensure that "rural people were not excluded from the benefits of our society's rising standard of living" (Deavers 1989b, p. 7). Now there seems to be no such national commitment to rebuilding rural America, and no political consensus that rural community development is important to the nation as a whole.

The very states where rural communities are in most stress and need most assistance are also states whose fiscal troubles have been quite severe because of problems in agriculture, mining, or lumbering. So, claiming there is little they *can* do, states are able temporarily to obscure the longer-range question of whether there is anything they *want* to or *ought* to do for their rural communities. Even without major budgetary commitment, though, much more could be done to root out antirural bias in funding and regulation and to make policies and programs more suited to the needs of small, rural communities. More vigilant attention should be paid to the equity question for rural areas, with a close monitoring of the rural-metropolitan gap, and monitoring of the rate at which rural spaces are being endangered, placed at risk of becoming the dumping ground of an urbanized waste-generating society. More careful social science research is needed to document, monitor, and help minimize such risks to rural spaces.

Though rural individuals will continue to struggle with the stresses of change that are sweeping across rural America, they can do so more effectively if they are embedded in and supported by a strong community, for "the outcome of the struggle is often determined by the characteristics of the community" in which the individual lives (Mazer 1976, p. 228). Community strength promotes individual strength; and rural communities can be places where pride in place engenders pride in self. To survive, communities will have to generate determination, innovative ideas, and energy from within, as these are unlikely to be delivered to them from state and federal governments. The communities that do the best in adapting to change will be those where residents make a full commitment to accepting the fact of change and the challenges that change implies. "The secret to survival for many of our rural communities seems to depend on whether the community is willing to clearly spell out the problems faced and creatively develop strategies of action for dealing with each of them" (Heffernan and Heffernan 1986a, p. 280). Social science research that documents effective community response to change could contribute to the creation of more proactive and comprehensive approaches to rural development (see Israel and Beaulieu 1990, and Christenson and Flora 1990).

Rural people cannot build a wall around themselves to prevent further change, to keep out the new trends they don't like, to isolate their children from drugs or their lands from dumps, for the changes are already within and among them, and they themselves are part of the changes. Inevitably, rural people are caught up in the national and global changes of the era, and contrary to the more traditional dichotomous rural thinking, most rural residents would admit that not everything rural is good and not everything nonrural is bad. Any attempt to wall themselves off from the rest of society would raise a question for which they have no ready answer, the question posed by the poet Robert Frost, who wrote: "Before I built a wall I'd ask to know/What I was walling in or walling out . . ."

In the absence of a wall, societal ills that rural people generally associate with urban places have appeared in rural communities, too, and rural people must marshal their personal and social resources to address them. Some rural people see their own handling of societal problems in their communities as setting an example for the nation. A county probation officer, asked whether he thought rural communities could or should be expected to solve problems that are clearly society-wide, such as drugs and crime, replied emphatically and confidently, "Oh, yes! If there's going to be any solution to the problems of our society, it will come from places like this little county, not from Albany and Washington. Here the problem is small enough that we can, if we are willing, face it and deal with it. And it's not just dollars that will solve the problem. It's people, people just like us in rural places and small towns, people who know how important community is to decent human life. We are the people who can begin to address these problems."

If society's problems are rural problems, too, then it is also the case that rural problems are society's problems. Eventually, nonrural Americans will realize that the neglected health of the rural areas *is* a problem for the whole of the nation, not just for rural people. The preservation of rural America, not as a romantic "living museum" but as a viable alternative to other patterns of living, should be an important issue for the nation. It is an uphill fight, however, because of a pervasive national assumption that "metropolitanization" is both good and inevitable and, consequently, that whatever can be done to move the transition along is good because it contributes to the sweep of progress and because rural is obsolete.

Most people in rural places in New York State and around the nation are anxious to preserve their rural communities, solve their own problems, and strengthen their social institutions. They still want to fulfill their role of raising both food and citizens for the nation and also of perpetuating some of the enduring values and institutions that provide a safe and sane environment for people. Rural people can offer the nation their rural communities as an alternative way of living that is not only attractive but increasingly necessary for the well-being of the wider society.

APPENDIX ONE

Anthropological Approach to Studying Change in Rural Communities

This research project emerged and grew as it went along, starting with one issue, then adding another and another as it became apparent that each change or issue was only one part of the total picture, just one piece of the puzzle. Overall, I conducted about 400 separate interviews and observation periods, mostly concentrated in four counties but expanding into eleven others from 1985 through 1990. Selection of the particular localities in which to conduct research evolved during the research process itself, and within any given site research proceeded on a snowball strategy. Selection of informants was purposive rather than random, and the kinds of informants or their roles in the community varied depending on the topic under study and the community or event being observed.

Three counties, Delaware, Allegany, and Chenango (see Map 1.2) formed the base of the research on farm issues and continued to be the core research counties of other topics as well, yielding over 250 of the total interviews and observation periods. For the farm study, I conducted long, unstructured interviews with members of forty farm families, about evenly divided among the three counties, in their homes, their barnyards, and their barns. I also interviewed over twenty local agricultural experts such as Extension agents, owners of local feed stores, implement dealers, veterinarians, auctioneers, and people in agencies or programs assisting farmers in coping with their financial and transitional problems. Several of the farm families first interviewed in 1986 were subsequently reinterviewed one, two, or three years later.

As research gradually moved from farm issues into a wider range of topics, and to enhance geographic distribution, Franklin County in the northernmost part of the state was added as a fourth core research county. Additionally, wherever there was a rural community facing significant changes and wherever there were good opportunities for on-site research, that locality, but not the county in its entirety, became a subsidiary research site. Thus, smaller amounts of research were conducted on specific topics or issues in eleven other counties (see Map 1.1).

The research strategy of networking out from a starting point and using "informants" in one locality as a source of ideas about people to contact and events to observe in other localities may play havoc with an original research design for selection of sites and informants—but it leads to research opportunities that would otherwise be missed. And because this project was conceived not as a comparative study of a few specific counties or communities but as a scoping endeavor, trying to catch and explore the whole range of changes, issues, and problems in rural communities, the anthropological tendency to let the research go where it will won out over considerations of elegance of research design.

Field research consisted of interviews conducted "on location," observation periods in communities, and collection of local data. Interviews, in most cases pre-arranged, generally lasted at least one hour. Each interview was tailored specifically to the respondent and focused on a preselected topic within that person's experience or knowledge. People selected for interviewing covered a gamut of local residents, sometimes singly, sometimes two together or several in a group. Some interviews were merely to collect factual information; others more nearly approached discussion, in that they were conducted in an informal manner with open-ended questions and were essentially interviewee-directed. Interviewees were told the purpose and focus of my inquiry. All were assured that interview material would be treated sensitively with regard to protection of sources: Privacy of individuals would be protected by omitting or changing names and, where appropriate, the identity of communities would be veiled. Actually, very few of the people interviewed seemed concerned about anonymity, although some appreciated being told that they could strike anything from the record if they had second thoughts about being quoted, even anonymously. In most cases I took notes during interviews; where this was not appropriate or convenient, I wrote notes immediately afterwards. I did not use tape-recording.

Observation periods involved a range of activities, from attendance at a variety of governmental meetings and participation in workshops for local teachers or human service workers, to spending several full days in elementary school classrooms, sitting in cowbarns, touring a small factory, riding a rural transit van or a Head Start bus, attending county fairs and local "old home days," and a certain amount of just hanging around in a variety of local places: the Friday night fish fry at the village restaurant, the courthouse cafe in the county seat, the local feed store on a rainy afternoon, the waiting room in a county welfare office, a local parade or protest demonstration, and a village flea market.

Secondary data were gleaned from a wide variety of sources, including agency reports and brochures, official municipal and institutional records and correspondence, grant proposals, statistical profiles. I perused back issues of local newspapers in libraries, purchased local papers on site, interviewed local editors and reporters, and subscribed to one local newspaper for a year and half. The newspapers not only kept me apprised of local events and doings but served as a source of people to contact for future interviews and provided a document of a community's self-image, its projection to the world.

Perhaps the best way to indicate the nature of this research is to present a few sample days of research. I did not take up residence at any of the research sites, preferring to use my centrally located home base from which to set out in any direction, for distances ranging from 30 to 280 miles. Depending on distances, activities, and interviews planned, some trips lasted a single day and others involved staying in a community for several days at a time. Each major research site has been visited and revisited dozens of times over the course of the five years.

July 8, 1987: I set out from home before 6 a.m. for a day of research in a nearby county. Two interviews at the start of the day had been scheduled ahead by telephone, and two at the end of the day had been arranged in person on a previous visit. The first appointment, at 7:30, was with a school superintendent of a rural district, who discussed a range of topics, from the apparently minor effect of the farm crisis on school children to the problems faced by children from rural poverty backgrounds. Next I drove to another village in the same county to interview the president of a large regional feed and seed company, who shared observations and information on the present status of dairy farming in the area and the impact of the farm crisis on agribusinesses such as his. At this man's suggestion, I stopped in at the office of the newly reorganized local newspaper and talked with the owner-editors, gaining insights into the social effects of some recent population changes. Then, on the spur of the moment, I contact the county Head Start staff, with which I had previously had several mutually fruitful interactions. I joined them for a buffet lunch they were having in one of the county's Head Start centers and steered the conversation into an impromptu focus-group discussion of certain topics related to rural poverty. Next, by the happy coincidence of getting my directions wrong, I ended up interviewing the president of a local building supply firm, who was eager to give not only the facts on changes affecting his business but also his philosophical (and pessimistic) overview of change in his hometown community. Next I arranged an impromptu interview with a village mayor, a longtime and knowledgeable resident. As we sat on his front porch sipping lemonade, he offered recollections and observations of many decades. Following a brief supper stop in a local diner (with good opportunities to observe and eavesdrop), I had a long-promised interview with a busy farm couple on a beautiful hilltop farm, an interview as interesting in its dynamics as in its information: No matter how hard I tried to direct some questions at the wife, the husband answered every question. Finally, the day ended with another farm family, where my attention was immediately called to a living-room shelf of trophies won for herd production. I enjoyed a cold glass of fresh, unpasteurized milk and spent the night in their spare bedroom. At 6 the next morning, I was watching the milking and promoting a free-floating discussion in the cowbarn.

June 1988: In another county, a three-day research visit included fifteen interviews and observation opportunities, as well as perusal of newspapers, agency reports, and other public documents collected on site. Research activities included interviewing public officials such as the chairman and one other member of the county board of legislators and the county's economic development director, and attending a county planning board meeting and a church-sponsored "rural crisis network" meeting. I interviewed the head of the county's office for the aging, the director of a housing and rural development agency, the principal of an elementary school, the owner-manager of a local small industry, an Extension agent, a social worker, and a job counselor. I attended a county government meeting, visited a school and interviewed the dynamic instigator of some innovative programs for "at risk" children, sat in on a class at the county's employment training center, and spent a happy evening with a farm family. In between, I made numerous calls from public phones to schedule more interviews, sweltered in my car jotting interview notes, drove back and forth through the county, and consumed a lot of coffee and soda pop in local restaurants and convenience stores.

Winter and spring 1989: On a rainy-snowy winter day, a specific issue beckoned me to another county: the imminent displacement of over a hundred low-income families so that the physically worn-down buildings they rented could be refurbished and converted into condominums to sell to more affluent people. I had been tracking this issue by telephone conversations with some agencies and through the newspaper since it broke, in January 1989, and felt a site visit was needed. I had pre-arranged interviews with various school personnel with whom I had previously been in contact on other issues, so that I could pick up any impacts they were seeing or forecasting among children. I then went to talk with some community residents who were working to help apartment tenants deal with this housing crisis. In the evening there was a village board meeting to attend, where this issue was the principal item on the agenda. Over the next several weeks, I kept up with the story through telephone conversations with these and other involved people. On a pouring rainy day in midspring, I visited the village again, to talk with the community agency people helping tenants search for and secure substitute housing, and especially to interview some of the residents of those substandard apartments. These latter, of course, were unannounced, potluck interviews— and my luck was good that day. In a few cases, no one was at home to answer my knock, and in one case the woman talked only briefly because she and her two young children were just departing to walk "downtown" to the bank because (as it was the first of the month) the welfare check and food stamp authorizations had just arrived in that day's mail. In four other apartments, after I explained my interest, residents interrupted their soap opera, housecleaning, supper preparations, or the packing of their belongings, to sit down and talk with me about the implications of this impending conversion to condos. Some with babies in their laps, some with older children just coming home from school, four women nonetheless obliged with long personal answers to my focused but wide-ranging questions, giving a lot of candid information about themselves as well as their housing crisis.

Sometimes research proceeded according to a plan, with interviews lined up ahead of time to make sure that certain topics would be systematically covered in the several locations, informants selected to ensure picking up various angles on an issue, and field observations carefully scheduled. But as the above passages illustrate, research also involved a great deal of flexibility and serendipity. Occasionally, but rarely, there were disappointments, as when a planned inter-viewee failed to show up or a long-sought interviewee turned out not to be very informative. Far more often there were useful and enlightening unanticipated opportunities: an unplanned event to witness and ask about, a chance meeting with a well-informed and talkative person, an unexpectedly penetrating insight from an informant. Even getting lost in the rural countryside can lead to good new contacts: Stopping to ask directions once turned into an impromptu roadside interview, with an invitation to come back for a real interview some other time.

The fast pace of changes occurring in these rural areas, and the variety of different changes, meant that, like a news reporter, I had to follow stories whenever and wherever they broke, throughout the year and throughout the region, and thereafter to follow up on them. Such unanticipated events, even if they caused interruptions in a planned schedule of work, are the stuff of anthropological research. Because I had been doing fieldwork all along in rural New York, when a new event occurred somewhere, in most cases I already had some background context for understanding it and some contacts in the community, people I could turn to for finding out more about the present event and local perceptions of it.

What these vignettes of typical research days may fail to get across must be said directly: That in all localities people were incredibly hospitable to my approach, willing to set up interviews even when they had no idea who I was or what, really, I wanted. People were willing to stop their work or their leisure activities for what often took well over an hour of their time, and in almost every case they were eager, interested, anxious to be helpful, knowledgeable, and talkative. Conducting this research has been exciting and fun, and I have genuinely enjoyed listening and probing. Many of my informants have enjoyed the interaction as well: Many commented that they were pleased to have the opportunity to tell their side of a story and seemed interested in the research and in the questions that were raised in their own minds as a result of the interview.

Change is without end, and some of the "stories" I have followed are still unfolding and unresolved. But at some point it is necessary to shift from concentration on data gathering into the work of analysis and writing. When the researcher begins to experience deja vu in the field, when research produces a high rate of redundancy, when new data seem only to substantiate that collected earlier, when no significant new points are added, only more examples of a point already sufficiently illustrated, then it is time to terminate research. As I reached this point, I also began to feel a responsibility—a debt, really— to those I had interviewed, a sense of commitment to write up the research in timely fashion. The bulging file drawers of research notes to be analyzed, integrated, and written up began to outweigh the appeal of spending more time in the field.

APPENDIX TWO

Selected Data on the Four Core Research Counties

Population and Settlement

	1970 Population	1980 Population	1970-80 % Change	Estimated 1986 Population	1980-86 % Change	1980 Density per sq. mi.	1980 % Population in Places < 2,500	1986 Largest Village or City	1986 Smallest Village or City	1986 % Population in all Villages/Cities
Allegany	46,458	46,954*	1.0	45,712*	-2.6	49	79.3	5,070	470	36
Chenango	46,368	49,344	6.4	50,000	+1.3	54	83.6	7,790	890	35
Delaware	44,718	46,824	4.7	47,100	+0.5	33	75.3	4,650	370	36
Franklin	43,931	44,929	2.2	43,800	-2.5	27	63.8	7,180	230	39
Comparison Figure for N.Y. State				17,772,000	+1.2					

* excludes college population

Demographic and Economic Characteristics

	1980 % Residents >25 with some College Education	1980 % Non-white Population	Age Distribution, 1980			1980 % Families in Poverty	1985 Per Capita Income Rank of the 62 Counties	% Per Capita Income Change 1979-85 (1985 Dollars Adjusted to 1979)
			% < 21	% 21-65	% > 65			
Allegany	30	1.3	39.9	47.5	11.6	16.4	62	- 2.0
Chenango	25	1.0	35.7	51.8	12.5	13.9	44	+ 3.7
Delaware	27	1.3	34.6	50.7	14.7	15.6	47	+ 1.7
Franklin	25	5.4+	37.1	50.1	12.8	18.4	60	- 1.5
Comparison Figure for N.Y. State		20.5				13.4		+ 5.6

+ includes approximately 4.5% American Indians

Employment, Manufacturing, and Agriculture

	1980 Number of Jobs	1980 % Unemployment	% Jobs in Agriculture, Mining, Forestry	% Jobs in Service	% Jobs in Manufacturing	Manufacturing Plants >100 Employees	Manufacturing Plants 20-99 Employees	1985 Number of Farms×	1988 Number of Farms	1988 Number of Commercial Farms	1988 Milk Production Rank in State
Allegany	19,132	9.5	6.3	68	26	5	7	920	850	240	24
Chenango	20,556	7.2	7.2	59	34	15	12	1,075	965	428	9
Delaware	18,260	7.6	9.6	64	27	10	12	1,090	1,000	360	12
Franklin	15,926	12.3	6.7	77	17	4	10	625	580	340	15

Comparison Figure for N.Y. State

70

× operations selling $1,000 or more in agricultural products

Sources: Eberts, 1984;
Economic Development and Technical Assistance Center, 1987;
New York Agricultural Statistics Service, 1989.

References

Albrecht, Don E., Steve H. Murdock, Kathy L. Schiflett, Rita R. Hamm, F. Larry Leistritz, and Brenda Eckstrom
    1988   "The consequences of the Farm Crisis for Rural Communities." *Journal of the Community Development Society* 19 (2):119–135.

Allen, John C.
    1989   *Against All Odds: Rural Community in the Information Age.* Ph.D. dissertation, Washington State University.
    1990   "Outsiders Versus Insiders: A Case Study of a Small Agricultural Community in Washington State." Paper presented at the annual meeting of the Rural Sociological Society, Norfolk, VA.

Apgar, William C., Jr., and H. James Brown
    1988   *The State of the Nation's Housing, 1988.* Cambridge, MA: Joint Center for Housing Studies of Harvard University.

Applebome, Peter
    1990   "Appalachia: Vast Change but New Challenges." *New York Times,* April 14.

Barlett, Peggy F.
    1986   "Part-time Farming: Saving the Farm or Saving the Life-style?" *Rural Sociology* 51 (3):289–313.

Bates, Steve
    1989   "Trade-Off Plan for Lorton Prison Called Long Shot." *Washington Post,* August 24.

Beale, Calvin
    1984   "Poughkeepsie's Complaint, or Defining Metropolitan Areas." *American Demographics* 6 (January):29–31, 46–47.

Beaulieu, Lionel J., ed.
    1988   *The Rural South in Crisis: Challenges for the Future.* Boulder, CO: Westview Press.

Bell, Earl H.
    1942   *Culture of a Contemporary Rural Community: Sublette, Kansas.* Rural Life Studies no. 2. Washington: U. S. Department of Agriculture.

Bergland, Bob
    1988   "Rural Mental Health: Report of the National Action Commission on the Mental Health of Rural Americans." *Journal of Rural Community Psychology* 9 (2):29–39.

Bloch, John
    1989   Testimony, U. S. House of Representatives, Select Committee on Children, Youth, and Families. April 11.

Bloomquist, Leonard E., Leif Jensen, and Ruy A. Teixeira
    1988   "Too Few Jobs for Workfare to Put Many to Work." *Rural Development Perspectives* 5 (1):8–12.

Bonanno, Alessandro
    1988   "The Capitalist Reorganization of America: Perspectives for the Creation of Emancipatory Political Strategies." Paper presented at the annual meeting of the Midwestern Sociological Society, Minneapolis, MN.

Borich, Timothy O., James R. Steward, and Harlowe Hatle
    1985   "The Impact of a Regional Mall on Rural Main Street." *Rural Sociologist* 5 (1):6–9.

Bouvier, Leon F., and Vernon M. Briggs, Jr.
    1988   *The Population and Labor Force of New York: 1990 to 2050.* Washington: Population Reference Bureau.

Breimyer, Harold F.
    1990   "Prospects for Rural America as the Nation Matures: An Agricultural Economist's Prognosis." *Rural Sociologist* 10 (3):3–9.

Brown, David L., and Kenneth L. Deavers
    1988   "Rural Change and the Rural Economic Policy Agenda for the 1990s." In *Rural Economic Development in the 1980s: Prospects for the Future,* 1–28. Washington: Economic Research Service, U. S. Department of Agriculture.

Brunner, Edmund de S., and Irving Lorge
    1937   *Rural Trends in Depression Years: A Survey of Village-centered Agricultural Communities, 1930–'36.* New York: Columbia University Press.

Bruno, Debra
    1990   "Dangerous Neighbors." *Rural Electrification* (February):64, 57.

Bryan, Frank, and Bill Mares
    1983   *Real Vermonters Don't Milk Goats.* Shelburne, VT: New England Press.

Bryant, F. Carlene
    1981   *We're All Kin: A Cultural Study of a Mountain Neighborhood.* Knoxville: University of Tennessee Press.

Buttel, Frederick H., Mark Lancelle, and David R. Lee
    1988   "Farm Structure and Rural Communities in the Northeast." In *Agriculture and Community Change in the U. S.,* edited by Louis E. Swanson, 181–237. Boulder, CO: Westview Press.

Butterfield, Fox
    1982   "Accustomed Poverty Intensifying in Rural Maine." *New York Times,* February 15.

Butler, L. M., Robert E. Howell, and Ronald Faas
    1979,   *Coping With Growth.* Corvallis, OR: Western Rural Development
    1980   Center.

Calta, Marialisa
  1989   "Blacks Start Church in 'Whitest' State." *New York Times*, February
            4.

Carlson, Katherine A.
  1986   "The Community of Clallam Bay Before the Opening of the Clallam
            Bay Corrections Center: The First Interim Report of the Clallam
            Bay Project."
  1988a   "Understanding Community Opposition to Prison Siting: More
            Than Fear and Finances." *Corrections Today* (April):84–90.
  1988b   "The Clallam Bay Corrections Center at Clallam Bay, Washington."
            In *Impacts of Washington State's Correctional Institutions on Com-
            munities*, edited by R. Lidman. Olympia: Washington State Institute
            for Public Policy.
  1989   "When A Prison Comes to Town: Community Benefits and Com-
            munity Problems." Paper presented at the Rural Sociological Society,
            Seattle, WA, August.
  1990   "Prison Impacts: A Review of the Research."

Cautley, Eleanor, and Doris P. Slesinger
  1988   "Labor Force Participation and Poverty Status Among Rural and
            Urban Women Who Head Families." In "Symposium: Rural Versus
            Urban Poverty." *Policy Studies Review* 7 (4):795–809.

Cervantes, Niki
  1988   "Out of the City: Urban Poor Seek Second Chance in Rural
            America." *San Diego Union*, August 28 and 29.

Charlier, Marj
  1988   "Small-Town America Battles a Deep Gloom as Its Economy Sinks."
            Wall Street Journal, August 4.

Christenson, James A., and Cornelia B. Flora, eds.
  1990   *Rural Policies for the 1990s.* Boulder, CO: Westview Press.

Cohen, Anthony P.
  1985   *The Symbolic Construction of Community.* London: Tavistock Pub-
            lications.

Cohen, Mark
  1990   "Adirondack Dilemma: Economic and Social Consequences of Using
            Zoning Regulations to Limit Regional Development." Department
            of Agricultural Economics, Cornell University.

Compass
  1988   "Compass: Charting Courses for Community Caring." Clinton
            County, NY.

Cornell Cooperative Extension
  1989   "A Home of One's Own: Housing Options for the '90s." Ithaca,
            NY: Cornell University.

Coughenour, C. Milton, and Louis E. Swanson
  1988   "Rewards, Values, and Satisfaction with Farm Work." *Rural Sociology*
            53 (4):442–459.

Cox, Jay
    1989   "Romulus Happy About Jobs, Boost Prison Offers." *Ithaca Journal*,
                August 8.

Cunningham, Neil, and Tom Grace
    1986   "Projects Offer Little Hope for Residents." *Daily Star* (Oneonta,
                NY), August 7.

Deavers, Kenneth L.
    1988   "Scope and Dimensions of Problems Facing Rural America." Address
                to the 46th Annual Professional Agricultural Workers Conference,
                Tuskegee, AL, December 5.
    1989a   "Economic and Social Trends in Rural America." Address to the
                Conference on Community Change and Economic Development,
                Burlington, VT, June 1.
    1989b   "Lagging Growth and High Poverty: Do We Care?" *Choices* 4
                (Second Quarter):4–7.

Deavers, Kenneth L., Robert A. Hoppe, and Peggy J. Ross
    1986   "Public Policy and Rural Poverty: A View from the 1980s." *Policy
                Studies Journal* 15 (2):291–309.

Dillman, Don A., and Daryl J. Hobbs, eds.
    1982   *Rural Society in the U. S.: Issues for the 1980s.* Boulder, CO: Westview
                Press.

Dubbink, David
    1984   "I'll Have My Town Medium-Rural, Please." *Journal of the American
                Planning Association* 50 (4):406–418.

Duncan, Cynthia M., and Ann R. Tickamyer
    1988   "Poverty Research and Policy for Rural America." *American So-
                ciologist* 19 (3):243–259.

Duncan, Greg J.
    1984   *Years of Poverty, Years of Plenty.* Ann Arbor: Institute for Social
                Research, University of Michigan.

Dunphy, Paul
    1988   "The Pastoral Paradox." *Harrowsmith*, May–June, 41–47.

Dyballa, Cynthia, Lyle S. Raymond, Jr., and Alan J. Hahn
    1981   *The Tug Hill Program: A Regional Planning Option for Rural Areas.*
                Syracuse: Syracuse Univerity Press.

Eberts, Paul R.
    1984   *Socioeconomic Trends in Rural New York State: Toward the 21st Century.*
                Albany: New York State Legislative Commission on Rural Resources.

Eberts, Paul, and Marwan Khawaja
    1988   "Changing Socioeconomic Conditions in Rural Localities in the
                1980s: Experiences in New York State." Rural Sociology Bulletin
                no. 152, Ithaca, NY: Cornell University.

Economic Development and Technical Assistance Center
   1987   "1986 Population Estimates and 1985 Per Capita Income Estimates
            for Subcounty Areas of New York State." Plattsburgh, NY: Economic
            Development and Technical Assistance Center.

Edelstein, Michael R.
   1988   *Contaminated Communities: The Social and Psychological Impacts of
            Residential Toxic Exposure.* Boulder, CO: Westview Press.

Ellwood, David T.
   1987   *Divide and Conquer: Responsible Security for America's Poor.* Occasional
            Paper number 1, Ford Foundation Project on Social Welfare and
            the American Future. New York: Ford Foundation.

Engel, David M.
   1984   "The Oven Bird's Song: Insiders, Outsiders, and Personal Injuries
            in an American Community." *Law & Society Review* 18 (4):551–
            582.
   1987   "Law, Time, and Community." *Law & Society Review* 21 (4):605–
            637.

Erikson, Kai
   1976   *Everything in Its Path: Destruction of Community in the Buffalo Creek
            Flood.* New York: Simon and Schuster.

Essex County (New York)
   1988   "Economic Development Zone Application."

Fessenden-Raden, June, Janet M. Fitchen, and Jenifer S. Heath
   1987   "Providing Risk Information in Communities: Factors Influencing
            What is Heard and Accepted." *Science, Technology, & Human Values*
            12 (3 and 4):94–101.

Fitchen, Janet M.
   1981   *Poverty in Rural America: A Case Study.* Boulder, CO: Westview
            Press.
   1987a   "Cultural Aspects of Environmental Problems: Individualism and
            Chemical Contamination of Groundwater." *Science, Technology, &
            Human Values* 12 (2):1–12.
   1987b   "The Importance of Community Context in Effective Risk Man-
            agement." In *Risk Assessment and Management,* edited by Lester B.
            Lave, 677–685. New York: Plenum Press.
   1987c   "When Communities Collapse: Implications for Rural America."
            Human Services in the Rural Environment 10 (4) and 11 (1):48–57.

Fitchen, Janet M., Jenifer S. Heath, and June Fessenden-Raden
   1987   "Risk Perception in Community Context: A Case Study." In *The
            Social and Cultural Construction of Risk,* edited by Branden B. Johnson
            and V. T. Covello, 31–54. Dordrecht, Netherlands: D. Reidel.

Flora, Cornelia Butler, and Jan L. Flora
   1988   "Implicitly Anti-Rural Policies and Rural Development in the 1980s."
            Paper presented at the Rural Sociological Society, Athens, GA.
   1989   "Rural Area Development: The Impact of Change." *Forum for Applied
            Research and Public Policy* 4 (3):50–52.

1990   "Developing Entrepreneurial Rural Communities." *Soliological Practice* 8:197–207.

Fuguitt, Glenn V., David L. Brown, and Calvin L. Beale
1989   *Rural and Small Town America.* New York: Russell Sage Foundation.

Furuseth, Owen J., and Mark S. Johnson
1988   "Neighbourhood Attitudes Towards a Sanitary Landfill: A North Carolina Study." *Applied Geography* 8:135–145.

Gates, Paul W.
1969   "Agricultural Change in New York State." In *New York History,* 115–141. Cooperstown: New York State Historical Association.

Gateway Community Services
1988   "Eaton Shelter Project, Year End Report." East Lansing, MI.

Gearing, Frederick O.
1970   *The Face of the Fox.* Chicago: Aldine.

Geisler, Charles C., and Hisayoshi Mitsuda
1987   "Mobile-Home Growth, Regulation, and Discrimination in Upstate New York." *Rural Sociology* 52 (4):532–543.

Ghelfi, Linda M.
1988   "About that Lower Cost of Living in Nonmetro Areas." *Rural Development Perspectives* 5 (1):30–34.

Gladwin, Christina H.
1989   "Rural Business Women in North Florida: How Different from Men Are They?" Paper presented at the Rural Sociological Society, Seattle, WA.

Graham, Katherine H.
1986   "A Description of the Transition Experiences of 28 New York Families Forced From their Farms: 1982–1985." M.S. thesis, Cornell University.

Greason, Michael C.
1989   "Here a Parcel, There a Parcel—Fragmented Forests." *The Conservationist* 44(1):46–49.

Greenhouse, Carol
1986   *Praying for Justice: Faith, Order, and Community in an American Town.* Ithaca, NY: Cornell University Press.
1988   "Courting Difference: Issues of Interpretation and Comparison in the Study of Legal Ideologies." *Law & Society Review* 22 (4):687–707.

Gwynn, Douglas B., Yoshio Kawamura, Edward Dolber-Smith, and Refugio I. Rochin
1989   *California's Rural Poor: Trends, Correlates, and Policies.* Davis: California Institute for Rural Studies.

Halpern, Sue
1989   "New Chain Store Splits Village in Adirondacks." *New York Times,* October 10.

Hardin, Garrett
1968   "The Tragedy of the Commons." *Science* 162:1243–1248.

Harrison, David S., and Jonathan Seib
n.d.   "Toward 'One Region': Strengthening Rural-Urban Economic Link-
        ages." In *A Northwest Reader: Options for Rural Communities*, 81–
        95. Seattle: Northwest Policy Center, University of Washington,
        Graduate School of Public Affairs.

Hedrick, Ulysses Prentiss
1933   *A History of Agriculture in the State of New York.* 1966 edition. New
        York: Hill and Wang.

Heffernan, William D., and Judith B. Heffernan
1986a   "The Farm Crisis and the Rural Community." In *New Dimensions
        in Rural Policy: Building Upon Our Heritage*, 273–280. Washington:
        Joint Economic Committee, U. S. Congress.
1986b   "Impact of the Farm Crisis on Rural Families and Communities."
        Rural Sociologist 6 (3):160–170.

Hill, Carole E.
1988   *Community Health Systems in the Rural American South: Linking
        People and Policy.* Boulder, CO: Westview Press.

Hirschl, Thomas A.
1987   "Agricultural, Economic and Family Organization in a Post-Indus-
        trial Society." Presentation to Chenango County Board of Super-
        visors.

Horowitz, Mitchell, and Jonathon Dunn
1989   "The 1989 Rural Economic Climate Report." *The Entrepreneurial
        Economy Review* (September–October). Washington: Corporation for
        Economic Development.

Housing Assistance Council
1989   "State Action Memorandum." Washington, July–August.

Israel, Glenn D., and Lionel J. Beaulieu
1990   "Community Leadership." In *American Rural Communities*, edited
        by A. E. Luloff and Louis E. Swanson, 181–202. Boulder, CO:
        Westview Press.

Ithaca Journal
1989   "Dairy Farmers Use Pizza to Attract Workers: U. S. Labor Crunch
        Takes a Bite out of Dairy Farm Labor Force." January 21.

Jensen, Leif
1988   "Rural-Urban Differences in the Utilization and Ameliorative Effects
        of Welfare Programs." In "Symposium: Rural Versus Urban Poverty."
        Policy Studies Review 7 (4):782–794.

Johansen, Harley E., and Glenn V. Fuguitt
1984   *The Changing Rural Village in America: Demographic and Economic
        Trends Since 1950.* Cambridge, MA: Ballinger Publishing Company.

Johnson, Kenneth
    1989   "The Nonmetropolitan Turnaround in the 1980s: Recent Population Redistribution Trends in Nonmetropolitan America." *Rural Sociology* 54 (3):301–326.

Johnson, Kirk
    1989a   "Incinerators Creating New Landfill Woes." *New York Times*, January 30.
    1989b   "Maverick Politician Wages Lonely Battle." *New York Times*, September 29.

King, Leslie, and Glenn Harris
    1989   "Local Responses to Rapid Rural Growth: New York and Vermont Cases." *APA Journal* 55 (2):181–191.

Kingsolver, Ann E.
    1989   "Toyota, Tobacco, and Talk: Who Has 'The Say' in Rural Kentucky" paper presented at the American Anthropological Association, Washington, D.C., November.
    forth-   "Tobacco, Textiles, and Toyota: Working for MNCs in Rural Kentucky." In *Anthropology, Industry, and Labor: Studies of the New Industrialization in the Late Twentieth Century*, edited by Frances Rothstein and Michael Blim. New York: Praeger.
    com-
    ing

Knop, Edward, and Patrick Jobes
    1988   "The Myth of Non-metropolitan Community Stability: Patterns and Implications of Turnover Migration in Montana and Colorado Cases." Paper presented at the Rural Sociological Society, Athens, GA.

Kramer, Mark
    1980   *Three Farms: Making Milk, Meat, and Money from the American Soil.* 1987 edition. Cambridge, MA: Harvard University Press.

Krannich, Richard S., and Thomas R. Greider
    1990   "Rapid Growth Effects on Rural Community Relations." In *American Rural Communities*, edited by A. E. Luloff and Louis E. Swanson, 61–73. Boulder, CO: Westview Press.

Kreis, Donald M.
    1989   "The Rhetoric of Doom: Round 2 of the Landfill Hearings in Machias Was Not for the Faint of Ear." *Maine Times*, March 17.

Kunstler, James Howard
    1989   "For Sale: Developers are Grabbing Huge Chunks of the Adirondacks, and Albany's Bumbling Has Already Put 100,000 Acres in Jeopardy." *New York Times Magazine*, June 18.

Lazere, Edward B., Paul A. Leonard, and Linda Kravitz
    1989   *The Other Housing Crisis: Sheltering the Poor in Rural America.* Washington: Center on Budget and Policy Priorities.

Leistritz, F. Larry, Brenda L. Ekstrom, and Richard W. Rathge
    1988   "Farm Families in Transition: Implications for Rural Communities." Paper presented at the Rural Sociological Society, Athens, GA.

Levitan, Sar A., and Elizabeth Conway
    1988   "Shortchanged by Part-Time Work." *New York Times*, February 27.

Lifton, Donald Evan
1988 "The Influence of 'Fiscal Will': Determinants of New York's Counties' Budget Priorities in Response to Fiscal Stress." Ph.D. dissertation, Cornell University.

Lisansky, Judith
1986 "Farming in an Urbanizing Environment: Agricultural Land Use Conflicts and Right to Farm." *Human Organization* 45 (4):363–371.

Luloff, A. E., and Louis E. Swanson, eds.
1990 *American Rural Communities.* Boulder, CO: Westview Press.

MacLeish, Kenneth, and Kimball Young
1942 *Culture of a Contemporary Rural Community: Landaff, New Hampshire.* Rural Life Studies no. 3. Washington: U. S. Department of Agriculture.

Martinez-Brawley, Emilia E.
1986 "Community-oriented Social Work in a Rural and Remote Hebridean Patch." *International Social Work* 29:349–372.
1989 "Community Oriented Social Work: Some International Perspectives." Address to the Rural Human Services Leadership Conference, Syracuse, NY, December 4, 1989.
1990 *Perspectives on the Small Community: Humanistic Views for Practitioners.* Silver Springs, MD: National Association of Social Workers Press.

Martinez-Brawley, Emilia E., and Joan Blundall
1989 "Farm Families' Preferences toward the Personal Social Services." *Social Work* 34 (November):513–522.

Mazer, Milton
1976 *People and Predicaments: Of Life and Distress on Martha's Vineyard.* Cambridge, MA: Harvard University Press.

McLaughlin, Diane K., and Carolyn Sachs
1988 "Poverty in Female-headed Households: Residential Differences." *Rural Sociology* 53 (3):287–306.

Mermelstein, J., and P. Sundet
1986 "Rural Community Mental Health Centers' Response to the Farm Crisis." *Human Services in the Rural Environment* 10 (1):21–26.

Moe, Edward O., and Carl C. Taylor
1942 *Culture of a Contemporary Rural Community: Irwin, Iowa.* Rural Life Studies no. 5. Washington: U. S. Department of Agriculture.

Momoni, Jamshid, ed.
1989 *Homelessness in the United States.* Vol. 1, *State Surveys.* New York: Greenwood Press.

Murdock Steve H., and F. Larry Leistritz, eds.
1988 *Farm Financial Crisis: Socioeconomic Dimensions and Implications for Producers and Rural Areas.* Boulder, CO: Westview Press.

Murdock, Steve H., F. Larry Leistritz, Rita R. Hamm, Don E. Albrecht, and
Arlen G. Leholm.
   1987   "Impacts of the Farm Crisis on a Rural Community." *Journal of
           the Community Development Society* 18 (1):30–49.

New York Agricultural Statistics Service
   1989   *New York Agricultural Statistics 1988–1989.* Albany: New York State
           Department of Agriculture and Markets.

New York State Department of Correctional Services
   n.d.   "Site Selection Criteria" and "Fact Sheet."

New York State Department of Economic Development
   1988   "Master Plan for North County Economic Resurgence Approved."
           Opportunity New York 2 (3):7.

New York Department of Health
   1988   "General Information on Low-Level Radioactive Waste Disposal in
           New York State." Albany: State of New York.
   1989   "Disposal Technologies, Low-Level Radioactive Waste Disposal in
           New York State." Albany: State of New York.

New York State Division of Housing and Community Renewal
   1984   "An Analysis of the Housing Needs of New York State." New
           York: New York State Division of Housing and Community Renewal.

New York State Legislative Commission on Rural Resources
   1985   *Rural New York in Transition: Report of the First Statewide Legislative
           Symposium on Rural Development.* Albany: Legislative Commission
           on Rural Resources.
   1987   *Rural Health Resource Guide: A Compilation of Data and Information
           on Rural Health in New York State.* Albany: Legislative Commission
           on Rural Resources.

New York State School Boards Association
   1988   "Teacher Recruitment and Retention in Rural School Districts." In
           *EDissues: A Special Research Report from the New York State School
           Boards Association* 2 (1).

Norem, R. H., and J. Blundall
   1988   "Farm Families and Marital Disruption During a Time of Crisis."
           In *Families in Rural America,* edited by R. Marotz-Baden, D. Henon,
           and H. Brubaker, 21–31. St. Paul, MN: National Council on Family
           Relations.

Northwest Policy Center
   n.d.   *A Rural Northwest Reader: Options for Rural Communities.* Seattle:
           University of Washington, Graduate School of Public Affairs.

Norwich, Chenango County (New York)
   1986   *City/County Data Book.*

O'Hare, William P.
   1988   *The Rise of Poverty in Rural America.* Washington: Population
           Reference Bureau.

Otto, Daniel
  1985a   "Analysis of Farmers Leaving Agriculture for Financial Reasons: Summary of Survey Results from 1984." Ames, IA: Iowa State University, Cooperative Extension Service.
  1985b   "Economic Linkages Between Agriculture and Other Sectors Within Rural America." *American Journal of Agricultural Economics* 68 (5):1175–1180.

Paulsen, Julie
  1988   "A Service Response to a Culture in Crisis." *Journal of Rural Community Psychology* 9 (1):16–22.

Petrulis, Mindy F., and Bernal L. Green
  1986   "Agriculture's Role in the Economic Structure of Rural America." In *New Dimensions in Rural Policy: Building Upon Our Heritage,* 200–213. Washington: Joint Economic Committee of Congress.

Porter, Kathryn H.
  1989   *Poverty in Rural America: A National Overview.* Washington: Center on Budget and Policy Priorities.

Ranney, Christine K.
  1989   "Rural Development Policy Issues in the Northeast." In *Focus on the Future: Options in Developing a New National Rural Policy: Rural Development Policy Workshops,* Ronald D. Knutson and Dennis U. Fisher, project coordinators, 60–66. College Station, TX: Texas Agricultural Extension Service.

Ravo, Nick
  1988   "It's Near Canada, but It's New York's Jail." *New York Times,* August 31.

Reiger, Jon, and Harry K. Schwarzweller
  1988   "Mechanization in the Western Upper Peninsula (MI) Pulp Industry." Paper presented at the annual meeting of the Rural Sociological Society, Athens, GA.

Roe, Daphne A., and Kathleen R. Eickwort
  1973   "Health and Nutritional Status of Working and Non-Working Mothers in Poverty Groups." Report to U. S. Department of Labor, Manpower Administration.

Rosenblatt, Paul C.
  1990   *Farming Is in Our Blood: Farm Families in Economic Crisis.* Ames: Iowa State University Press.

Ross, Kathryn
  1989   "County's Planning Board: Thumbs up to Prison Idea." *Wellsville* (NY) *Daily Reporter,* November 16.

Rowe, Corinne
  1988   "Migration Choices: Compound Decisions in a Complex Society." Paper presented at the Rural Sociological Society, Athens, GA.

Rural Futures: News of Interest About Rural New York.
  1988–   Albany: New York State Legislative Commission on Rural Resources.
  1990

Sanderson, Dwight
  1937   *Research Memorandum on Rural Life in the Depression.* New York: Social Science Research Council.

Scheidt, Rick J., and Carolyn Norris-Baker
  1989   "Small Town to Ghost Town: Rural Elderly at Risk?" Paper presented at the American Psychological Association, New Orleans, LA.

Shapiro, Isaac
  1989   *Laboring for Less: Working but Poor in Rural Amercia.* Washington: Center on Budget and Policy Priorities.

Slesinger, Doris P., and Eleanor Cautley
  1988   "Determinants of Poverty Among Rural and Urban Women Who Live Alone." *Rural Sociology* 53 (3):307–320.

Slovic, Paul, Baruch Fischoff, and Sara Lichtenstein
  1979   "Rating the Risks." *Environment,* 21:14–39.

Smardon, Richard C., and Emanuel Carter, eds.
  1990   "Rapid Growth Impacts Rural Communities: The Fort Drum Case." Special issue, *Small Town* 20 (5):3–31.

Smith, Michal
  1989   *Behind the Glitter: The Impact of Tourism on Rural Women in the Southeast.* Lexington, KY: Southeast Women's Employment Coalition.

Stanton, Bernard F.
  1987   "The Quest for Improved Agricultural Data: Concepts and Measurement." In *Relevance of Agricultural Economics: Obsolete Data Concepts Revisited.* Proceedings of a symposium at the annual meetings of the American Agricultural Economics Association, East Lansing, MI, August 2–5.

Stone, Kenneth E.
  1987   "Impact of the Farm Financial Crisis on Retail and Service Sectors of Rural Communities." *Agricultural Finance Review* 47:40–47.

Stone, Kenneth, and James C. McConnon, Jr.
  1982   "The Effect of Shopping Centers on Host Town and Outlying Areas." Paper presented at a meeting of the American Agricultural Economics Association, Logan, UT.

Strange, Marty
  1988   *Family Farming: A New Economic Vision.* Lincoln: University of Nebraska Press.

Summers, Gene F., and Thomas A. Hirschl
  1988   "Retirees as a Growth Industry." In *Community Economic Vitality: Major Trends and Selected Issues,* edited by Gene F. Summers et al., 49–54. Ames, IA: North Central Regional Center for Rural Development.

Thernstrom, Stephan
  1970   *Poverty and Progress: Social Mobility in a Nineteenth Century City.* New York: Atheneum.

Tomaskovic-Devey, Donald
   1990   "Back to the Future: Human Resources and Economic Development
             Policy for North Carolina." Raleigh: Department of Sociology,
             Anthropology, and Social Work, North Carolina State University.

Uchitelle, Louis
   1987   "Wage Increases Are Sluggish Despite a Scarcity of Workers." New
             York Times, September 8.

U. S. Senate
   1986   Governing the Heartland: Can Rural Communities Survive the Farm
             Crisis? Washington: Committee on Governmental Affairs, Subcom-
             mittee on Intergovernmental Relations.

Varenne, Herve
   1977   Americans Together. New York: Teachers' College Press.

Vaughan, Lawrence M.
   1929   "Abandoned Farm Areas in New York." Agricultural Experiment
             Station Bulletin, no. 490, Ithaca, NY: Cornell University.

Vidich, Arthur J., and Joseph Bensman
   1958   Small Town in Mass Society: Class Power and Religion in a Rural
             Community. Princeton, NJ: Princeton University Press.

Voss, Paul R., Thomas Corbett, and Bernard Stumbras
   1986   "The Migration Impact of Wisconsin's AFDC Benefit Levels." Report
             of the Welfare Magnet Study Committee. Madison, WI: Wisconsin
             Expenditure Commission.

Wagenfeld, Morton O.
   1988   "Mental Health, Community Psychology, and Rural America: A
             Look Back and a Look Forward." Journal of Rural Community
             Psychology 9 (2):85–93.

Wardwell, John M., and Corinne M. Rowe
   1988   "Economic Recession and Nonmetropolitan Migration." Paper pre-
             sented at the Rural Sociological Society, Athens, GA.

Warren, Barry P., and Thomas A. Banks
   1988   "Summary Report, 1988 Survey of Non-Resident Property Own-
             ership in Delaware County." Delhi: State University of New York,
             College of Technology.

Warren, Roland L.
   1963   The Community in America. Chicago: Rand McNally.

West, James
   1945   Plainville, U.S.A. New York: Columbia University Press.

Wilkerson, Isabel
   1990   "With Rural Towns Vanishing, States Choose Which to Save." New
             York Times, January 3.

Wilkinson, Kenneth P.
   1988   "The Community Crisis in the Rural South." In The Rural South
             in Crisis, edited by Lionel J. Beaulieu, 72–86. Boulder, CO: Westview
             Press.

Willits, Fern K., Robert C. Bealer, and Donald M. Crider
    1985   "Persistence of Rural/Urban Differences." In *Rural Society in the U.S.: Issues for the 1980s*, edited by Don A. Dillman and Daryl J. Hobbs, 69–76. Boulder, CO: Westview Press.

Wright, Sara E., and Paul C. Rosenblatt
    1987   "Isolation and Farm Loss: Why Neighbors May Not Be Supportive." *Family Relations* 36: 391–395.

Wylie, Laurence
    1964   *Village in the Vaucluse.* Revised edition. New York: Harper and Row.

About the Book and Author

Rural America as a place and a way of life is undergoing major transformation. The farm crisis and the decline of manufacturing dealt a double blow to the rural economy in the 1980s. Rural communities continue to lose farms, factories, and young people. Rural lands are increasingly being sought as places for vacation homes, state prisons, and waste dumps. Rural people are ambivalent about new residents and activities that are coming in and unsure of their own rural identity. Old assumptions about rural life and rural community are now open to question.

Based on years of field observations and hundreds of interviews in fifteen rural counties in upstate New York, Fitchen's book explores these interconnected changes. It describes the financial stress in dairy farming and the efforts families made to hold onto their farms. It records the stunned disbelief and difficult adjustment of rural factory workers and small communities as local plants shut down. The author chronicles the struggles of communities plagued by toxic chemicals in their drinking water and of young families slipping farther into poverty. She reports on some communities that are campaigning to "win" a state prison and others that are protesting against a proposed radioactive waste dump.

The book illustrates the persistence of rural ingenuity and determination but argues that these alone cannot solve the problems of rural America. A well-informed federal and state commitment is necessary. With policies and programs appropriate for rural situations, most communities could adapt creatively to the changes, integrate around a new rural identity, and survive into the twenty-first century as enduring social settings for their residents.

Janet M. Fitchen is an associate professor of anthropology at Ithaca College and frequently leads training workshops and public discussions on rural issues. Her earlier book, *Poverty in Rural America* (Westview), remains one of the few descriptive case studies of rural poverty.

Index